CIVIC QUARRY LIBRARY
LEEDS METROPOLITAN UNIVERSITY

Items should be returned on or before the last date shown below
All items are subject to recall if required by another reader. The loan
period may be shortened from that given below and, in these
circumstances, you must return the item by the revised due date
indicated on the recall notice which we send you.

Charges are levied for the late return of items.

Renewal may be made by personal application, in writing or by telephoning
(0113) 283 3164 and quoting the barcode number below.

Pers

Date Due	Date Due	Date Due	Date Due
2. JAN 01		19. JAN 04	
MAR 08.	14. DEC 01	08. JAN 04	
AY 01	29. APR 02	23-1-04	
NV 01	21. MAY 02.	05. FEB 04.	
	22/8/02	13. MAY 04.	
	19. NOV 02		
	08. MAY 03		
	27. NOV 03	04. JUN 04	

For Andrea

Personnel in Practice

Donald Currie

The right of Donald Currie to be identified as author of this work has been asserted in accordance with the Copyright, Designs and Patents Act 1988.

First published 1997
Reprinted 1998

Blackwell Publishers Ltd
108 Cowley Road
Oxford OX4 1JF, UK

Blackwell Publishers Inc
350 Main Street
Malden, Massachusetts 02148, USA

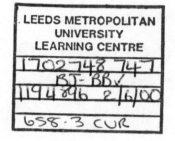
British Library Cataloguing in Publication Data
A CIP catalogue record for this book is available from the British Library

Library of Congress Cataloging in Publication Data
Currie, Donald
Personnel in practice / Donald Currie
p: cm.
Includes bibliographical references and index.
ISBN 0–631–20089–4 (alk. paper)
1. Personnel management. I. Title.
HF5549.C843   1997-11-24 658.3—dc21

Typeset in 10 on 12pt Bookman
by Photoprint, Torquay, Devon
Printed and bound in Great Britain
by TJ International Ltd, Padstow, Cornwall

This book is printed on acid-free paper

Contents

List of Figures

List of Tables

List of Exhibits

List of Abbreviations

16PFI	Sixteen Personality Factor Inventory
AAF	appointment authority form
ACAS	Advisory Conciliation and Arbitration Service
AJF	appointment justification form
ATR	authority to recruit
CPIS	computerized personnel information system
CPSG	creative problem-solving group
CRE	Commission for Racial Equality
CV	curriculum vitae
EOC	Equal Opportunities Commission
EWS	experienced worker's standard
HASAWA	Health and Safety at Work Act
HEA	Health Education Authority
HRD	human resource development
HRM	human resource management
HRP	human resource planning
HSC	Health and Safety Commission
HSE	Health and Safety Executive
IT	industrial tribunal
LPC	least preferred co-worker
MRS	minimum required standard
O&M	organization and methods
OCR	optical character recognition
OD	organizational development
OMR	optical mark recognition
PBR	payment by results
P-rP	performance-related pay
STC	systematic training cycle
TNA	training needs analysis
WAIS	Wechsler Adult Intelligence Scales

Introduction

The idea for this book came from the needs of students undertaking the Certificate in Personnel Practice (CPP) course, which is a nationally recognized award of the Institute of Personnel and Development (IPD). The content has been specifically designed to meet the precise needs of CPP students, although it may prove useful to those undergoing other courses of a similar level that involve study of the same subjects.

The aim of the book is to present the reader with the basic knowledge requirement, to explain how fundamental personnel skills may be developed and, hopefully, to encourage the building of self-confidence and improvement of work performance. People who develop a skill in a classroom are sometimes reluctant to try it out in the workplace, often because they lack the confidence. Confidence is the most essential ingredient of success in the transfer of knowledge and skills to a practical situation.

The book is in six parts, each of which represents a major aspect of the Certificate Course. Most of the theories referred to are well known and may be found in other texts, the idea here being to consolidate into a single text the theories and practices that CPP students need to understand. To achieve this, I have drawn on a variety of personnel-related approaches and disciplines which are applied in actual practice, and which, it is hoped, will also serve as an introduction for those who subsequently wish to take their studies further. First, students will benefit from a brief historical sketch of management thought, which will enable them to understand more clearly the role of the personnel management function in today's organizations. Second, experience shows that they will also gain from an

understanding of the relevant parts of such disciplines as occupational psychology and industrial sociology, which have made
significant contributions to personnel practice. The principal
focus here is on six main areas of study:

Part I, *The Context of Personnel Practice*, is designed to provide
the student with knowledge, understanding and awareness of
the role of the personnel function in organizations. This includes
corporate awareness, management processes and functions, elements of corporate strategy, objective setting, policy formulation
and resource allocation and structuring. This involves studying
the different kinds of organization in which personnel is prac-
tised; the history of the various approaches to management,
including present-day thinking; and how personnel fits in to the
structures of organization and management.

Part II, *Planning the Human Resource*, explains how personnel
specialists ensure that the future human resource needs of the
organization will be met through the implementation of human
resource strategy, recruitment, selection and induction. This
part introduces students to the writing of job descriptions and
personnel specifications, recruitment and recruitment advertising, interviewing and selection methods, selection decision making and induction. These are areas in which it is expected that
the reader, who normally is a part-time student aspiring to or
working in personnel, will be involved and which will be most
useful at this stage of study and career development.

Part III, *Developing Employees*, explains how people learn
individually and what they need to learn in the workplace. It also
examines the 'systematic training cycle', the techniques of
training, and how learning and training are evaluated and
related to workplace performance. The reader is also introduced
to instruction techniques, the delivery of training, and self-
development.

Part IV, *Performance Management*, provides an explanation of
why individuals behave as they do in the workplace, in terms of
their personalities, perceptions, intelligence levels, attitudes and
motivations. We then go on to explain systems of appraisal,
individual objective-setting, systems of payment, and wage and
salary administration.

Part V, *Personnel Information Handling*, covers the use of basic
computer packages to facilitate effective personnel decision

making, and the role of information technology in general personnel activities – gathering, storing, retrieving, interpreting and presenting information, information security and data protection.

Part VI, *Employee Relations*, discusses the relationship between the organization, its managers and its employees. This includes such legal issues as those of the contract of employment and equal treatment; relevant procedures, such as those for handling grievances and disciplinary matters, and related interviewing; conflict; discrimination; meetings; negotiation; the status and role of today's trade unions; and health and safety at work.

The main purpose throughout is to explain the relevant concepts and the knowledge and skills that are required for an effective performance at the interface of personnel practice.

Part I

The Context of Personnel Practice

The aim of this part of the book is to provide an understanding of the personnel function, within the context of the organizational environment. Organizations are defined and their purposes are described and categorized; the several approaches to the management of organizations that have arisen during the twentieth century are examined, and the processes and functions of management are discussed. Part I concludes by describing the role and function of personnel as a specialism in the organization

1

Organizations

Introduction

It is sometimes held that those who work at the operational level in organizations need only be educated and trained in the knowledge and skills that are needed exclusively at that level; this is not a view that is shared by everyone. The alternative approach is to show those at operational level how their work fits in to the overall strategies and plans of the organization. If the organization's objectives are understood by the operational workers, they are more likely to be achieved. The purpose of this chapter, therefore, is to introduce you to the various types of organization and the different theoretical approaches to them, so that you will have a clear picture of how the personnel department and the activities of its specialists contribute to the meeting of objectives and the fulfilment of strategy. This is not an exhaustive analysis; what follows is a synopsis of the major theories of organizations.

The Purposes of Organizations

We live in a society that is dominated by organizations. Our birth, health, education, marriage, employment – even our death – are all influenced or handled by one kind of organization or another. So why do we create organizations? The fundamental answer is that we do so in order to survive. Man is a rational creature who is able to reflect upon the past, assess the current situation and make plans for the future. Human beings are aware of their survival needs of the future and they organize themselves to ensure that those needs will be met. Thus, there is a vast industry surrounding each of our basic needs, such as those for food, drink, shelter, rest and security. We grow crops, rear animals, fish the seas, process liquids, build houses and manufacture comfortable furniture. There is a large industry engaged in the manufacture of safes, locks, alarm signals and other security devices, and we have armed services and the police to protect the country and maintain our personal security.

We build hospitals, schools, shops and places of entertainment, not merely in order to survive, but so that we may survive for longer, in greater comfort, and, of course, so that we may derive pleasure from life. To ensure that the provision of all of our needs will continue, we create organizations that exist to produce the necessary goods and services.

Public Sector Organizations

In an economy such as ours, some organizations are directly controlled by central government; for example, government departments and local authorities, which provide us with essential services such as those for health, education, policing, dealing with fires and other emergencies, social services, transport and so on. These organizations are said to be in the *public sector*. The provision of drinking water, drainage services, gas and electricity were in the public sector, but the current government policy of privatization has transferred them to what we call the *private sector*.

In the public sector, organizations are directly or indirectly responsible to central government for meeting public needs. Public sector organizations exist to provide services. Those who ultimately are responsible for running the public sector organizations are politicians, who are accountable to the public, who elected them. It is said, therefore, that their authority to make decisions and take actions is derived from *public trust*. If the public is dissatisfied with the way the politicians manage, they can be replaced at the next election. Usually, politicians are amateurs in terms of the specific responsibilities they are given, and the decisions they make are actually implemented by employed experts, who also act as advisers to the politicians. These experts, who actually are senior civil servants, remain in their positions, regardless of any political changes that the electorate makes; hence the term, *permanent* secretary.

Private Sector Organizations

The private sector is made up of industrial and commercial undertakings which have evolved to respond to the natural and changing demands of the market. In the private sector, the company's shareholders are the main beneficiaries and the organizations exist to make a profit. The directors, who are responsible for managing private sector organizations, do so on behalf of the shareholders, since it is the shareholders who own the organization. In the private sector, therefore, it is said that directors' authority to make decisions and take actions is derived from the *ownership* of the organization.

Today in the private sector, most shareholders' only connection with the organization is their shares. Like the politicians, they employ experts (the company's directors), not only to implement policy, but to formulate it too. If the shareholders do not approve of the way the organization is being managed, they can vote the directors out of office; at least, that is the theoretical position. The shareholders' opportunity to vote arises at the organization's Annual General Meeting (AGM), where the directors report on the past year's performance and state their plans

Figure 1.1 Basic organizational structure.

for the future. In reality, however, shareholding has become scattered widely among individuals and institutions, and many shareholders never attend AGMs (see figure 1.1).

Definitions of Organizations

There have been several definitions of organizations. Stephen P. Robbins (1996), the American writer, says that organizations are 'a consciously coordinated social entity, with a relatively identifiable boundary, that functions on a relatively continuous basis to achieve a common goal or set of goals'. Robbins (quite rightly), goes on to say, 'That's a mouthful of words', but then he breaks the definition down into its component parts and explains each of them, which turns the 'mouthful of words' into something meaningful.

How an academic defines organizations is usually determined by *why* he or she is defining it in the first place. Many definitions have arisen from theorists who have produced new and different ways of looking at organizations, while other definitions have been produced by management theorists, social scientists and organizational psychologists. Theorists study organizations through the framework of their own particular science; each will study different aspects and not surprisingly, they all define them differently. Academics and practising managers have been studying organizations and how they should be managed for more than 100 years and some of them say that the study of organizations and the study of 'management as an organizational process' are inextricably linked. Indeed, E.F.L. Brech (1965) describes organizations as 'the framework of the management process'.

Edgar Schein (1980) defines the organization as 'the planned coordination of the activities of a number of people for the achievement of some common, explicit purpose or goal, through division of labour and function, and through a hierarchy of authority and responsibility'. This is another complex definition that has been analysed and explained by its author.

As well as defining organizations, theorists also classify them. Above, we classified organizations into *public* and *private* sector undertakings. In 1966, Blau and Scott classified them further in terms of who are the *prime beneficiaries* of the organization. They proposed four categories:

1 *Mutual benefit organizations*, in which the members are the prime beneficiaries. A trade union is one obvious example. Others include sports and social clubs, some building societies and professional institutions, such as the IPD.
2 *Business concerns*, in which the shareholders are the prime beneficiaries. These are commercial/industrial profit-orientated organizations.
3 *Service organizations*, in which the prime beneficiaries are its users: customers and clients. Examples of such organizations are health and educational institutions.
4 *Commonweal organizations*, in which the general public are the prime beneficiaries. Examples are the armed services, central and local government.

The social and economic status of organizations is undergoing change, especially in Britain, and they are the subject of continuous study. Theorists, therefore, continue to produce new definitions and classifications of organizations.

The Pressures on Organizations

The main purposes of every organization are to survive and develop. To survive, the organization must continue to perform functions, such as the production of goods or services, which are demanded by their customers and clients. Organizations also have to operate within the law and are subjected to pressures from the environment, to which they must respond, either by resisting those pressures or conforming to them, whichever is appropriate.

Such pressures can be analysed into four broad categories:

1 *Political interventions.* These occur when new laws that affect the way in which companies operate are introduced, or when codes of practice relating to particular aspects of that law are published. Company law, mainly through the Companies Acts, is a principal example of law affecting how companies operate. Other examples include the Health and Safety at Work Act and its associated Regulations and Code of Practice, and the laws relating to employment protection and sex and race discrimination. In a sense, a change of the governing political party may be regarded by organizations as a political intervention. For example, it may be well known that the employment and economic policies of a current government are quite different from those of the party in opposition.

History has taught us that when a change does take place, we can safely anticipate new legislation that will affect organizations' business and employment policies. Organizations respond to political interventions by staying within the law and operating according to the codes of practice.

2 *Economic changes.* The influence of regional, national and international economic situations plays a very large part in the fortunes of organizations. Sometimes, as in the 1980s, the economy appears to be buoyant and in a state of boom and plenty, unemployment is low, industrial and high street spending is high and property values soar. At other times, the economy dips and most of the 'highs' that are mentioned above go into reverse. Clearly, all organizations are affected by the alternate peaking and dipping of the economy and must prepare themselves accordingly.

3 *Social trends.* The influence of social trends on the organization are many and varied. Firstly, there is the influence of fashion and fad. Market demands change, but organizations tend to influence these changes themselves by developing new goods and services or modified versions of existing ones and then deliberately creating the demand for them. Secondly, people are becoming more environmentally conscious and they form themselves into groups which monitor the activities of organizations to ensure, for example, that atmospheric and waterborne pollution levels are minimized and the countryside is preserved.

4 *Technological innovation.* This occurs on two broad fronts, firstly in terms of *process innovation*, which include modifying or replacing machinery and the methods of production because new and better manufacturing systems have been developed, giving greater cost-efficiency and effectiveness, and secondly in terms of *product innovation* in which new products and services are developed and/or modifications to existing ones made. Organizations tend to develop their own product innovation. So far as process innovation is concerned, they are largely 'users' of technology developed by manufacturers of capital equipment and computer software.

PEST is a mnemonic that may help you to remember these four main external factors that exercise influence and exert pressures upon organizations.

The Process of Organizing

Everyone wants the organization to achieve its purposes of survival and development, and it is the task of those at the very top, the chief executive and the members of the board, to ensure that it does. If an organization is to fulfil its purposes, its future must be planned. Someone has to be at the steering wheel making decisions about the direction in which the organization must go. Such decision making is complex and sometimes involves considerable risk. The person at the wheel, making the decisions that shape the future direction of the organization, is engaged in *strategy*.

In order to reach its strategic goals, the organization is given objectives to achieve, which means that certain milestones need to be reached at pre-planned times. Organizations achieve their objectives within the limits of the *policies* they formulate. A policy is a statement of intent about how the organization proposes to achieve its strategic objectives. Once the organization knows where it is going in the future (it has a strategy), what it has to do to get there (it has objectives) and how it is going to achieve those objectives (it has policies), attention can be turned to resources.

The organization needs resources in the form of money, materials, machinery and the human resource. Decisions concerning the human resource are extremely important, since someone has to do the work that leads to the achievement of objectives. This means that policy decisions have to be made about how to attract the right people to the organization and encourage them to stay. By now you will understand that those responsible for strategy, objective setting, policy formulation and resource allocation live at the top end of the organization. In some organizations there is a whole department of people employed specifically to advise the board of directors on these matters. In addition to the *strategists*, however, there is another level of managers who are responsible for *operations*. As the word implies, they are called *operational managers*, alternatively referred to as *line managers*. Line managers are responsible for ensuring that all of the tasks that are necessary for the achievement of objectives are actually carried out.

In yet another managerial role we find the *staff managers*, sometimes referred to as *functional specialists*. They are responsible for advising and guiding the board of directors, and senior and line managers through those parts of their jobs that involve the staff manager's specialism. For example, a personnel executive who specializes in, say, recruitment and selection, will advise and guide the line manager who needs to take on a new member of staff. The line manager may be an engineer, who is not experienced in recruitment and selection. Other functional specialists who advise the line managers are involved in research and development, accountancy, marketing, production engineering, information technology and whatever other specialism it takes to run a particular organization. The number, variety and size of the specialist departments are determined by the organization's specialist needs.

Every manager and supervisor has responsibility for the performance of his or her staff and has, therefore, a personnel role to fulfil. Personnel responsibilities and activities have become very complex in recent years. Managers need to be aware of the implications of equal opportunities, health and safety at work, individual rights and other legislative requirements. In addition to ensuring that the law and its related regulations and codes of practice are adhered to, managers are expected to motivate, counsel, coach, train and develop their staff as well as appraise their performance and make recommendations that affect the rewards they receive and their future careers. Furthermore, the operational manager is responsible for resolving employees' grievances, disciplining them when necessary and handling disputes about working practices and the terms and conditions of employment.

When the complexity of all of these responsibilities is considered, it is hardly surprising that managers need the advice and assistance of personnel experts, especially since they have to fulfil those responsibilities within the context of their main job as operational managers.

References

Blau, P.M. and Scott, W.R. 1966: *Formal Organisations*. London: Routledge and Kegan Paul.

Brech, E.F.L. 1965: *Organisation: The Framework of Management*, 2nd edn. London: Longman.

Robbins, S.P. 1996: *Organisational Behavior*, 7th edn. Englewood Cliffs, NJ: Prentice Hall.

Schein, E.H. 1980: *Organisational Psychology*, 3rd edn. Englewood Cliffs, NJ: Prentice Hall.

2

A History of Management
Thought

Introduction

This chapter sets out to explain the major approaches to the study of management that have emerged during the twentieth century, and the theories within each approach. The overall aim is to provide insight into how organizations were managed in the past and how they are managed today (see table 2.1). Some of the writers to whom we refer were academics and others were practising managers. Rather than cover the work of these writers in detail, we explain the broad concepts underlying their

Table 2.1 The history of management thought

Classical (1990s)	Bureaucracy (1920s)	Human relations approach (1930s+)	Systems and contingency (1960s)	Human resource management (1980s/90s)
H. Fayol F.W. Taylor F. and L. Gilbreth E.F.L. Brech	Max Weber	Elton Mayo and the Hawthorne Studies A.H. Maslow F.W. Herzberg Douglas McGregor Chris Argyris Rensis Likert	Trist and Bamforth Burns and Stalker Joan Woodward Katz and Kahn Lawrence and Lorsch Pugh, Hickson et al. (the 'Aston Group')	Numerous theorists

theories and throw some light on the approaches that have led management to its current ways of thinking.

Classical Theories

This section provides a brief summary of the works and theories of F.W. Taylor, H. Fayol, F. and L. Gilbreth and Max Weber. These are the main classical theorists; certainly they are the most well known among those who founded the study of organizations and management.

FREDERICK WINSLOW TAYLOR AND SCIENTIFIC MANAGEMENT

Taylor was born in 1856 and started his working life as a labourer at the Midvale Steel Company in the USA. Several years later, after qualifying as an engineer, he moved to the Bethlehem Steel Corporation, as a management consultant, where he carried out the work for which he is most well known. Even in those early days of the industrial revolution, he could see that business and industry were afflicted by problems that were rooted mainly in a severe lack of knowledge. 'Management,' he said, 'is ignorant of what men can produce . . . and they make no effort to find out, or even to define what a day's work is.' The workers took it for granted that there would be delays, poor machinery, 'down-time' and so forth, and they did not appreciate that there might be a better way of doing things; nor did they know how to improve their own productivity; they had not been shown.

Taylor developed a set of principles which he claimed would solve most of the problems he saw. This system was later called, 'scientific management' (Taylor, 1911, 1947). The central principles of scientific management were:

1 Apply scientific methods to management, by using work measurement as a basis for accurate planning and production control.
2 Establish the best work methods; give each worker a clearly defined task.
3 Select, train and instruct subordinates scientifically.
4 Pay people fairly; high pay for successful completion of work.
5 Obtain cooperation between management and men and divide responsibility between them.

Unfortunately, many of the managers who followed Taylor adopted his scientific methods, but rejected his more humane provisions. This rejection resulted in the tainting of scientific management, and opposition to it became so fierce that in 1911 he was called before a Congressional Committee to explain himself. This may seem surprising, since, even today, much of what he said is regarded as normal practice in most countries in the western, industrialized world.

For the purposes of applying his main theory, which was to remove the guesswork and replace it with facts, he studied the human body and its capabilities, the interactions between men and machinery, and the length of time it took to perform certain functions. In other words, he invented Work Study. Armed with such knowledge, he also devised the incentive systems of payment which have come to be known as 'payment by results' or PBR schemes. Today, about a third of all manufacturing organizations in western industry still use PBR schemes, although they are much more sophisticated than those originally developed by Taylor.

HENRI FAYOL AND HIS GENERAL PRINCIPLES OF MANAGEMENT

Fayol was a French mining engineer who worked in the same company all of his working life, rising to the position of managing director, a post which he occupied for almost 30 years, retiring at the age of 77. The company was on the verge of liquidation when he took over, but under his leadership it thrived and flourished, earning him popularity with the community, employees and everyone else who had anything to do with the company. Fayol was an entrepreneur who had many ideas about how organizations should be run, but most attention was given to his *General Principles of Management*, which he published in France in 1916. The English translation, published in 1949, was entitled *General and Industrial Management*.[1]

Fayol's career was concurrent with that of Taylor, both were engineers and managing directors, but their perspectives on management were, with one or two exceptions, quite different. While Taylor concentrated on the application of science to management methods (indeed, he was dubbed the 'Father' of Scientific Management) and the use of work measurement as a basis for accurate planning and production control, Fayol emphasized the importance of management. He saw management as a process and not as a set of activities that were the sole province of some elite group at the top of the organization. Rather, management was a process, needed throughout the organization. Today, we say that management is something you do, rather than something you are.

(Underlying Fayol's general principles were six activities which he regarded as the fundamental activities of all organizations (table 2.2). Fayol separated the sixth set of activities by describing management as: forecasting, planning, organizing, commanding, coordinating and controlling]

He saw forecasting and planning as developing a plan of action for the future, organizing as producing a company structure, and commanding as 'maintaining activity among the personnel', coordinating as combining people's activities, while controlling indicated that the activities were carried out in accordance with company policy and established practices.

Table 2.2 Fayol's six groups of organizational activity

Activity	Description
Technical	Related to the work system and productivity, maintenance work and general duties
Commercial	Buying, selling and other related activities
Financial	Activities covering matters relating to capital, such as ensuring sufficient working capital and managing the financial aspects of the organization
Security	Safeguarding the company's property, including information relating to future plans, products, research and development
Accounting	The provision of financial information, invoicing, issuing statements, receipts and so forth
Managerial	Fayol treated this group of activities differently, saying that the other five groups were all interrelated, but that none of them, nor the combination of them, dealt with the general processes of planning the future and resourcing the activities

Central to Fayol's ideas were his 14 'Principles of Management' (see table 2.3). He did not claim the 'Principles' to be all that was needed for success; he simply said that these were principles by which he abided when he was running the company. The comments alongside each item in the table are those of Fayol himself; those in parentheses are mine.

Reading through Fayol's 'Principles', one should bear in mind what is said above about the nature of past management theories: they are a product of the way people thought at the time. Theories such as those of Taylor and Fayol obviously were the products of a time when formality ruled social relations. Also, the concepts of 'fairness' and 'equity' that were applied were those of the managers; in those days, it did not occur to anyone to consider employees' perceptions of such concepts.

FRANK AND LILIAN GILBRETH AND THE SCIENCE OF MANAGEMENT

This husband and wife partnership were contemporaries of Taylor; in fact, Frank Gilbreth used to consult Taylor about the possible application of the principles of scientific management to skilled crafts and, in particular, to bricklaying. The Gilbreths experimented with Taylor's principles and fed information back to him, reporting, for example, that they had managed to reduce the number of movements in laying bricks from 18 to 5 per brick. The Gilbreths analysed and redesigned the methods employed by bricklayers. After studying Taylor's ideas, they analysed and timed the movements of the bricklayers, and this 'motion study', as it became known, was the basis of the Gilbreths' work (1917).

It is particularly interesting to note that while modern theorists maintain that there is no 'one best way' to do anything in organizations, the Gilbreths were convinced that through their perception of the concept of 'measurement', it would be possible to identify 'one best way' of doing things. They followed Taylor's principles and developed them further in their own organization, persistently looking for the attainment of the 'ideal' way to do things. The methods of the Gilbreths were very detailed indeed, and it is believed that this reduced the number of people who were attracted to the methods. Nevertheless, the basic techniques caught on and it is the Gilbreths, through their further development of Taylor's ideas, that we should thank for what has become known as 'method study'.

Table 2.3 Fayol's 14 principles of management

Principle	Description
1 Division of work	Reduces the span of attention or effort for any one person of group. Develops practice and familiarity
2 Authority	The right to give orders. Should not be considered without reference to responsibility. (On the other hand, if one has to use that right in order to get things done, one's leadership skills may be in question)
3 Discipline	Outward marks of respect in accordance with formal or informal agreements between the firm and its employees
4 Unity of command	One man superior!
5 Unity of direction	One head and one plan for a group of activities with the same objective
6 Subordination of individual interests to the general interest	The interests of one individual or group should not prevail over the general good. This is a difficult area of management
7 Remuneration	Pay should be fair both to employees and the firm. (This coincides with Taylor's pronouncements on pay)
8 Centralization	Is always present to a greater or lesser extent, depending on the size of the company and the quality of its managers
9 Scalar chain	The line of authority from top to bottom of the organization
10 Order	A place for everything and everything in its place
11 Equity	A combination of kindliness and justice towards employees
12 Stability of tenure of personnel	Employees need to be given time to settle into their jobs, even though this may be a lengthy period for managers
13 Initiative	Within the limits of authority and discipline, all levels of staff should be encouraged to show initiative
14 Esprit de corps	Harmony is a great strength to an organization; team work should be encouraged

Max Weber and bureaucracy

Unlike the writers mentioned above, Weber was an academic. He was a sociologist and was interested in discovering why people obeyed the instructions of those in the positions above them. His chief interest was in organizational structures and his most well-known work was *The Theory of Social and Economic Organisation* (1964). The publication resulted from his study of the German civil service; it was in that book that he first used the term 'bureaucracy'. He said that to some extent, bureaucracy existed in all organizations, in the private as well as the public sector. Weber drew distinctions between three types of organization in terms of the kinds of authority that existed within them: *traditional*, *charismatic* and *legal–rational*. In describing the three types Weber used the term 'legitimate authority' and defined them as follows:

- *Traditional.* Authority is accepted as legitimate through custom and long-term tradition, or belief that those in authority have a natural or inherent right to rule. This 'right' comes from the result of traditional procedures or rites being exercised. Examples are: royalty, the Dalai Lama, the Pope or a paternalistic employer.
- *Charismatic.* Authority is given legitimate status by belief and trust in the personal qualities of the leader. There are some exceptional people with appealing personalities who are capable of developing a loyal and trusting following. The main problem with this kind of authority is that in the event of the demise or dethronement of the leader, the organization may disintegrate. Even if a legitimate successor is found, he or she will exercise authority on the basis of a different set of personal qualities. The loss of a charismatic leader can transform the organization into a traditional or bureaucratic set-up.
- *Legal–rational.* Acceptance is derived from the position or office of the person exercising authority. In contrast to the personality-driven example of charismatic authority, legal–rational authority stems from the position of the person. Government departments and local authorities are typical examples.

The contrast between charismatic and legal–rational authorities is similar to that made in theories of 'power in organizations', in which it is said that people have 'position' power or 'personal' power. Here, however, we are principally interested in the legal–rational concept, because this is seen as synonymous with bureaucracy, to the extent that the same organizations are alternately referred to as 'bureaucratic' and 'legal–rational' organizations.

Most people associate bureaucracy with 'red tape' and they dread dealing with an organization that is bound by rules and regulations. Indeed, one of the criticisms of the concept is that the organization's mass of rules, regulations and paperwork may be seen by the employees to be more important than the overall purposes of the organization itself. It should be said that Weber did not *invent* bureaucracy; he *discovered* it when he studied the German civil service, although to some degree he did advocate bureaucracy and predicted that it would become the most popular (frequently found) form of organization. Weber said that the main features of a bureaucratic organization are as follows:

1   A hierarchy of offices and positions, arranged in descending order of importance and degree of authority.
2   A high level of specialization and clear divisions of labour. Specialization applies to the job and not the person, so that the efficient execution of tasks is not influenced by staff turnover.
3   Selection of staff to occupy the offices and positions is based on technical competence and qualifications.
4   Tasks are allocated downwards to the various positions.
5   Interactions with subordinates and clients are impersonal, an attitude which is designed to produce rational judgement in decision making.
6   Employees are separated from the ownership of the organization.
7   All rules, decisions and resulting actions are recorded in writing.

There is a formal list of criticisms of bureaucracy, the following five of which are the most frequently cited:

1   The rules that are supposed to facilitate efficiency can become more important than the main purposes of the organization.

2 The systems discourage creativity in so far as decisions are governed by pre-programmed limited choices; no one considers possibilities outside of the predetermined alternatives. The ultimate result of this is that bureaucracies tend not to attract creative people as employees.

3 As a result of their inflexible rules and procedures, bureaucracies experience great difficulties when attempting to adjust to external changes.

4 The impersonal nature of relationships can adversely affect relationships between the organization and its clients and between managers and staff.

5 The 'knowledge base' that is a requirement of those who occupy the positions has led to a burgeoning of so-called experts, whose frames of reference for decision making may conflict with those of the managers.

Gerald Cole (1986), commenting on bureaucracy as the most frequently found form of organization, says that the question to be asked is not 'Is this organization a bureaucracy?' but 'To what extent *is* this organization bureaucratized?'

The Human Relations Approach

While the classical theorists were largely interested in organizational structures, physical working conditions, work methods, measurement and proposing formal 'rules' of management, it became evident in the 1920s that attention should be paid to social aspects within the workplace. It was the study of employees' social interactions, their attitudes and values that gave rise to the human relations approach. One study in particular that is said by many writers to have stimulated managers' and academics' interest in the motivations of human beings at work is the now famous *Hawthorne Studies*, which took place between 1924 and 1936 at the Hawthorne plant of the Western Electric Company in Chicago. The studies were carried out in five main stages: (1) the lighting experiments, (2) the relay assembly test room, (3) the interview programme, (4) the bank wiring observation room and (5) personnel counselling.

THE LIGHTING EXPERIMENTS

The lighting experiments began in 1924 and lasted for three years. Tests were carried out by two members of Western

Electric's staff, Pennock and Dickson, who were interested in the effects of lighting on productivity. Two groups, each in different parts of the plant, were selected for study. Measurement had shown that the groups put in parallel performances. It was decided that one group should be the 'control' group and the other the 'experimental' group.[2] The control group operated in consistent lighting conditions, while the lighting in which the experimental group operated fluctuated from high to low levels.

Pennock and Dickson were surprised to discover that apparently, the lighting had no effect whatsoever on productivity. In other words, productivity in the experimental group varied without any observable relationship to the level of lighting; in fact, productivity increased, not only in the experimental group, but in the control group too. It seemed to the researchers that productivity was influenced by factors unconnected with the physical working conditions. Pennock and Dickson decided to consult Elton Mayo, a Professor of Industrial Research at the Harvard Business School. The results of the lighting experiments gave rise to the subsequent stages of the studies (Mayo, 1933).

THE RELAY ASSEMBLY TEST ROOM

Research here began in 1927. The researchers consulted six female workers and involved them in the experiments, adopting a friendly attitude and keeping them up to date with their progress. The women were isolated from their colleagues and placed in a separate work area. The objective was to find out the effects on productivity of varying physical working conditions. The researchers imposed 13 changes to the working conditions, including the introduction of rest pauses and refreshments, variations in the timing and duration of lunch breaks and alterations to the working week. Regardless of the changes, productivity increased. Eventually, the researchers realized two things. Firstly, the increases in productivity were due to the extra attention that the workers were receiving. It made them feel special and important. This phenomenon came to be known as the 'Hawthorne Effect'. Secondly, rather than observing physical working conditions, they had been studying the attitudes and motivations of the workers.

THE INTERVIEW PROGRAMME

These results prompted the company, in 1928, to introduce an interview programme, the objective of which was to discover employees' attitudes towards their physical working conditions and towards their supervisors. During the interviews, employees were encouraged to discuss these matters inside a period of what was originally intended to be 30 minutes. In fact, the friendly and sympathetic attitudes of the interviewers drew out the employees' feelings to the extent that the 30-minute schedules tripled in length. The programme had to be abandoned in the end, but not before 20,000 interviews had taken place. The objective of gaining a wealth of information was certainly achieved. Workers had spoken freely, giving their opinions of working conditions and the quality of supervision, but had also held forth on a host of other issues too. The main message that came through from the interviews was that interpersonal relations were a significant factor in the study of employees' attitudes.

THE BANK WIRING OBSERVATION ROOM

The study of 14 men working in the bank wiring room took place in 1932 and had an extremely interesting outcome. They too were removed and placed in a separate observation room, where the physical working conditions of their usual working area had been replicated. The study lasted for six months and the objective was to observe them working under normal conditions. It soon became clear that the group had its own norms and had developed its own rules and patterns of behaviour in terms of social relations. They were offered more money for extra productivity, but despite this incentive their output was markedly below their obvious capabilities. Clearly, informal group pressures on individual members counted for more than the perceived value of the incentives. The men had formed themselves into cliques in which informal leaders emerged naturally, leading with the consent and approval of their fellows. Undoubtedly, these observations had worrying implications for managers. 'Informal' or 'social' groups such as these could easily undermine the authority of the managers and supervisors, who had thought previously that what was produced was the result of their exhortations, coupled with the skills of the workers and the conditions in which they operated. Now, it was clear that there was another source of power in the organization.

Personnel counselling

The final stage of these famous studies took place in 1936 and was based on what had been learned from the first four stages. The objective was to improve employee relations, and the method of achieving this was to introduce a programme of personnel counselling. In this, the counsellors invited employees to express any problems that they had at work, with a view to helping them to resolve them. Eventually, the programme led to improvements in the relationships between the employees and the managers and supervisors.

One of the most important aspects of the human relations approach is an understanding of the major theories of motivation. Remember that we are discussing *management* theories and that the main interest of managers is to achieve the objectives they have been given, by maximizing on their resources, and this includes the human resource, since it is only through the work performance of their staff that managers can achieve their objectives. Principally, therefore, managers are interested in how they can get the best possible work effort from employees; in other words, how to motivate them to work to the best of their ability. Those who study human motivation are trying to gain an understanding of what makes people do what they do (see chapter 5).

System Theory and Contingency Approaches

These two approaches are grouped together because of the strong conceptual relationship between them. It is safe to say that in terms of management development and managerial practice, systems and contingency approaches have superseded the classical and human relations approaches, although elements of the earlier works have been subsumed into modern management strategies, particularly into human resource management ideas, which are still developing.

ORGANIZATIONS AS SYSTEMS

The main principle upon which this approach is based is that the organization is seen as sets of interacting, interdependent systems and subsystems. The structure of the theory draws an analogy with human physiology. In both cases, the organization and the human body, the complete system contains a number of subsystems. The human body's main subsystems include, for example, the central nervous system, the circulatory system, the respiratory system and so forth, all of which interact and are interdependent. Functional changes that take place in any one system will affect the functioning of the others. In the case of the organization, the subsystems include, among others, production, marketing and the accounting system.

It is important to consider the question of the boundaries between systems and subsystems, because it is in this context that the human–organization analogy becomes slightly less clear. Obviously, if we are looking at human beings, aeroplanes or motor cars, there are no problems in distinguishing one total system from another and, indeed, in the case of, say, the motor car, it is easy for us to distinguish one subsystem from another: 'here is the carburettor and there is the cooling system', and so forth – almost as easy as finding geographic boundaries on a map. In such overt cases, the boundaries are matters of fact, but the boundaries between organizational subsystems are not so visible and can be changed by internal strategic decisions, perhaps to restructure the total system. What makes them less visible, however, is that the location of the boundaries is based on *relationships* as well as physical fact. According to this theory, therefore, what we should see is a total system (the whole organization), which interfaces with the environment, and a set of subsystems that are contained within the whole organization's boundary. In system theory, boundaries are referred to as *interfaces*. The location of interfaces determines where one subsystem ends and another begins. The interactions and interdependencies of subsystems often create a 'grey' area between the two which needs to be managed. Interfaces can be very sensitive and ambiguous areas in terms of the roles and responsibilities of individuals. People working at these internal boundaries relate to other subsystems, such as the various departments. Others working at the external boundaries relate to the environment in terms of either 'inputs' at one end of the total system or 'outputs' at the other.

OPEN AND CLOSED SYSTEMS

Whether a system is *open* or *closed* depends on whether or not it interacts with its environment. As the terms imply, open systems interact with their environment and closed systems do not. A closed system is one that is self-contained and self-supporting and does not need to interact with the environment. Here, we are mainly interested in open systems and, in particular, with open social systems, such as the business organization. The main characteristics of the business organization as an open system are that it takes things in from its environment, such as raw materials, information and people, changes them and then returns them to the environment. A manufacturing plant, for example, takes in the necessary supplies of metals, plastics or whatever it needs to make its products, subjects them to a change process that turns them into the products and then returns them to the environment by selling them. A simple model of such an organization as an open system is shown below in figure 2.1).

The 'change process' in the centre of the figure refers to the internal organizational systems that are there to combine human skills, machinery and raw materials and convert them into the products and services that are the organization's output. The organization changes the people in that it adds to their wealth, which they spend on other organizations' products and services, develops them in terms of knowledge, skills, ideas and so forth, and exposes them to its unique culture, so that the changed individuals return to the environment and influence it in a new way.

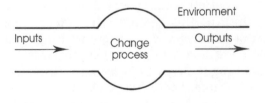

Figure 2.1 A simple model of an open system.

While undoubtedly the organization as a whole, interacting with its environment, is an open system, since it depends upon its environment for a continuous supply of inputs and for the continuous receipt of its outputs, the subsystems within it can be seen as open or closed, depending on their purpose and the nature of their activities. If, for example, an organization produces a new product, it needs to make that product known to its customers. This is the job of the marketing department, which actively deals with the environment, largely by importing and exporting information. In this way, the marketing department can be seen as an open system. Similarly, the personnel department makes known the organization's vacant positions and interacts with the environment as it handles the recruitment and selection processes that lead to the import of people. There are subsystems, however, that do not interact with the environment. These are the subsystems that serve the organization's internal processes: the system of payment, accounting, quality assurance and so forth. Some writers see these subsystems as 'closed' in that they are relatively independent of the external environment, while others see them as 'open' in that the whole internal organization is the environment with which they interact. As we said above, subsystems within an organization have interfaces (the boundaries), some of which butt against those of other subsystems, while others overlap where interaction takes place.

Writers on systems theory include Katz and Kahn (1978) and Trist et al. (1963). The work of these writers points to the complex nature of organizations and the degree of understanding that is required if those who manage them are to succeed.

CONTINGENCY THEORIES

No one would argue with the assertion that this approach has resulted from the findings of the system theorists; indeed, some writers do not draw a distinction between system and contingency approaches. Like system theorists, contingency theorists accentuate the complexity of organizations, especially in relation to the subsystems within them. They are, however, concerned with identifying effective and appropriate managerial styles and designs for organizations. Contingency theorists point out the differences between organizations in terms of the internal activities that have to take place in order to convert inputs to outputs. These activities, they say, will vary in nature and scale from one organization to another, according to the interrelationships between: (1) technological factors, (2) human skills and motivation, (3) organizational design and (4) the external environment.

While classical theorists endeavoured to find *the best way* to manage organizations, contingency theorists say that there is *no single best way* to manage all or any part of an organization. They say that the interrelationships between and among a large number of situational factors, within and without the organization, influence performance and that these interrelationships are different for all organizations. How, therefore, can there be a 'best way' to manage? These interrelationships produce a situation for the organization that demands a particular organization design and a particular managerial style. 'Style' and 'design' are all important, since they have to be appropriate to the situation. Situations change, of course, and managers need to be flexible so that they can adapt to those changes. Theorists produce models that accentuate differences between organizations; managers can use these models to examine their own organizations and make adjustments where necessary. The most well-known contingency theorists are: Lawrence and Lorsch (1969), Woodward (1980), Burns and Stalker (1966) and Perrow (1967).

Human Resource Management

Nobody 'invented' HRM. It has evolved from the fundamental principles that are rooted in past approaches, and it is still developing. The principles that have been selected for inclusion in HRM are those that are regarded as appropriate for the management of *today's* organizations. The original, classical approaches, such as those of Taylor and Fayol, are held together by sets of firmly stipulated principles, each of which was based on the ideas of a single individual. HRM has many proponents and is more flexible. The approach has created considerable confusion among managers and academics, some of whom believe that HRM is just another name for personnel management. Others believe that it is a new way of seeking out and tackling personnel-type problems and that, as such, it will eventually displace personnel management as an organizational function. Symptomatic of this lack of understanding is the sign on the door, which used to read 'Personnel Manager', and now reads 'Human Resource Manager', even though the duties and responsibilities of the incumbent have not changed.

Armstrong (1988) clarifies the HRM concept, by saying that it is based upon four fundamental principles:

1   Human resources are the most important assets an organization has and their effective management is the key to its success.
2   Organizational success is most likely to be achieved if the personnel policies and procedures of the enterprise are closely linked with, and make a major contribution to, the achievement of corporate objectives and strategic plans.
3   The corporate culture and the values, organizational climate and managerial behaviour that emanate from that culture will exert a major influence on the achievement of excellence. This culture must be managed, which means that continuous effort, starting from the top, will be required to get the values accepted and acted upon.
4   Continuous effort is required to achieve integration – getting all the members of the organization involved and working together with a sense of common purpose. This point was originally made by Douglas McGregor (1960), when he defined his principles of integration as: 'The creation of conditions such that the members of the organization can achieve their own goals best by directing their efforts towards the success of the enterprise.'

Certainly, HRM is a theory that has more to do with the perception of individuals in their own right, rather than through group representation in the organization-wide context, and rather than with 'people management' in the exclusive personnel management context. HRM regards the employees as an asset in which the organization has invested; a resource, rather than a cost that has to be kept to a bare minimum. HRM theorists see the success of the organization as a *mutuality of interest*, between the organization and its employees. In fact, mutuality of interest is emphasized as an important feature of the theory, in terms of goals, rewards and responsibilities. HRM managers set goals, provide rewards and allocate responsibilities which are in the mutual interests of the organization and its employees.

The organization's human resource strategy should be a reflection of its main business strategy. This implies a comparative assessment of corporate and employee values, with a view to achieving compatibility through the management of the culture, to make it more conducive to the achievement of objectives. The most well-known approach in these respects is organization development (OD), which is based on the values and beliefs of the behavioural sciences, as are some other strategies designed to achieve business success.

We said earlier that there is no one best way to do anything in organizations, and that includes management. All situations demand their own relative methods of managing, and HRM, despite its obvious flexibility, will not be relevant in all organizations. It is true to say, therefore, that while HRM as the main influence that determines how the organization will be managed is new, there is nothing new within it. It is a hybrid that has just begun to flower, although it may look out of place in some gardens.

Summary of the History of Management Thought

One of the most noticeable features of the history of management thinking is the gradual departure from the rigid and mechanistic approaches of the classical school. Everything, it is said, is a product of its time, and it is obvious that as the century has progressed, organizations have proliferated, increased in variety and grown in size, thereby becoming progressively more difficult to manage. The reader should try to understand the variety of approaches, without seeing them as discrete entities, with one cutting off another's existence as it arose. Aspects of all of these approaches still operate in organizations today: for example, F.W. Taylor's work led to the advent of PBR schemes, and updated versions of these schemes are still used in today's manufacturing organizations. The human relations approach, in the wake of the work of Elton Mayo and others, followed the classical school and, it is said, was itself superseded by system theory; and yet it is hard to find an organization that totally ignores the findings of the human relations approach. Perhaps it is best to regard each approach in its own right, with its own value and appropriateness for a particular situation. Certainly, they should not be seen to be in competition with each other, as if one is 'better' than another.

Notes

1 Clearly, it is not expected that readers will be able to obtain this book, but since Fayol is referred to so frequently in management texts, it is not necessary.
2 In an experiment such as this, a control group is a group that is subjected to normal conditions, while the experimental group, as its name suggests, is the one that experiences the varied conditions. The control group is included so that any variations in outcomes within the experimental group can be measured against the norms of the control group.

References

Armstrong, M.A. 1988: *Handbook of Personnel Management Practice*, 3rd edn. London: Kogan Page.

Burns, T. and Stalker, G.M. 1966: *The Management of Innovation*. London: Tavistock.

Cole, G.A. 1986: *Management Theory and Practice*. DP Publications.

Fayol, H. 1949: *General and Industrial Management*. London: Pitman.

Gilbreth, F. and Gilbreth, L. 1917: *Applied Motion Study*. New York: Sturgis and Walton.

Katz, D. and Kahn, R.L. 1978: *The Social Psychology of Organisations*, 2nd edn. Chichester: Wiley.

Lawrence, P.R. and Lorsch, J.W. 1969: *Organization and Environment*. Homewood, IL: Irwin.

Mayo, E. 1933: *The Human Problems of an Industrial Civilization*. New York: Macmillan.

McGregor, D. 1960: *The Human Side of Enterprise*. Maidenhead: McGraw-Hill.

Perrow, C. 1967: *Organisational Analysis – A Sociological View*. London: Tavistock.

Taylor, F.W. 1911: *The Principles of Scientific Management*. New York: Harper & Bros.

— 1947: *Scientific Management*. New York: Harper & Row.

Trist, E.L., Higgin, G., Pollock, H.E. and Murray, H.A. 1963: *Organisational Choice*. London: Tavistock.

Weber, M. 1964: *The Theory of Social and Economic Organisation*. London: Macmillan.

Woodward, J. 1980: *Industrial Organisation – Theory and Practice*, 2nd edn. Oxford: Oxford University Press.

3

Management Processes and Functions

Introduction

For the personnel specialist to be effective in advising and assisting managers, knowledge, understanding and awareness of what managers actually do is an essential prerequisite. The twentieth-century approaches to managing organizations that are described in the first two chapters hopefully will provide a setting for the contents of this chapter, which describes management processes and functions in today's organizations.

Definitions

We said earlier that management is a process; that it is something you *do*, rather than something you are. E.F.L. Brech (1975) defines management as, 'A social process entailing responsibility for the effective and economic planning and regulation of the operations of an enterprise, in fulfilment of given purposes or tasks, such responsibility involving:

(a) judgement and decision in determining plans and in using data to control performance and progress against plans
(b) the guidance, integration, motivation and supervision of the personnel composing the enterprise and carrying out its operations'.

Drucker (1977), says that managers have three tasks to perform: '(i) to fulfil the specific purpose and mission of the organisation, (ii) to make work productive and the worker achieving, and (iii) to manage social impacts and social responsibilities.'

Some writers believe that it is fallacious to attempt to define management, since it is 'so amorphous and shifting' (Heller, 1972). Others say that management is, 'achieving results through people', but that is only a part of it. It is true that managing the human resource probably is the most important function that managers have, since they cannot achieve their objectives without their employees' cooperation, but, as we shall see, the manager is also involved in other tasks. Finally, it has been said that management is 'The accomplishment of desired objectives by establishing an environment favourable to performance by people operating in organised groups' (Koontz and O'Donnell, 1955). This implies that the manager's main function is not to dash about giving orders, but to create and sustain a working environment in which people will want to work, which is a reference to the climate of the place and the manager's style.

According to Edgar Schein (1980), the main purposes of any organization are to survive and develop: 'The survival and development of any organisation, ultimately is determined by its ability to continue to be of use to its prime beneficiaries.' Also, organizations survive and develop only when they continue to perform some useful function for their customers and clients. These statements have strong implications for managers. They imply that the environmental needs that are met by the organization should be analysed continually and new needs identified. Managers then will know what has to be done if the enterprise is to meet those needs and, thereby, succeed. What *needs* to be done, however, may turn out to be more than what *can* be done when the manager has assessed the resources that he or she can call upon. Resources are scarce, and no matter how good the manager may be at achieving an optimal distribution of resources, there still will be a discrepancy between what needs to be done and what actually can be done.

When managers look outside of the organization to identify the demands of the environment, they will have created some of those demands themselves. New products and services come on to the market frequently. Sometimes they are modified versions of existing goods, or they may be totally new. 'Product life cycle' is a marketing concept, that describes the rate at which various goods and services become obsolete.

Part of the concept of management then, means that managers are involved in four major areas of responsibility; they have to:

1   Discover what *needs* to be done (to meet demands from the external environment)
2   Assess available resources and decide what *can* be done
3   *Get* things done (through people)
4   Assess what *has been done*.

These responsibilities hold true for managers at all levels. Top managers adopt them when they are formulating strategy, middle managers when they are running their departments and functions, and first line managers when they are running their sections of the enterprise. To carry out these responsibilities efficiently and effectively, managers need to be skilled in a variety of functions, which include, *planning*, *organizing*, *directing* and *controlling*. These four functions are linked together by *coordination*.

- *Planning*. This includes setting objectives and making decisions about how those objectives are to be achieved. The decisions that are made now are designed to determine what will happen in the future. Plans, therefore, will include the formulation of strategies, objectives, policies and procedures.
- *Organizing*. In this context, organizing means developing a structure through which the work may be carried out, allocating the work to various staff members, delegating tasks and giving people commensurate authority to carry them out. Organizing also involves decision making and, along with the planning function, gives the manager his or her main coordinating thrust.
- *Directing*. It is within this function that the manager 'gets things done' through people. It means actually 'directing' – showing the way. Directing, therefore, includes the use of such skills as leadership, motivation, communication, training, coaching and counselling people.
- *Controlling*. Under this heading, the manager monitors and assesses the degree to which the predetermined objectives have been met. This function identifies any gaps there may be between the work that was planned and the work that was actually completed. Decisions then have to be made about how to close those gaps in the future.

From what we have said about these four functions, it is clear that decision making is extremely important, and we will discuss this further. Other activities, such as communicating, leading and motivating, are examined in later chapters.

Decision Making

In the field of management studies, decision making is an important and complex subject. When asked what managers do, some say, 'They make decisions'; when we look at the four managerial functions outlined above, we can see that decision making must feature strongly in carrying them out. Managers, however, also have to be effective, and their effectiveness is usually determined by the quality of the decisions they make. The kinds of decision that managers make vary from one level of responsibility and from one function to another. Decisions may be categorized, and when we do that we begin to see their importance in terms of say, the consequences of making poor decisions, and the effect that managers' decisions have on other people.

Decisions may be categorized in several ways. Firstly, we can place them on a dimension, ranging from simple to complex. Simple decisions are those that are made on the basis of a quick assessment of an immediate situation that needs to be dealt with. These are often referred to as 'on the hoof' decisions, such as allowing a minor expenditure, or agreeing a day off for a key worker. They are needed quickly, made on the basis of very little information – just a few clues and cues – and usually form part of the manager's day-to-day duties. Complex decisions are those that are made about important, and usually longer-term, issues. A good quality complex decision may be made after gathering and weighing the significance of a considerable amount of relevant information. When, for example, an issue has been thoroughly investigated by a specialist who has written a report that contains recommendations for action, a number of managers may read the report and then get together to make decisions about the best way forward. A high-level complex decision may affect the organization's strategy: 'Should we enter this or that market?' or 'Should we merge with this or that company'. A middle-level complex decision could be related to changing a supplier, or delegating a project. It should be emphasized that the 'simple-to-complex' concept, is a dimension and not a dichotomy, and that decisions, therefore, may be more or less simple or more or less complex, according to where they appear on the dimension.

Decisions also may be *strategic* or *operational*. Strategic decisions are usually complex, affecting the medium- and long-term future of the organization. Such decisions are made by the top managers of the organization, usually on the advice of its senior specialists, such as the finance, marketing, technical and personnel managers. They are, in other words, the decisions that determine the corporate strategy: identifying goals, setting objectives and formulating policy. Decisions relating to the selection, promotion and transfer of staff are part of the human resource strategy. Operational decisions are made by line managers and are related to achieving objectives and managing within the policy framework. Typical operational decisions are about work methods, productivity, grievance handling, budgeting, work allocation, and so forth.

Decisional Risk

When we make decisions, we have to live with them afterwards. Poor quality decisions at strategic level can cost millions, while at operational level, the cost may be less, although still unacceptable. Launching a new product or service, for example, is always a risk; even when the decision was made after long-term research into the market, the production of prototypes, dry runs, pilot studies and so forth, there is always the risk of a flop. Betamax video cassette tapes and the Sinclair electric car are examples of risk-taking that resulted in costly flops. There is also an element of risk in personnel decisions. Consider, for example, the cost of making a poor quality selection decision. Recruitment advertising is expensive; so is administration and the time of the managers and specialists involved, occupational tests, medical examinations, and interviewees' travelling expenses. And having borne those costs, there is then the cost of severing the wrongly selected individual, which is followed by the cost of going through the whole procedure again, when we try to recruit the *right* person.

It is safe to say, however, that decisional risk reduces as we move down the organization. Usually, costs are not so high and often the decisions are not of the kind that normally are associated with risk.

How Decisions are Made

The manner in which decisions are reached varies from public to private sector and from one organization to another. Inevitably, however, such variations are greatest in the private sector, where decision making may vary even from one part of an organization to another. In the public sector, decision making is governed by rules and regulations, while the private sector, which contains a much larger number and wider variety of organizations, enjoys considerable freedom. These differences may be in who is involved in decision making. The culture of the organization and the managerial style of the chief executive are important determinants of who becomes involved. In some companies, especially small to medium-sized set-ups, a small group at the top will make all important decisions, while in others, individual managers decide things for themselves. Managers who lead groups and teams may bring decision making into their leadership style, when, for example, they consult the group members before making decisions that affect them.

DECISION MAKING PROCESS

The process contains three main stages. (1) Firstly, *why* is the decision needed? It may be that a problem needs to be solved. The most important aspect of this stage is the correct and accurate identification of the problem. Sometimes, this involves an investigative sub-stage. (2) Once the problem is known, it should be analysed in order to clarify its nature. (3) The various possible solutions should be examined and the possible consequences of each weighed before deciding which is to be used. Going back to the 'simple-to-complex' dimension, we can see that where the decisions are simple, the process may be carried out speedily, while complex decisions will take more time. Managers are well advised to adopt this three-stage process, no matter how simple or obvious the problem may appear to be.

References

Brech, E.F.L. 1975: *The Principles and Practice of Management*, 3rd edn. London: Longman.
Drucker, P. 1977: *People and Performance: The Best of Peter Drucker on Management*. London: Heinemann.
Heller, R. 1972: *The Naked Manager*. London: Barrie and Jenkins.
Koontz, H. and O'Donnell, C. 1955: *Principles of Management*. New York: McGraw-Hill.
Schein, E.H. 1980: *Organisational Psychology*, 3rd edn. Englewood Cliffs, NJ: Prentice Hall.

4

Communication

Here, we aim to provide an understanding of the importance of effective communication in the organization. We examine the various kinds of communication, including official and informal channels and structures, interpersonal, written, verbal and non-verbal communication. We explain how and why people sometimes withhold information and create barriers to effective communication, and why attempts at communicating sometimes fail.

Definition

Communication takes place when a message or idea is *transmitted* by one person and *received and understood* by another, *without loss of integrity*. It is something which, superficially, seems simple but in fact is hard to achieve with consistency.

In all organizations, there is a structure that indicates the division of labour and a set of superior–subordinate relationships. In addition, the structure indicates the official communication system, in terms of who is accountable to whom. There is, therefore, a need for cooperation and coordination, particularly between those who plan the work and those who do it: senior managers and middle managers, line and staff managers and operators. Experience shows, however, that efforts to pass on information often fail.

The Communication Process

To understand why this is, we need to attain a deeper appreciation of the concept of communication. The above definition tells us that communication is a two-ended concept. There is a sender and a receiver. The channel between the sender and the receiver is called the medium. Media may be vocal, written, graphical or 'implied', and should be selected to suit the purpose. This is not always easy, indeed there are people in the field of communication who specialize in media selection.

FORMULATING AND SENDING

Someone gets an idea and wishes to communicate it to someone else. Firstly, the idea has to be turned into a message. Next, the message is transmitted, usually using words, which are spoken, written or both. The recipient of the message then has to interpret its meaning, which is the stage at which integrity can be reduced, or even totally lost. The term 'integrity' refers to the true meaning of the message, and it can be lost if:

- the wrong medium is chosen;
- the sender fails to allow for the ability of the receiver to understand it;
- the receiver is distracted by something;
- the credibility or authority of the sender is low in the perception of the receiver;
- the receiver regards the message as unimportant.

The intention of the sender is that the receiver should turn the message back into the original idea, but this cannot happen unless the receiver's perception of the message is the same as that of the sender. Sometimes, the individual is both the sender and the receiver. For example, when an artist gets an idea, he or she attempts to produce it in some graphic or other tangible form, but artists are never totally satisfied with their work. Most of them will tell you that when you are holding something in your hand, it is never so beautiful as it was when it was in your mind. Transmission reduces integrity. Good communication takes place when genuine efforts to reduce the harmful effects of transmission are successful.

INTERPRETATION

Listening is just as important a part of communication as sending. It is important, therefore, for the receiver of a message to be 'tuned in' to the sender. For example, we sometimes switch on the radio and find that it is tuned between two channels. We can hear the noise of both channels, but cannot interpret the meaning of either. There is nothing wrong at the sender's end of the process, but to get the message we want, we have to turn the appropriate knob, until the sender can be heard clearly. In the same way, managers and subordinates need to be on the same wavelength if communication is to be effective. This means that they need to get to know each other, so that each understands the other in terms of their verbal styles, knowledge of what is going on around them, and the meanings behind their facial expressions.

Receivers attribute credibility and importance to a message in accordance with their perception of the sender. Rosabeth Moss Kanter (1984) points out that the first thing that senior managers do when they receive an idea from below is look at how far down the line the idea originated. If it is 'too far down', they dismiss it, saying, 'after all, if the idea was any good at all, we up here would have thought of it first'. What they should be doing, says Kanter, instead of considering where the idea has *come from*, is to examine where it might be capable of *going to*. Thus we can see that personalizing a message in this way can inhibit progress and reduce effectiveness.

Barriers to Good Communication

Above, we have seen reasons why communication sometimes fails, but there are many more, including:

Motivation, in which the reason for the communication is to initiate action. The message may be understood fully, but nothing happens because the receiver is not motivated to take action. This kind of message, then, should contain an element of motivation.

Indifference, in which the receiver is not interested in the meaning of the message. Sometimes this is a feature of the recipient's personality, and, difficult though it can be, the sender has to try to overcome this barrier by indicating persuasively that the message carries importance for the receiver.

Sensitivity, in which the sender and the receiver are insensitive to the non-verbal reactions of each other. A solo performer, for example, is sensitive to the reactions of his or her audience and may modify the routine accordingly. In the same way, a lecturer has to be sensitive to the students' level of interest in, and understanding of, what he or she is talking about, and this is assessed by their non-verbal reactions. There is no difference between these examples and that of a manager talking to a subordinate. Without such sensitivity, communication will not take place.

Distraction, in which the medium is distorted by extraneous noise or other interference. In this sense, *where* the message is delivered can be important. Would you attempt to talk about an important issue on a noisy factory floor? Or would you choose the comparative peace of an office environment? Where there is distraction, the receiver usually gets only part of the message, which can be more harmful than if the message was not delivered at all.

Interpretation, in which the receiver, by projecting his or her own feelings into the interpretation of the message, corrupts its true meaning. Often, this is done without conscious control, and the antagonism that results is attributed to an attempt at confrontation, while the true intention was to be fair and reasonable. This seldom happens between people who are on the same wavelength.

Formal Communication

This generally takes place up and down the hierarchical order of the organization, from superior to subordinate and vice versa, often referred to as *vertical* communication; and horizontally, from one department or person to another, both of whom are around the same hierarchical level, which is referred to as *lateral* communication. Both have problems.

The effectiveness of vertical communication varies with what we call *organizational distance*, which is the distance created by the number of levels, or strata, through which the message has to pass. Messages lose their integrity at every level, where they are 'filtered', 'embroidered' or altered in some other way. Individuals, as they pass on the message, alter the form of words to suit their own purposes, which may be to play down or exaggerate the importance of particular aspects of it. Recent 'delayering' or 'flattening' of organizational structures has helped to solve these problems, although the determined efforts of those with an internal political axe to grind still find a way of creating barriers.

In the case of lateral communication, barriers are produced by departmental loyalties causing information to be withheld, in the misplaced belief that 'knowledge is power'. The saying certainly is true, but what is described above represents the use of power for illegitimate purposes, whereas it is the purposes of the organization as a whole that are legitimate and, of course, of supreme importance. For this last reason, it is vital for good quality lateral communication to be established and maintained.

I People should be trained to communicate effectively. Modern approaches include training in interpersonal skills, including non-verbal communication; understanding formal systems of communication; and team or group briefing, in which messages are cascaded down, through the organization's structure, group by group. If the structure is formulated to be complementary to good communication, a briefing system can be extremely effective.

Communication Methods

The methods used to communicate may take any of the forms referred to at the beginning of this chapter. Firstly, we will look at written and oral communication, which can appear in the shape of memoranda, letters, incoming telephone messages, project reports, the annual report and accounts, house journals, posters, notice-board messages and training instruction booklets, casual conversations, interviews, training sessions, briefing sessions, project presentations, work allocation sessions, meetings, negotiations and appraisal reviews.

The advantages of written communications are that they:

- do not lend themselves to politically motivated alteration;
- represent a clear record of the message(s);
- allow a longer period for the recipient to assess the meaning;
- can be re-read if the recipient forgets the content of the message;

- can be read at the recipient's convenience.

The disadvantages are that they:

- are easily ignored;
- can be lost, or placed in the pile that the recipient 'will sort out one day';
- can be misunderstood;
- may be seen by outsiders;
- are cold and impersonal.

It has been said that face-to-face interaction is the most superior form of communication and obviously, written methods lack the advantages of this. But in cases where the content of the communication is long or complicated, putting it in writing offers a distinct advantage. Oral communication, on the other hand has the following advantages:

- it allows for verbal and non-verbal feedback between the communicating parties;
- the message can be altered immediately, where necessary;
- the personal contact offers human relations advantages;
- more of the message is received and understood;
- the message can be repeated in several ways to confirm understanding.

The disadvantages are:

- the contact can worsen a poor relationship;
- there is no record of the message having been delivered;
- the recipient has nothing to refer to afterwards;
- often there are limitations on the time taken to deliver the message;
- it can be costly in terms of employees' time.

Experience shows that if the same message is delivered using both written and oral media, more of the integrity is retained. Delivering a message face-to-face and following it up with a confirmatory memo should be regarded as good communication. Two of the essentials of effective communication, therefore, are good writing and interpersonal skills.

At this stage, it is worth reviewing the reasons why communication sometimes fails:

- People hold on to information in order to achieve power over others, so that actions and decisions may be taken only on the basis of the information as they care to issue it, which usually is in a piecemeal fashion. This prevents people from knowing why they are doing what they are doing; managing their time, because they do not know when the task will finish; and cooperating with the total intention behind the task. With-holding is a demotivator that inhibits effectiveness.

- People playing the role of the person who never makes a mistake, by thinking (usually wrongly) that keeping information from a superior provides self-protection when a mistake has been made.
- Inept handling of interpersonal relations.
- Protecting one's personal image by concealing potentially embarrassing information.
- Poor command of one's own language, creating misunder-standing.
- Failing to pass on information on the grounds that it would put a competing colleague at an advantage.
- Wrongly assuming knowledge on the part of others.

Listening

Earlier, we mentioned the importance of people being sensitive to each other's reactions. Such sensitivity is an essential ingredient of effective listening. Firstly, the situation has to be created in which effective, or *active* listening can take place. Active listen-ing occurs when one person hears and understands what another is saying, because he or she genuinely wishes to under-stand. In a one-to-one situation, active listening, coupled with what is called the *client-centred* approach, can be very effective. The client-centred approach allows one person to listen while the other talks, for most of the time. In this way, the talker 'talks out' his or her problems, while the listener adopts an open and encouraging attitude, putting in the odd word of agreement or guidance towards a solution. It takes considerable practice to achieve this kind of situation, but it is a high-quality method of solving problems, and of drawing information up through the organization.

Anyone can sit behind a desk issuing directives to staff, telling them what to do. The difficult feat is to draw information and ideas upwards, from the staff. If a manager wishes to do this, he or she must learn to listen actively to the employees.

Exhibit 4.1 Active listening skills

1   Keep your input to the conversation brief and simple, without being discourteous
2   Do not interrupt the speaker; you may divert him or her away from their true intention
3   Do not attack the speaker. If something is unclear, rephrase the statement, ideally in the form of a question, and wait for an answer
4   Be sensitive to the emotional as well as the factual content of what the person is saying, but do not attempt to rationalize things on the person's behalf
5   Wait until the speaker has finished before contradicting what has been said
6   Avoid confrontation – it puts people on the defensive
7   Study the person and observe what has *not* been said (avoidance, by the person, of some relevant fact or issue, may indicate his or her state of mind)
8   Ensure that there is mutual understanding of what is being said. Every now and then, briefly summarize your understanding and wait for the confirmation that you have got it right
9   Be honest. Do not search for reasons why the person could be wrong
10 Do not be judgemental about anything the person says, or says he or she thinks
11 Be non-directive; that is to say, avoid giving advice or instructions; ask questions and just nod or smile to encourage the person to speak further
12 Remain as unemotional as you can. Be supportive and encouraging, but beware of emotions; they are contagious and can cloud your understanding

In the group context, this can be done in joint consultative committees or works councils, but at an individual level, it becomes more personal. One of the greatest compliments that managers and subordinates can pay to each other is to give 100 per cent attention to what they are saying. Not only should people actively listen to each other, they should appear to be listening.

The brief set of guidelines in exhibit 4.1 might be useful to those who wish to develop listening skills. At first, these may appear to be difficult guidelines to follow. They call for consider-able restraint, especially from a listener who has a powerful personality, strongly held views of his or her own, and a position of some status. It should be remembered, however, that one learns little by talking. In some circumstances, the ability to adopt a calm and non-aggressive stance can be pushed to its limits, but with practice, and experiencing the value of its out-comes, the approach that these guidelines describe will develop, and become a valuable tool in your human relations, problem solving and decision making kits.

Summary

The communication process involves one person delivering a message to another, via an appropriate medium. Media vary from the written word, to face-to-face interaction, non-verbal commu-nication and graphical methods. All communication media have their advantages and disadvantages. When defined, communica-tion seems simple, but it is difficult to achieve in the light of interference from both natural and deliberately contrived sources. People withhold information in the mistaken belief that it gives them power over others, or to protect themselves from harm, embarrassment or a reduction in status. Communication fails because people are not trained in the appropriate skills, they select wrong media and do not all have a good command of their own language. In such circumstances, problems are created when recipients of messages misinterpret their meaning.

Client-centred approaches are recommended, when one is seeking information to solve a problem, make a decision or draw information up through the hierarchical order of the organization. On a group basis, joint consultation between managers and workers is recommended for the improvement of a healthy, two-way flow of information. On a one-to-one basis, communication becomes a personal issue which can have human relations value.

References

Kanter, R.M. 1984: *The Change Masters*. London: Allen and Unwin.

5

Motivation

Introduction

Motivation is the willingness to apply one's best efforts towards the achievement of a goal that satisfies an individual need. *Work motivation*, therefore, is the willingness to apply such efforts towards the achievement of the organization's goals; also at the same time, an individual need is satisfied.

One of the most important aspects of the human relations approach to management is an understanding of motivation. The main interest of managers is to achieve the objectives they have been given, by maximizing on their resources. This includes the human resource, since it is only through the work performance of their staff that managers can achieve their objectives. Principally, therefore, managers are interested in how they can get the best possible work effort from employees; in other words, how to motivate them to work to the best of their ability. Those who study human motivation are trying to gain an understanding of what makes people do what they do. After more than sixty years of study, both early and modern theories have produced just two basic motivational concepts. The first espouses what we can call *content theory* and the second, *process theory*. Research into work motivation is still ongoing but, so far, the results have been either extensions to, or modifications of, the two main theoretical approaches. Content and process theories are both valid and they go together. Modern theorists are preoccupied with integrating theories of motivation, which means that someone who is just beginning to study the subject first needs an understanding of the early theories.

Early Theories of Motivation

Motivation should be seen as an individual psychological phenomenon. It is something that happens internally when the
individual (1), is aroused by some stimulus and (2), makes a
decision about the style and direction of any action that might
result. Motivation is not to be confused with behaviour; indeed,
behaviour results from internally induced motivation. An understanding of both of the main approaches to motivation enables
one to predict behaviour with a reasonable degree of accuracy.
Content theories describe and categorize the environmental factors that generate 'arousal' in individuals, while process theories
– or 'choice' theories, as they are sometimes called – describe the
mental *processes* that take place when an individual is choosing
what action to take.

CONTENT THEORIES

Content theorists point to environmental factors as principal
motivators. When examining the workplace, for example, they
list the environmental factors that make up the total job situation, categorize them as 'extrinsic job factors' and 'intrinsic job
factors', and say that the individual is more or less motivated by
the presence or absence of desired factors. The degree to which
an individual is motivated to work will be determined by how
much he or she is aroused by particular job factors. Arousal is
an important concept in this respect and, indeed, some writers
refer to content theories as *arousal theories*. The most widely
known content theories are those of the American academics,
Abraham Maslow, Frederick Herzberg, Douglas McGregor and
Clayton P. Alderfer, whose research and publications took place
between the 1940s and the late 1980s.

When reading the following explanations of these theories, you
should notice that each theorist has his own terminology for
describing particular aspects of his theory. The theories have
some elements in common and yet different terms are used to
describe what appears to be the same concept. These differences
of expression are important in the sense that, firstly, their use in
general conversation identifies the theorist under discussion
and secondly, the relationship between one particular concept

and another within a theory is often different from its relationship with concepts within other theories.

Maslow's theory of growth motivation   Central to Maslow's theory is what he calls the 'hierarchy of needs'. Figure 5.1 is a familar sight in organizations' training areas, classrooms and textbooks on management and organizational behaviour. Maslow studied human motivation during the Second World War and first postulated a hierarchy of needs in 1943. He continued his research, however, for several years and his book, *Motivation and Personality*, was first published in 1951, with subsequent editions in 1972 and 1987.

Maslow says that we are motivated by the desire to satisfy particular needs. Studying the figure, we can see that he placed the needs in an order of priority, starting at the bottom of the hierarchy, saying that our motivations start with the desire to satisfy our physiological needs, such as those that are triggered by thirst, hunger, fear, fatigue and sexual arousal. When we are sure that our physiological needs will be met to our satisfaction, we will turn our attention to our need for 'safety', meaning our need to be in a secure, non-threatening environment. Next, we turn to 'love needs', by which he meant our need to know where we stand in terms of relationships with others. This is followed by the meeting of our 'esteem needs', which include the needs for self-esteem and for the respect of others. Finally, we try to satisfy

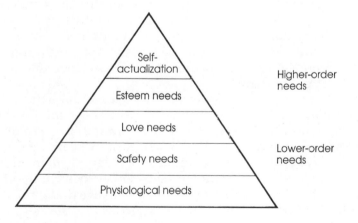

Figure 5.1 Maslow's hierarchy of needs.

our need for 'self-actualization', which Maslow equates with the need for self-fulfilment.

He said that our behaviour is motivated by our desire to have our needs met and that we try to achieve this progressively, in line with the 'bottom-up' order of priorities, hence it is 'a theory of *growth* motivation'. He put the needs he described into two categories: lower order needs and higher order needs.

The main theme of the theory is growth. Until we are sure that a particular set of needs is satisfied, or is going to be satisfied, the desire to have those needs met is the main cause of our behaviour. Once they have been met, we move on; as Maslow said, 'A satisfied need is no longer a motivator.' In his later deliberations, he modified his approach to the satisfaction of self-actualization needs, when he said that the achievement of self-actualization gave rise to a need for further achievement.

There are several criticisms of Maslow's theory. The structured progression through the lower order to higher order needs seems not to occur for many people. Research has shown that in the workplace a significant number are happy to accept the satisfactions provided by the meeting of lower order needs. People need to fulfil themselves, yes, but in many cases, that fulfilment is achieved by pursuing interests outside of the workplace.

It is also important to remember that individuals differ in their perceptions of what is 'satisfying'. For example, one person's perception of the quality and quantity of the factors that would satisfy their physiological needs will be different from that of another person. Levels of quality and quantity that would satisfy one person might be insufficient for another. Furthermore, people have different values and different perceptions of job factors, which cause them to have their own individual priorities. A job factor that is important to one person might be irrelevant to another.

Before moving on, it is worth noting that the satisfaction of lower order needs is probably not always at the forefront of our consciousness. As we said at the beginning of Chapter 1, we have organized things so that such needs will be met, and we tend to take them for granted. It is only when they are threatened that our attention is consciously focused upon them; whereas the case is different for those who live in the third world countries, many of whom do not know where the next meal is coming from. Despite these criticisms, Maslow's theory is still used as a starting point by those who teach and study theories of motivation, especially work motivation. Much of what he said provides useful material for discussion.

Frederick Herzberg and the motivation–hygiene theory   Herzberg was principally interested in job satisfaction. He wanted to know which job factors created feelings of satisfaction within employees and which created feelings of dissatisfaction. The information on which he based his 'motivation–hygiene' theory came from interviews with 220 accountants and engineers (Herzberg et al., 1957). The subjects were asked to recall things that had happened at work that produced feelings of satisfaction and dissatisfaction. The analysis indicated that some job factors produced satisfaction, while others led to dissatisfaction. Herzberg labelled the factors that produced satisfaction *motivators*, and those that produced dissatisfaction *hygiene factors*. These initial results prompted Herzberg to extend the studies to manual and clerical workers and the results were very similar to those for the accountants and engineers.

One of the important features of Herzberg's theory is that while the motivators induced positive feelings of satisfaction, the hygiene factors could only prevent dissatisfaction. Herzberg said that in this context, satisfaction and dissatisfaction were not opposite in meaning, in the sense that while the motivators provided satisfaction, the hygiene factors at best, were capable of producing a condition that he termed 'the absence of dissatisfaction'. What Herzberg's team discovered was that people will never say that they are totally satisfied with a particular set of working conditions. 'If they are not asking for more of anything, then they are not dissatisfied with the way things are.' Herzberg's research, which led to his postulation of the motivation–hygiene theory, produced several important motivators – 'important' because they featured most frequently in the subjects' responses. Remember that subjects were asked which job factors created feelings of satisfaction and which created feelings of dissatisfaction.

The most frequently occurring motivators (job factors that produced feelings of satisfaction), were:

- achievement
- recognition
- the work itself
- responsibility

- advancement

The most frequently occurring hygiene factors (those that can produce feelings of dissatisfaction or the absence of dissatisfaction) were:

- company policy and administration
- supervision – the technical aspects
- salary
- interpersonal relations – supervision
- working conditions

A distinction needs to be drawn between the individual's perceptions of the working environment on the one hand and the nature of the job itself on the other. Most workers see the work environment as the context in which the job is set; not only the physical environment but the *context* too, in terms of what motivation analysts call *extrinsic* job factors. That is to say that these factors are outside of the 'job–person unit' (see exhibit 5.1). Factors that the content theorists list in this respect we will call List A, and they include:

- salary
- general terms and conditions of employment
- the state of the working environment (clean, safe, etc.)

Exhibit 5.1 Extrinsic and intrinsic job factors

The factors in *List A* are contained within the work environment and the context in which the job is set
The factors in *List B* are contained within the job itself

- how the workforce is affected by company policy
- peer relationships
- the length of the working week
- the holiday entitlement
- the quality of the super-annuation scheme

Note that none of these factors is a central feature within the 'job–person unit'. Within the 'job–person unit' are what the content theorists call *intrinsic* job factors. These are not just the tasks that the individual has to carry out in order to do the job. They also include other things, as follows in List B:

- authority (the right amount for what I do)
- responsibility
- autonomy
- variety
- recognition
- prospects

We should see the person, therefore, as a unique individual working at a job, and whose perception of that job is different from his or her perception of the total working environment. If we relate Maslow's lower order needs to Herzberg's hygiene factors, we can see that both are 'extrinsic' job factors; likewise, when we relate Maslow's higher order needs to Herzberg's motivators, we see them both as 'intrinsic' job factors.

Douglas McGregor and Theory X and Theory Y X and Y are essentially a theory made up of two analyses of the attitudes of managers towards their staff. McGregor (1960) highlighted two types of assumption that managers made about employees.

The first type of manager he referred to as the 'Theory X' manager, who saw employees as lazy, indolent and work-shy, in need of constant prodding and continuous control and who were interested only in achieving security and avoiding responsibility.

The second type of manager he referred to as the 'Theory Y' manager, who saw employees as self-starters, to whom work was as natural as rest or play. Normally, they are committed to the achievement of organizational objectives and are willing to apply their initiative and creativity to those ends. They do not need constant supervision and will seek out challenges and responsibility.

The terms 'Theory X' and 'Theory Y' have become widespread in the field of management, and, probably more readily than academics, practising managers have accepted the underlying principles of McGregor's theory. McGregor's ideas were published in 1960 and have received considerable attention from academics. McGregor did not see managers as *either* Theory X or Theory Y; rather, X and Y were at each end of a dimension, on which all managers were to be found. Thus, managers were *more* or *less* inclined towards one end or the other. Other researchers and writers, particularly those in the field of leadership styles, have followed a similar principle.

Clayton P. Alderfer III and ERG Theory   Clearly, Alderfer's ideas are based on Maslow's need hierarchy. Essentially, what he did was to draw a parallel between Maslow's five categories of need and three categories of his own, which he referred to as Existence, Relatedness and Growth (E, R and G; Alderfer, 1972). His theory is often referred to as Alderfer's modified need hierarchy.

Existence needs are concerned with physiological, safety and security needs and cover all needs of a material nature that are necessary for human survival.

Relatedness needs mean those for love and belongingness (Maslow), and also mean social needs, such as relationships within the environment, including meaningful interpersonal relationships and affiliation needs.

Growth needs relate to achievement, recognition, the realization of potential and what Maslow called self-actualization.

While Alderfer saw motivation as a mechanism involving an individual's progress through the various categories, from the meeting of existence needs to those of growth, the principal difference between his ideas and those of Maslow was that the needs were more of a continuum than a hierarchy, and he also suggested that an individual's motivations to meet several needs can be activated concurrently. Another area of difference lies in his suggestion that individuals may also move *down* the continuum. In a case, for example, where an individual's striving to meet his or her growth needs is frustrated, the lesser category of need (relatedness), assumes a greater importance. Alderfer proposed further ramifications to his theory, some of which were in line with Maslow's ideas while others conflicted with them. The studies that were carried out to examine his proposals, with one main exception, produced results that neither supported nor refuted Maslow's need hierarchy. The exception that draws the distinction between Maslow and Alderfer is that lower order needs do not have to be satisfied before the motivation to reach a higher order need is activated. Earlier, we noted Maslow's premise that 'A satisfied need is no longer a motivator', and the research that was undertaken to examine Alderfer's ideas provided support for this, in that it found that lower order needs decrease in strength as they are satisfied.

Other content theories include McLelland's achievement motivation theory (1975), which identified motivational factors that were related to Maslow's love, esteem and self-actualization needs. These he called affiliation (N_{Aff}), power (N_{Pow}) and achievement (N_{Ach}), in which N = need.

R. Likert and participative management   Likert's theory had a significant impact on practising managers and academics. He proposed a theory in which he said that managers should encourage employees to participate in the decision making and problem solving processes, thus adding to their goals and giving them a sense of responsibility for the quality of the outcomes of the decisions to which they contributed. Unlike the 'authoritarian' manager who strictly separates 'planning' and 'doing' work (see Chapter 6), Likert's 'System 4', as he called it, integrates the planning and the doing of the work.

It is noticeable that there are aspects of some theories that can be related to others. Across time, theorists have improved and expanded upon the work of their predecessors, although even those who shared the same era seemed to share similar ideas. One favourite model through which many writers express this notion of similarity is shown in figure 5.2.

In principle, all of the content theorists relate motivation to the natural human desire to reduce emotions. We are born with the need to have all of our lower needs met; if we fail in that respect, we die. The motivated behaviour that leads to the satisfaction of our lower order needs is said to arise from our *primary drives*. As we learn, grow and become experienced, we develop other, secondary motives, which are referred to as *acquired drives*. While

Maslow	Herzberg	Alderfer
Self-actualization	Motivators	Growth
Esteem needs		Relatedness
Love needs	Hygiene factors	
Safety needs		Existence
Physiological needs		

Figure 5.2 Comparison of three 'content' theories.

everyone's primary motives are alike (we all need to survive), the socialization and personality development processes cause our acquired motives to be unlike each other's.

We develop prejudices and preferences, expectations and secondary needs, all of which are extremely influential in the determination of our behaviour. It would be easy to fall into the trap of thinking that a manager's job is made easy by the existence of theories of motivation. After all, cannot he or she simply manipulate the extrinsic factors until everyone is satisfied, or at least until they are not dissatisfied? Obviously, the answer to this is no. Extrinsic factors make up the situation, but individual differences determine how people will react to it. Next, we turn our attention to a set of motivation theories that focus more upon the individual's internal decision making processes, through which they make conscious choices about how they wish to behave.

Later Theories of Motivation

PROCESS THEORIES

The more we develop, the more we come to understand that our behaviour has consequences. Sometimes we enjoy the outcomes of our behaviour and sometimes we are hurt or saddened by them. This process of learning gives us the ability to predict the outcomes of our behaviour with a reasonable degree of accuracy, and we develop a set of expectancies that are related to the results of our actions. We learn that if we behave in a certain way, the likelihood of a particular expected outcome is raised

Exhibit 5.2

Jerry Reed was an hourly paid worker on a 40 hour, five-day week. One fine summer's morning, Jerry decided that instead of going to work, he would go to the seaside. He knew that as a result, his next pay packet would contain 20% less than usual, but he didn't mind that, because at the time, going to the seaside was what he preferred (and therefore chose) to do. In other words, it was the expected outcome that motivated Jerry to do what he did. Mind you, Jerry knew that he could not make a regular habit of going to the seaside. Why?

and, in fact, we learn that by varying our behaviour, we can pretty well vary the outcomes. The more experienced we become, the more accurate are our outcome predictions and, therefore, the more able we are to gain some element of control over them (see exhibit 5.2).

Expectancy theories of motivation According to what is said above, people are influenced by the outcomes they expect from their behaviour. What motivates us towards a particular course of behaviour, therefore, is a mental *process* through which we speculate or predict outcomes before we act. But we are multi-motivated and we are opportunistic. We have many concurrent needs and goals, and while our behaviour is motivated by our needs and goals, the opportunities to achieve them in accordance with our orders of priority do not arise in the same convenient order. It would be fallacious, therefore, to assume that the current behaviour of an individual is designed to meet his or her most pressing need.

The most well-known theories in work motivation are Victor H. Vroom's expectancy theory, which was further developed by L.W. Porter and E.E. Lawler; J.S. Adams's equity–inequity theory; and goal theory, sometimes referred to as goal-setting theories, postulated by E.A. Locke and G.P. Latham. We will start with Vroom's expectancy theory, since it provides a clear basis for understanding the main underlying principles of the various process theories.

Victor H. Vroom's expectancy theory While the content theorists are mainly concerned with the degree to which people are aroused by particular job factors, process theorists focus upon individuals' perceptions of, and preferences for, expected outcomes. Process theories are so called because they describe the individual's internal motivational processes. Expectancy theory was developed in the 1960s by Vroom, working in the United States.

Central to expectancy theory is the individual's selective perception of the relationships between his or her own *effort*, *performance* and the *rewards*.

Individuals differ in terms of the kinds of reward they value and, therefore, in terms of how strongly they are attracted to particular rewards, or outcomes. Vroom refers to this 'strength of attraction' as the *valence*. To some extent, the individual will believe that his or her behaviour will produce the desired outcome, and the strength of that belief he refers to as the *expectancy*. We know, from what was said above about how we learn to predict or *expect* outcomes through our experiences, that outcomes can be positive or negative – desirable or undesirable. If an item of behaviour produces a positive outcome, then we will try to repeat the behaviour in order to enjoy the outcome again. On the other hand, if the outcome is negative, then we will avoid the behaviour that produced it. In this context, according to Vroom, a *positive* valence is where an individual's preference is to achieve, rather than not to achieve, the outcome; a *negative* valence is where the individual prefers to avoid the outcome. *Zero* valence occurs when the individual feels unconcerned about or indifferent towards the achievement or non-achievement of the outcome.

There are variations on this theme which occur when an individual's experience of an outcome differs from his or her expectancy – where, for example, a person who expects to gain satisfaction from an outcome experiences little or no satisfaction from it; or conversely where a person who fails to avoid a particular outcome experiences satisfaction from it. Vroom said that valence is the strength of the anticipation of satisfaction from an outcome. In this context, Vroom says that *valence* and *value* are distinct from each other. From this point on, explanations of the theory become a little complex and, to the novice, may even seem cumbersome. To aid understanding, it is a good idea to learn and internalize the terminology that relates to the theory.

One outcome leads to another An individual who aims for excellence at work may experience satisfaction from putting in what is deemed to be an excellent performance. In this way, the quality of the performance, seen perhaps, in the form of high productivity, can be regarded as an outcome. But it is a *first-level* outcome; that is to say, it is an outcome that can lead to the achievement of a *second-level* outcome, which could be reward-related, in the form of money or promotion, which relates to the satisfaction of a need. A person who gains satisfaction from his or her (first-level) performance-related outcome may do so knowing that the achievement will lead to the (second-level) need-related outcome. Vroom's (1970) description of expectancy theory is as follows:

> Whenever an individual chooses between alternatives which involve uncertain outcomes, it seems clear that his behaviour is affected not only by his preferences among these outcomes but also by the degree to which he believes these outcomes to be possible. An expectancy is defined as a momentary belief concerning the likelihood that a particular act will be followed by a particular outcome. Expectancies may be described in terms of their strength. Maximal strength is indicated by subjective certainty that the act *will* be followed by the outcome, while minimal (or zero) strength is indicated by subjective certainty that the act *will not* be followed by the outcome.

Finally, it should be borne in mind that the valence, which is the strength of the expectation, is not enough to produce behaviour. Experience has taught people to expect certain outcomes as a result of certain behaviour, but the person has to *desire* the first-level and/or the second-level outcomes if action is to occur. After all, if an individual can predict the consequences of his or her own behaviour, possible undesirable outcomes will inhibit behaviour. Also, to achieve a desired performance-related, first-level outcome, an individual has to have the ability as well as the motivation.

On the basis of what has been said about expectancy theory, the model of behaviour that is depicted in figure 5.3 might further aid understanding.

The Porter and Lawler model of expectancy While the content theorists attempted to show that job satisfaction leads to improved performance, this further development of Vroom's

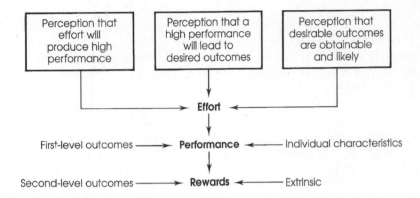

Figure 5.3 Expectancy theory – a model of behaviour.

ideas indicates that it is in fact performance that produces satisfaction. Porter and Lawler (1968) point out that effort alone is not enough to produce a good performance; the person has to be equipped with the right skills and have the kind of personality that is attracted by the second-level outcomes. They say that while there is a relationship between motivation, satisfaction and performance, all three are discrete variables and that the *levels* of motivation, satisfaction and performance are determined by the individual's perception of the outcome.

In the Vroom and the Porter and Lawler models of expectancy, rewards may be intrinsic or extrinsic, and different behaviours produce different expectancies. Depending on their personality characteristics and their ultimate aims, individuals variously prefer intrinsic and extrinsic rewards. One individual may behave in a particular way because he or she is aiming for an extrinsic, need-related reward, while another individual will behave differently because his or her aim is for an intrinsic, need-related reward. Also, one person may vary his or her behaviour to produce alternate intrinsic and extrinsic rewards.

J.S. Adams's equity–inequity theory This theory is based on the concept of fairness, or, more accurately, *a fair exchange*. We know that people expect certain outcomes from their behaviour, but what is their perception of those outcomes? In the work situation, for example, how does the value of the worker's input compare to the value of the related outcome? This is a question of *perceived* value. The individual has a perception of both values, intrinsically and extrinsically, and might ask himself: 'Is the reward worth the effort I put in?'

Adams (1961) maintained that the person's perception of the fairness, or the equity of this exchange is the determinant of his or her motivation. In the work situation, an individual's perception of the value of the rewards that go with the job may be that they are greater than the value of his or her input. This, says Adams, raises feelings of guilt or inadequancy within the individual, and as a result he or she puts in a greater effort to compensate for the perceived inequity. If, on the other hand, the reverse is the case, then the effort (the value of the input) will be reduced to a perceived equitable level. An alternative to the latter case might be that the individual seeks equity by trying to have the value of the rewards increased, but this might fail. The theory maintains that in such a case, the person might seek employment elsewhere, in an organization in which he or she perceives that there is equity between the paired values.

Yet another alternative is rationalization, in which the individual's perceptions of the values are modified. What Adams is saying here is that the person might look at the rewards that others are receiving in return for a similar effort and then adjust his or her perceptions accordingly. There is a classic example of this theory in action, in which two new buildings were being erected, one on each side of a street in New York. Different contractors had been engaged for each building. In the lunchbreak one day, a worker looked across the street and saw his neighbour working on the building opposite. He picked up his lunch box, crossed the street and joined his friend. As they ate, they chatted and the conversation got around to pay. The first worker discovered that his friend's wage was higher than his to the tune of 50 cents an hour, for doing similar work. He also discovered that there were no vacancies on that site. For the rest of the contract's duration, the first worker remained on his own site, among co-workers who were receiving the same wage as himself.

Adams's central theme, therefore, is that it is the quest for perceived equity that motivates the work effort; where reward values exceed input values, the work effort will increase; where the reverse is the case, the work effort will reduce, or rationalization will occur. It is likely, however, that the individual's perceptions of fairness and of *fair exchange* in the above respects will be more likely to influence his or her *behaviour* rather than exclusively the work effort. An alternative to feelings of guilt or inadequacy, for example, could be fear, especially where the perceived value of the reward is considerably greater than the value of the worker's input. The worker may decide to *look* busy, as if he or she is overloaded with work, without actually putting in any extra work effort.

Goal theory: G.P. Latham and F.A. Locke   This is a theory that relates the quality of performance to 'goal-setting'. That is to say that if the manager sets specific goals for individuals, performance will be higher. The goals, they said, should be difficult but attainable and accepted as such by the workers, and the manager should provide the workers with feedback on their performance. If the workers participate in the goal-setting process, the likelihood that they will accept the goals will be raised and they will also feel committed to achieving the goals. Latham and Locke (1979) say that it is essential to obtain agreement on difficult goals and the prospect of their achievement should be supported by guidance, advice and, where necessary, training. The individual's perception that he or she is developing by learning new skills is a motivator and the feedback given by the manager will help to sustain motivation and generate aspirations towards the achievement of further, higher goals.

Clearly, the success of goal theory depends very much on the nature of the 'boss–subordinate' relationship, which is reminiscent of the central principles of Drucker's management by objectives (1955).

Integration of Theories

In very broad terms, early theories focused upon the degree to which people were aroused by extrinsic and intrinsic job factors, while later theories place more emphasis on the importance of individual choice, and the mental process that leads to the decision to behave in a particular way. These approaches do not compete with each other; there is no context in which one is better than another; rather, they are related, they act concurrently and are equally valid.

The whole motivational concept is clarified when we consider its central purpose, alongside current knowledge. The purpose is to get the best possible performance from the human resource.

We know that motivation leads to performance, that performance is goal-directed and that goal attainment leads to satisfaction. But individuals are all different from each other. We employ them for their skills, knowledge and experience, but when they come to work, they bring with them all of their individual values and beliefs, preferences and prejudices, attitudes and perceptions. The extrinsic job factors are what they are, no matter who is doing the job. But individuals have their own unique attitudes towards organizations, work, jobs and job factors, and these attitudes arise from perceptions that form part of their personalities, which they carry about with them from job to job. Personality will determine the degree to which an individual is prepared to become involved in a job. It is almost as if the person turns up and says, 'OK, I'm here, so motivate me.' What the manager presents as a motivator will or will not turn the person on. Much of this kind of potential complication can be foreseen at the recruitment and selection stage, and careful use of selection techniques can help us to tease out personality factors that will help us to predict what will and will not motivate particular people.

References

Adams, J.S. 1961: Toward an understanding of inequity. In R. Likert (ed.), *New Patterns of Management*, Maidenhead: McGraw-Hill.

Alderfer, C.P. 1972: *Existence, Relatedness and Growth*. New York: Free Press.

Drucker, P. 1955: *The Practice of Management*. London: Heinemann.

Herzberg, F.W., Mausner, B and Snyderman, B. 1957: *The Motivation to Work*. New York: Wiley.

Latham, G.P. and Locke, F.A. 1979: Goal setting – a national technique that works. *Organisational Dynamics*, 8.

Likert, R. (ed.) 1961: *New Patterns of Management*. Maidenhead: McGraw-Hill.

Maslow, A.H. 1987: A theory of growth motivation. In A.H. Maslow, *Motivation and Personality*. New York: Harper & Row.

McGregor, D. 1960: *The Human Side of Enterprise*. New York: McGraw-Hill.

McLelland, D.C. 1975: *Power, The Inner Experience*. New York: Irvington.

Porter, L.W. and Lawler, E.E. 1968: *Managerial Attitudes and Performance*. Homewood, IL: Irwin-Dorsey.

Vroom, V.H. 1970: *Management and Motivation*. Harmondsworth: Penguin.

6

Leadership

Definition

Leadership is the ability of one individual to influence the behaviour of others towards the achievement of a particular task or set of tasks. Good leaders are those who can get things done in the way that they wish them to be done.

Some people seem naturally to be influential over others. They possess the kind of personality that induces a following. Others get things done in a matter of fact way, simply by issuing directives under the authority that their organizational position gives them, while yet others get things done through the use of various kinds of power they hold. This implies that leadership is a *social* process, since it involves interaction between and among people. The situation in which leadership typically is portrayed is that of a work group, in which one of the members has responsibility for what the group does and what happens within it.

Sometimes, there is confusion between the knowledge, skills and attitudes required for management and those required for leadership. Undoubtedly, the confusion arises because managers are in positions of responsibility, which includes responsibility for the behaviour of subordinates. In this sense, managers are in leadership positions, but the mere fact that they are in such positions does not automatically turn them into good leaders. Also, not all leaders are in managerial positions. A shop steward, for example, is elected by trade union colleagues to represent them in the workplace and there are times when they look to him or her to lead them through difficult situations that affect their terms and conditions of employment. The shop steward usually is a good leader, but he or she is not a manager.

In this chapter, we examine the knowledge and skills required for effective leadership. It is as well, however, before going into detail on leadership, to provide a very brief description of the main responsibilities of managers, so that the reader may more readily appreciate the differences between these two sets of knowledge, skills and attitudes.

A manager has responsibility for the achievement of objectives in a clearly defined area of the organization. He or she reviews the objectives that are to be achieved, organizes the work that needs to be done in order to achieve them and then allocates the tasks to the employees. Even though the manager delegates the work to the groups and individuals under his or her control, accountability for what happens stays with the manager. In terms of getting things done, the personal quality that is possessed by the most effective managers is that of leadership, since things only get done through people.

Since the beginning of the twentieth century, when organizational leadership was first identified as an important issue, a considerable amount of time and ingenuity has been devoted to researching the subject. The questions that have been asked include: What is leadership? Is it a personality characteristic? Is there a set of personality traits that leaders possess and that others do not? Are leaders born or are they made? Answers to these questions have produced five main approaches to the study of leadership (see table 6.1).

The Traits Approach

There is a belief that 'leaders are born and not made'; that leadership traits are inherited. In fact, research has failed to find that so-called great leaders, such as Alexander the Great, Genghis Khan, Abraham Lincoln, and many more, shared common characteristics. Byrd (1993) studied research that had revealed numerous traits that were said to separate leaders from non-leaders, but found few that were *actually shared* by the leaders that were studied. What we are saying here is that while early research failed to identify traits that are common to successful leaders and which, thereby, would have explained why they were

Table 6.1 Five approaches to leadership

Approach	Content
The traits approach or 'Great Man' theory	In this approach the researchers investigated the notion that successful leaders share common physical and personality characteristics. If these characteristics could be identified, then through training, we would be able to turn a poor leader into a good leader. The approach assumes that 'leaders are born and not made' and that leadership traits are inherent.
Functional leadership	Here, attention turns away from personality traits and towards the actual task of leadership. The approach sees the person as the leader of a group of followers and it studies the effects of the interactions between the leader and the group members. The actual behaviour of the leader and the members of the group is also studied and conclusions are drawn about what the leader should be doing in order to get the job done through a good work performance. it is believed that people can develop leadership qualities through training.
The behavioural approach	This approach is concerned with the behaviour of the leader and the effect of that behaviour on the followers, in terms of work performance. It concentrates on the kinds of behaviour that lead to particular performance outcomes.
Leadership styles	This approach is a study of the leader's attitude towards the group members, which causes the leader to behave as he or she does. The approach is also concerned with the effects of the leader's attitude upon the group members and how they may regard him or her as a result.
Situational leadership and contingency models	In these approaches, the focus is upon the situation in which the leader operates. Situational variables, and their effects, are identified. It is believed that there is no 'one best way' to lead a group, since the leader's behaviour is determined by the influence of the variables.

successful leaders, later research has shown that there is a positive relationship between effective leadership and certain personality characteristics, such as intelligence, social skills, integrity, initiative, and so on (Byrd, 1993). The apparent lack of success of research into trait theories of leadership, largely has caused researchers to concentrate their efforts on other approaches.

Functional Leadership

This approach examines the task of leadership and what it is that the leader should actually be doing in order to accomplish the tasks that need to be done. In Britain, the most well known explanation of functional leadership is given in John Adair's theory of action centred leadership (1973). Adair identifies three areas of need within the work-group situation: task needs, group needs and individual needs. Central to Adair's theory is a model that has become very familiar in most, if not all leadership training situations, the functional leadership model, in which the three overlapping circles indicate the needs (see figure 6.1).

Obviously, a manager cannot achieve the objectives for which he or she has been given responsibility without the active assistance and cooperation of the subordinates. Most writers cast the leader in the role of leading a group of followers, and essentially

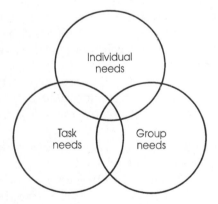

Figure 6.1 Functional leadership model (Adair, 1973).

what Adair is saying is that leaders can improve their performance (in achieving their objectives) through the actions they take in order to meet the needs in these three areas: 'Basically, our effectiveness as leaders depends on our ability to influence and be influenced by the members of our team in the implementation of a task. In practice, this means ensuring that the required tasks are always done; building and reinforcing the team and fostering teamwork and team spirit, [and] developing each individual member of the team.'

Adair says that anyone who can do these three things is an effective leader. Obviously, the actions that are needed are more easily said than done, but for those who wish to improve their performance as leaders, he provides guidelines that cover all three areas (see exhibit 6.1).

The Behavioural Approach

Research into this approach studies the behaviour of leaders in a variety of leadership positions, resulting in the placing of leaders into behavioural categories. One of the most far-reaching and well-known studies of this approach was carried out by the Bureau of Business Research at the Ohio State University in the USA (Fleishman, 1974). Questionnaires containing particular items of leadership behaviour and an analysis of the information revealed two main dimensions of leadership behaviour: *consideration* and *initiating structure*.

Consideration includes a human relations style of leadership behaviour that leads to the establishment of trust and respect between the leader and the group members, and that shows concern, warmth and support for them.

Initiating structure includes leadership behaviour in which the leader takes complete charge, organizing the group activities and directing intra-group behaviour towards the achievement of the task.

Consideration and initiating structure are widely regarded as separate and distinct kinds of leadership category and they produce four kinds of leadership behaviour (see figure 6.2). The model shown in the figure typifies several two-dimensional representations of research results in this approach to leadership. Mullins (1993) summarizes them as shown in table 6.2.

Exhibit 6.1 Guidelines for effective leadership

1 Achieving the task:

- being quite clear what the aim is, putting it over with enthusiasm, and reminding people of it often
- understanding how the task fits in with the overall plans of the organization, in both the short and the long term
- planning how to accomplish the task
- determining and providing the required resources, including human resources, time and authority
- doing everything possible to ensure that the organizational structure allows the task to be done efficiently
- pacing progress towards achievement of the task
- evaluating results and comparing them with the original plans and with the overall objectives of the organization.

2 Developing individuals:

- must be able to get satisfaction from personal achievement in the job they are doing
- must feel that they are making a worthwhile contribution to the objectives of the team and the organization
- must feel that the job itself is challenging, is demanding the best of them and is giving them a degree of responsibility that matches their abilities
- must receive adequate recognition for their achievements
- must have genuine control over those aspects of the job that have been delegated to them (that is, once you have delegated something, do not interfere unless you really have to)
- must feel that they, as human beings, are developing and advancing in experience and ability.

3 Building the team:

- setting and maintaining the team's overall objectives and standards
- involving the team as a whole in the achievement of objectives
- maintaining the unity of the team, and making sure dissident activity is minimized
- communicating efficiently with the team by briefing them face-to-face at least once a month on matters that affect them at work
- consulting the team members (unless time really does make it impossible) before taking any decision that affects them.

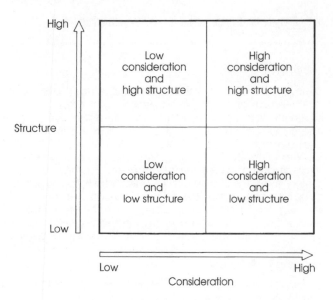

Figure 6.2 Ohio State University – four types of behaviour.

Table 6.2 Two-dimensional models of managerial leadership (Mullins, 1993)

Study	Dimensions	
Group interaction analysis	Task functions	Maintenance functions
Ohio State University leadership study	Initiating structure	Consideration
University of Michigan study	Production-centred supervision	Employee-centred supervision
McGregor, assumptions about people and work	Theory X	Theory Y
Blake and Mouton leadership grid	Concern for production	Concern for people

Leadership Styles

The research products of the behavioural approach undoubtedly put the spotlight on the importance of 'leadership style'. The

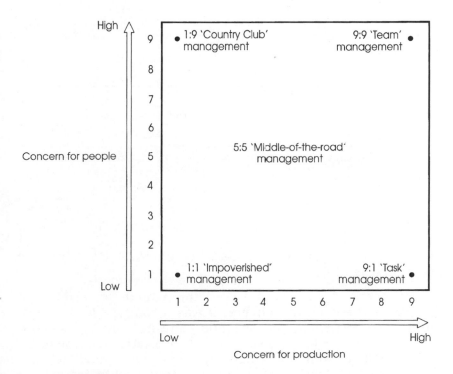

Figure 6.3 The managerial grid (adapted from Blake and Mouton, 1964).

managerial grid, originated by Blake and Mouton (1964), is one of the most popular frameworks for analysing and describing managerial styles, which are also depicted as two dimensions, as in Blake and Mouton's 'concern for production' and 'concern for people'. The grid is divided into 81 squares, 9 on each dimension. The manager's style is measured from an analysis of his or her responses to a questionnaire and the results are then plotted on the grid.

Some items on the questionnaire relate to the manager's drive for productivity and goal attainment, while others relate to the degree to which the manager regards the subordinates' human needs as important. The relationship between the two dimensions is one of emphasis; that is to say, managers are seldom totally concerned for productivity or totally concerned for people. Typically, they are fairly well balanced on both dimensions (see figure 6.3).

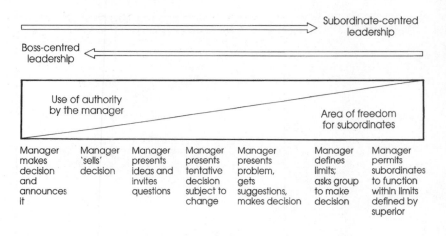

Figure 6.4 Continuum of leadership behaviour (Tannenbaum and Schmidt, 1973).

The popularity of the grid grew throughout the 1960s and 1970s, particularly in industry. It was a comparatively simple device to understand and use, and individual managers genuinely were interested in discovering their positions on the grid.

Information from working colleagues, who have studied the manager in action, may be added to that obtained via the questionnaire, with a view to increasing the accuracy of the findings, and thus the final position on the grid.

'How to choose a leadership pattern' (Tannenbaum and Schmidt, 1973) is one of the best known works on leadership style and it is not difficult to relate it to McGregor's Theory X and Theory Y (1960). McGregor's ideas concerned managers' assumptions about workers which, to a high degree, influenced managers' behaviour towards their staff. An 'authoritarian' leader, for example, will make all of the decisions and, as a 'Theory X person', will take over control of his subordinates and strictly separate the *planning* from the *doing* of the work. As we move along the continuum from left to right, the less authoritarian and the more 'democratic' the leader becomes (see figure 6.4). Democratic leaders are seen in a much more favourable light than authoritarians, although there is no empirical evidence to suggest that democratic leaders derive greater productivity from workers. It has been shown that morale is higher and that employees are happier working for democratic leaders, but there is no scientific evidence to support the view that a happy ship is a productive ship. On the other hand, workers who are employed in the relatively benign atmosphere that is fostered by the democratic leader are less likely to leave the organization and more likely to come in to work regularly. It could be said, therefore, that a democratic style of leadership reduces absenteeism and staff turnover. Other studies, including those that produced the famous managerial grid, are also based on McGregor's ideas.

Situational Leadership and Contingency Models

There is no doubt that the factors that make up a situation have a significant bearing on the kind of leadership that is required. The notion here is that all situations are different to the extent that they are made up of a combination of factors that is unique, and demand leadership behaviour that matches the situational needs. Mary Parker Follet (1971), thought that the situation was the most significant factor and even went to far as to say that the situation, rather than a person, issues the orders as to what (tasks) should be done. In this context, she advocated the depersonalization of giving orders: 'One person should not give orders to another *person* but both should agree to take their orders from the situation.' In this respect, it is clear that the situational approach attempts to ignore the interpersonal interaction within the group and between the group and its leader. Since interpersonal communication, particularly *informal* communication, is a natural and uninhibitable human inclination, it is folly to believe that one can base a theory upon it that amounts to a recommendation for effective leadership. Nevertheless, there is no doubt that situational factors are important to leadership requirements in terms of behaviour and style. There are examples in fiction and from real life in which changed situations have brought about changes in leadership. Shortly after the outbreak of the Second World War, for example, prime minister Neville Chamberlain was replaced by Winston Churchill, who was regarded as the right person for the situation. Commenting upon this, long after the war, something of Churchill's charitable nature was revealed in his response to being called 'lion-like': 'It was the nation and the race dwelling all round the globe that had the lion's heart. I had the luck to be called upon to give the roar.'[1]

The more recent contingency theories of leadership also cite situational variables as significant considerations in matching leadership behaviour to the demands of the situation. Here, however, the theory is based on the principle that there is no 'one best way' to lead in a situation and that leader behaviour should be influenced by the changing nature of the situational variables. This, of course, is a reference to leadership styles, and one of the most well-known contingency models is that of the American, F.E. Fiedler (1967).

Fiedler, investigating 'the type of leader attitude required for effective group performance', analysed group situations and placed them on a dimension that determined the degree to which the group situation was 'favourable' or 'unfavourable' to the leader, which he called the 'least preferred co-worker (LPC) scale' (Fiedler, 1964). According to Fiedler, therefore, performance depends upon the degree to which the leader is able to adopt a style that is appropriate to the favourableness of the situation. He says that 'favourableness' is determined by three major factors: (1) leader–member relations, (2) task structure and (3) power of position.

LEADER–MEMBER RELATIONS

Fiedler says that the degree to which the leader is liked and personally accepted by the group members, in terms of their esteem for, and loyalty to, him or her, are the most important factors influencing interaction between the leader and the group. Personal power such as this, he suggests, may be measured by asking the group members to name the individual whom they would most prefer as a leader, who has the best ideas and who contributes most to the group's achievements. Leader–member relations may also be assessed, says Fiedler, by presenting the leader with an LPC scale, but scoring the group, rather than his or her least preferred co-workers; this represents an indirect measure of the leader's acceptance by the group.

TASK STRUCTURE

This is an attempt to answer the question: What characteristics of the task determine the best type of leadership? Fiedler suggests that 'task structure' – the degree to which the task is defined – is the main dimension to be used to obtain an answer to this question. He points out that if a task is highly structured, every group member knows what he or she has to do, and does it. If a member makes a mistake it is immediately spotted and corrected. But the task is not always structured and precisely defined. Where the task is vague or unstructured, such as the development of a new product or a new policy, the leader is not aware of a precise set of steps to take, nor can he or she control the route to success.

It seems that when a task is vague and unstructured, the leaders are in the same kind of position as the editor of a national daily newspaper, in that they do not really know what they want until they see it. Task structure, suggests Fiedler, may be measured by rating the task on four aspects: (1) decision verifiability – the degree to which the correctness of the solution can be demonstrated, (2) goal clarity – the degree to which the desired outcome is clearly stated, (3) goal path multiplicity – the number of possible methods for performing the task, and (4) solution specificity – the degree to which there is more than one correct solution.

POWER OF POSITION

This considers the power that is attributed to the leader's position, apart from how much he or she is liked and able to command respect and loyalty, etc. Fiedler suggests that while position power is often signified by rank and the 'perks' that go with the position itself, it is frequently less important than the structure of the task. Powerlessness, in respect of position, does not always imply the inability to achieve the task. When I, for example, as a mere principal lecturer in a higher education institution, take the senior management team away on a residential workshop, I usually can achieve the workshop's objectives, because even though I am aware that I am leading my superiors, in terms of their rank, I know (and so do they) that I have the full backing of the managers at the very top.

There is a strong implication in Fiedler's work that it is legitimate to admit the leader's personality characteristics when assessing his or her style on a 'task orientated–considerate' dimension, or on the managerial grid. His original work was published in 1964, and in the following year, he published a reading entitled 'Leadership: a new model'.

The LPC scale attempts to measure the leader's assessment of the group, in terms of with whom he or she least prefers to work.

There are about twenty pairs of single-word items of opposite meaning on the questionnaire, with an eight-point scale ranged between each pair (see figure 6.5).

Pleasant	8	7	6	5	4	3	2	1	Unpleasant
Friendly	8	7	6	5	4	3	2	1	Unfriendly
Rejecting	8	7	6	5	4	3	2	1	Accepting
Helpful	8	7	6	5	4	3	2	1	Frustrating
Unenthusiastic	8	7	6	5	4	3	2	1	Enthusiastic
Tense	8	7	6	5	4	3	2	1	Relaxed
Distant	8	7	6	5	4	3	2	1	Close
Cold	8	7	6	5	4	3	2	1	Warm
Cooperative	8	7	6	5	4	3	2	1	Uncooperative
Supportive	8	7	6	5	4	3	2	1	Hostile
Boring	8	7	6	5	4	3	2	1	Interesting
Quarrelsome	8	7	6	5	4	3	2	1	Harmonious
Self-assured	8	7	6	5	4	3	2	1	Hesitant
Efficient	8	7	6	5	4	3	2	1	Inefficient
Gloomy	8	7	6	5	4	3	2	1	Cheerful
Open	8	7	6	5	4	3	2	1	Guarded

Figure 6.5 An example of Fiedler's LPC scale.

Summary

From these five approaches to the ways in which leadership has been studied, we know the difference between the knowledge, skills and attitudes required by the leader and those required by the manager. Good leadership is not just a question of 'If they like you they'll do things for you'; nor is it a question of using one's senior position to get things done. We can see that the factors that determine good leadership are varied and complex, and that a leadership style that proved effective in one situation may not be equally effective in another.

Most trainers believe that knowledge and skills can be 'trained into' people, but that there needs to be at least a trace of 'natural leadership ability' within the person to begin with. It is easy to distinguish between those with natural ability and those who are strictly the 'products of training'.

Note

1   Winston Churchill, speech at the Palace of Westminster on his 80th birthday, 30 November, 1954.

References

Adair, J. 1973: *The Action-Centred Leader.* London: McGraw-Hill.
Blake, R.R. and Mouton, J.S. 1964: *The Managerial Grid.* Houston, TX: Gulf.
Byrd, C. 1993: Social psychology. In L.J. Mullins (ed.), *Management and Organisational Behaviour*, 3rd edn. London: Pitman.
Fiedler, F.E. 1964: *A Contingency Model of Leadership Effectiveness.* New York: Academic Press.
— 1967: *A Theory of Leadership Effectiveness.* New York: McGraw-Hill.
— 1969: Leadership – a new model. In C.A. Gibb (ed.), *Leadership.* Harmondsworth: Penguin (originally published in 1965).
Fleishman, E.A. 1974: Leadership climate, human relations training and supervisory behaviour. In E.A. Fleishman and A.R. Bass (eds), *Studies in Personnel and Industrial Psychology*, 3rd edn. Homewood, IL: Dorsey.

Follett, M.P. 1971: The giving of orders. In D.S. Pugh (ed.), *Organisation Theory*. Harmondsworth: Penguin.

McGregor, D. 1960: *The Human Side of Enterprise*. New York: McGraw-Hill.

Mullins, L.J. (ed.) 1993: *Management and Organisational Behaviour*, 3rd edn. London: Pitman.

Tannenbaum, R. and Schmidt, W.H. 1973: How to choose a leadership pattern. *Harvard Business Review*, May/June.

7

General Personnel Activities

Introduction

This chapter describes what goes on in a personnel department. Its purpose is to introduce you to the fundamental nature of personnel activities – what personnel people actually do. The idea at this stage in your studies is to draw you into the personnel arena, show you around and provide answers to your questions. Also from this chapter, you should derive an understanding of the role of the personnel function in the organization, how it fits in structurally, and with the work of other managers.

In general terms, it is correct to say that personnel *management* is a strategic function. The department's senior experts formulate the personnel policies and strategies of the organization and have them accepted at the top level of management, while the department's personnel specialists are given responsibility for advising, assisting and guiding managers on matters affecting the employment of their staff. These 'middle-level' personnel managers and specialists, therefore, provide an expert service to other functional specialists and line managers, advising and assisting them in carrying out the human resource aspects of their roles efficiently, effectively and within policy and the law. Specialists in personnel administration are responsible for running the day-to-day activities of the personnel department and for the development of the department's systems and procedures, which include maintaining personnel records, gathering and collating information and presenting it in a form that can be generally understood. The department also provides advice, assistance and guidance to all employees on matters affecting them in their jobs. Table 7.1 shows an analysis of personnel responsibilities and specialisms at their various levels in the department.

The personnel function embraces a broad range of specialisms, based on the needs of the organization. What generally happens is that the senior personnel executives formulate policies and develop systems for all of the activities that are related to the specialisms. In this way, the organization has a recruitment and selection policy with systems for engaging people; a training and development policy with systems for training and developing the staff; a remuneration policy with systems for paying and rewarding the staff for their work efforts; and so on across the whole spectrum of personnel work.

Personnel staff, therefore, have a detailed knowledge of policies and systems, and they apply that knowledge when they are advising and guiding other managers through the human resource elements of their jobs. When, therefore, a line manager is engaging a new member of staff a personnel specialist will be available to guide him or her through the preliminary stages, such as drafting the job requisition, writing the job description, then later checking the recruitment advertisement, and eventually scrutinizing the shortlist of the candidates who are to be interviewed. Personnel will arrange the times, dates and interview locations, and are usually present at the interviews themselves to ensure that they are conducted in accordance with company policy, legal requirements and best professional practice.

In many organizations, one person takes responsibility for a specialism and all of the related sub-specialisms. The employee relations manager, for example, may be responsible for negotiating terms and conditions of employment, advising on the handling of grievances, disputes and disciplinary matters, and employment law, while the training and development manager handles induction, analyses training needs and organizes the training, manages career development and adopts responsibility for the performance management system.

Ultimately, it is the line managers who make the decisions that affect their staff. The recruitment and selection specialist may advise on the selection decision making *process* and will point

Table 7.1   Analysis of personnel responsibilities

Level	Responsibility and specialism
Senior personnel managers/ directors	Formulation of personnel strategy and policies and having them accepted at top management level Advising other managers on the implementation of policies and procedures
Middle-level personnel management specialists	Employee relations Employment law Handling grievances, disputes and disciplinary matters Negotiating terms and conditions of employment Manpower planning Staff recruitment and selection Induction systems Training and development Performance appraisal Career management systems Systems of payment and other rewards Welfare and counselling services Health and safety at work
Personnel administration specialists	Day-to-day administration of the personnel department Developing and implementing personnel systems and procedures Maintaining secure and confidential personnel records. Ensuring the efficient organization of training courses, induction sessions, interviews, career events and events involving external organizations and individuals Producing statistical analyses for the purposes of corporate and manpower planning Maintaining and servicing the manpower plan Handling information relating to manpower supply and demand Providing an employment law update service

out relevant factors from each candidate's experience, qualifications and past employment record, but it is the line manager who decides who is to get the job.

In that light, it is a good idea to train line managers in certain personnel skills. We said earlier that line managers have responsibility for the performance of their staff, and rather than call upon the expertise of personnel specialists every single time that personnel-type skills are needed, the line managers should be competent in several relevant skills, including handling grievances, administering the early stages of the disciplinary procedure, appraising people's performance and making recommendations concerning their rewards and readiness for promotion. Many line managers already carry out such tasks anyway, but proper training would help to keep them up to date with policies, the law and procedures. Line managers who are capable of carrying out these tasks are in a good position to relate to and influence their staff; as we shall see in later chapters, the relationship between the manager and the staff member is very important in terms of trust-building, team-building, mutual confidence and understanding.

Structuring the Personnel Department

Like most departments of an organization, personnel is structured to reflect the levels of seniority and the different specialisms in which people work. This is not to say that all personnel departments are similarly structured. The framework of the department is determined by many factors: the size of the whole organization, its geographic scope and spread and the amount of importance that the top managers attribute to the personnel function. In some organizations, certain personnel specialisms are more important than others and this may be reflected in the structure in terms of their size and level of seniority within the department. In the 1970s and 1980s, for example, Employee Relations was regarded as extremely important and in many cases a separate department was set up for it, with the Employee Relations Manager and the Personnel Manager at the same hierarchical level. Also, the training department sometimes breaks away from the personnel department, but this is most often due to its size and/or the establishment of a purpose-built training school. Figure 7.1 depicts the structure of a personnel department, while Figure 7.2 shows how an organization with several different geographic locations might organize its personnel function.

Organizations vary in size, from those that are too small to justify having a personnel department, to those that are very large and complex, with a Corporate Personnel Manager or Director and a personnel staff who have a 'headquarters' type of personnel function to carry out. In such a large organization, personnel managers also operate at *divisional* levels, reporting to the senior divisional manager on divisional personnel issues and to the corporate personnel manager on such issues as personnel policy and strategy.

The Personnel 'Parish'

We have seen that the personnel department can be organized to show the levels of seniority and the way the various specialisms are arranged. While some personnel departments extend this kind of structuring concept by further dividing the sub-specialisms, others have an entirely different approach, which calls for personnel 'all-rounders', rather than functional specialists. The all-rounder is a personnel officer who can function effectively, up to a particular level, in most personnel specialisms.

The 'personnel parish' concept is depicted in figure 7.3. On a single-site organization, for example, the personnel manager may delegate responsibility to one person for all personnel matters in one area of the organization, instead of having a staff consisting of a recruitment specialist, a training specialist, an employee relations specialist, and so on. In this kind of structure, each senior member of the personnel staff is an all-rounder and will attend to all personnel needs on his or her own 'patch'.

The personnel parish framework can be criticized on several grounds; firstly, that nobody can be 'all things to all men', and secondly, that the demands that are made upon the all-rounder can be met only one at a time. The 'specialist' type of framework, however, is also criticized on the grounds that if someone spends several years in just one area of personnel work, they will lose touch with developments in the other areas and become 'rusty'. Looking at it from the line manager's position, he or she may

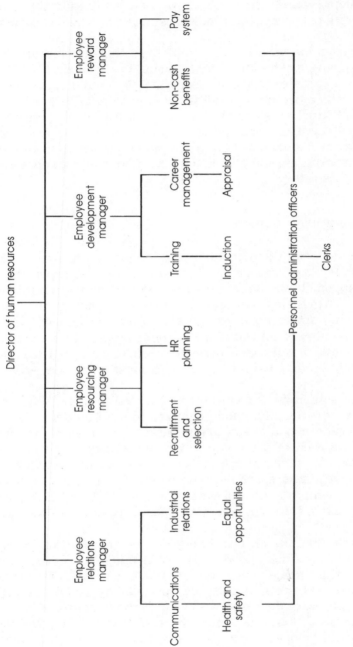

Figure 7.1 An example of a personnel department's structure.

prefer to deal exclusively with one personnel executive for all matters. In this way they would see each other more frequently

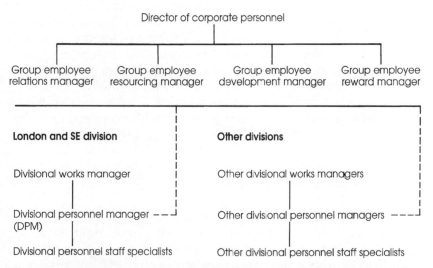

The DPM of each division has a line responsibility to the divisional works manager for the provision, welfare and administration of divisional staff. He or she, however, also has a 'dotted line' responsibility to the corporate personnel director, through the various corporate specialists, for the implementation of corporate personnel policy and the conduct of the personnel staff under his or her control.

Figure 7.2 An example of a multi-site organization's personnel department.

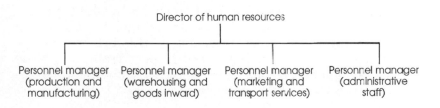

This is a single-site organization, and each personnel manager is responsible to the director of human resources for all personnel matters relating to his or her own 'parish', or area of responsibility. In a small or medium organization, just one manager with a couple of administrative staff will be in position.

Figure 7.3 An example of a 'personnel parish' structure.

and could build a relationship of trust and mutual under-standing. Another line manager may feel more confident with the advice and assistance of someone who specializes solely in the nature of the problem he or she has at the time.

These concepts of *specialist* and *generalist* personnel workers have been the subject of an ongoing debate among the members of the IPD for several years. It is clear that in organizations today, there is a demand for both. Obviously, newcomers to the personnel function need a generalized educational and training grounding of a kind that may be used as a floor upon which to build a specialism, should the person decide to specialize after several years' experience.

Personnel and Change

In order to remain competitive, organizations are always on the look-out for new approaches to ensuring that their strategic objectives will be met, and in order to do so they reorganize, usually to achieve a 'leaner, flatter structure'. This means strip-ping out layers of management, which in turn means making the remaining managers responsible for a larger number of employ-ees. In overall terms, it may also mean operating with a smaller workforce, and in this situation, individual employees find them-selves exercising new skills and working in areas with which they are unfamiliar.

Obviously, the personnel department becomes deeply involved in making changes such as those described above, and those working in the rest of the organization look to its personnel people for solutions to their problems. In this respect, therefore, today's personnel practitioners find themselves involved in man-aging change, especially in the areas of restructuring, developing flexible working practices, and working on the further develop-ment of the new culture that emerges as a result. In these respects, personnel specialists work more closely with line man-agers than they have in previous years.

Structure

Organizations are designed to reflect the relationships between the various positions and employees. The structure shows the logic behind the division of the organization's expertise and how functions are placed to work coordinatively. 'Structure makes possible the application of the process of management and creates a framework of order and command through which the activities of the organization can be planned, organised, directed and controlled' (Mullins, 1993). Strategy and structure are inextricably linked, and the question of restructuring has become a topical issue in the light of the organization's need to develop new strategies in the face of fierce domestic and international competition. In this context, restructuring may be seen as a reflection of the need to make internal changes in order to continue to meet the changing needs of the external environment. In Chapter 2, we examined early ideas on structure, bureaucracy and the classical approaches; while some of these ideas remain relevant for particular organizations, new approaches have emerged.

SPAN OF CONTROL

This term relates to the number of employees that falls directly under the control of one manager. Given that the organization has a particular number of employees, the total number of layers in the overall structure will be determined by the size of the spans of control within it. Organizations with 'tall' spans of control will have many layers and those with 'flat' ones will have fewer layers (see figure 7.4).

The late 1980s saw tall structures begin to disappear, and new, 'flatter' frameworks emerged in their place. The general effect of this trend was to reduce the number of managers and increase the number of subordinate staff reporting to each manager. This changed employees' working situations, in that in addition to changes in the work itself, they found themselves reporting to different managers and working with different colleagues.

MATRIX ORGANIZATIONS

This form of organization design may be introduced in organizations in which there is a need for teams to work on projects, such as those in the construction industry, civil engineering and other forms of commissioning firms. Matrix structures can also be found in enterprises in which there is a need to set up a temporary unit in order to carry out a specific internal project.

Managers and specialists are seconded from different parts of the organization for the duration of the project. On completion, the team may be disbanded, or assigned to another project. An organization may be running several projects concurrently. A civil engineering concern, for example, may be building a bridge

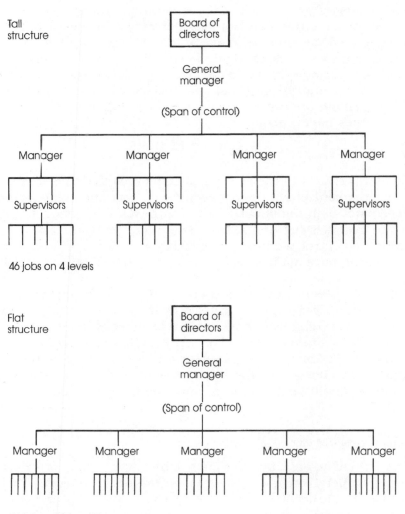

Figure 7.4 Span of control influencing structure.

in the Midlands, a tunnel in Scotland and an outfall for a water company on the east coast.

A matrix design is typified by a grid, which depicts a two-dimensional track of authority and responsibility (see figure 7.5). Authority and responsibility in the functional departments, track downwards, while from the project manager, authority and responsibility track laterally, across the main structure. In this way, project managers may share the resources of the organization, a concept that produces economic as well as practical advantages.

Matrix structures have drawn criticism from those working in the functions, who say that frustrations occur, largely as a result of their having two bosses: the functional heads to whom they report and the project managers who make demands on their

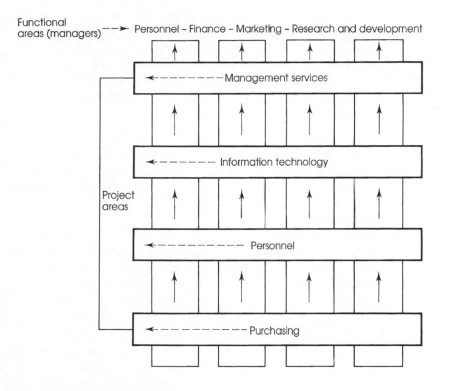

Figure 7.5 A matrix organization.

services. Indeed, it has been known for such frustrations to arise as a result of conflicting priorities and time constraints.

FLEXIBLE WORKING

The current attitudes of many senior managers has produced the increasing tendency for them to introduce new patterns of flexible working by drawing distinctions between *core* and *peripheral* workers. Core workers are those who are regarded as being particularly important to the organization and who are, therefore, encouraged to stay, by virtue of attractive prospects and rewards. Core staff are recognized as highly skilled and motivated technical, scientific or professional people, and organizations understand that they have to take positive steps to retain them. Peripheral workers, on the other hand, are not treated so generously, and in some cases, are actively encouraged to seek employment elsewhere. This attitude towards different categories of worker is reflected in the reward management structure. These ideas have grown in popularity for several reasons: (1) the rate of technological change, (2) the need for greater economic efficiency, (3) the need for a more flexible and speedy response to external demands and (4) the need for a greater degree of involvement, and thereby satisfaction, on the part of employees.

CULTURE

Senior managers' recognition that organizational culture has a significant bearing on efficiency and effectiveness is relatively recent, and it has brought with it the notion that the culture can be 'managed'.

Many factors influence organizational culture; principally, these are the climate, or the 'atmosphere', in which workers operate, the style of leadership and management, the nature of the industry and its technology, and the history of the organization. The concept of culture is that it is something that has evolved historically, through the media of these factors, producing a unique combination of values, beliefs and unwritten rules. It has been said that 'what it's like to work in this place', and 'the way we do things around here' are indicative of the culture, but these are terms that do not provide an adequate explanation. For example, those almost imperceptible changes that take place as the organization evolves are reflected in cultural change, and it is only when we look back several years that we realize that things have become different. If culture arises from 'the way things are', then clearly the introduction of changes will result in a changed culture, *for better or for worse.*

If change is not managed with honesty and understanding, culture may become *hostile*, in which the climate is ridden with fear and suspicion, is detrimental to motivation and satisfaction and, therefore, inimical to the overall purposes of the organization. Conversely, well-managed changes may result in a *benign* culture, in which the climate is pleasant, the managerial style encouraging and supportive, leading to raised levels of achievement and motivation, and the general value orientation that the organization's achievement of its goals is a good thing.

Certainly it is possible to manage the culture and, in doing so, it may be fruitful to encourage the development of a managerial style and working climate that lead towards a culture that is benign, and conducive to the achievement of objectives. Culture that has evolved historically is based on very deeply-rooted sets of assumptions about how things are. Such assumptions, which refer to job security, the way things are done, what would be 'good (or bad) for the company', what the company is for and so forth, are often held unconsciously, but they still are powerful determinants of attitude and behaviour. A fair example of the effect of this species of unconscious assumption became evident on the privatization of the public utilities, in which the employees of the newly privatized companies were the same people who had been employed in the 'authorities', some for many years. Many were oblivious to the need for the organization to ensure its own survival, and the 'job-for-life' syndrome remained in evidence long after the change in corporate status. The employees possessed long-term assumptions about obligations to the public, rather than to shareholders, and were resolute in the belief that nothing would change. Awareness of these assumptions has led to a conscious and rational process of culture change, across the medium to long term, rather than a direct 'unfreeze–change–refreeze' approach. This longer term approach, coupled with the improvement of managerial skills in introducing planned change, and the natural turnover of staff, is beginning to show positive results in terms of culture.

Summary

It is hoped that from this chapter you have gained some insight into how the personnel department is organized and the kind of work that personnel people do. As change continues to dominate the organizational scene, the activities of the personnel department and its specialists become more and more important, since they are also active in the determination of new structures and in providing advice and assistance in managing the culture.

Reference

Mullins, L.J. (ed.) 1993: *Management and Organisational Behaviour*, 3rd edn. London: Pitman.

Part II

Planning the Human Resource

Having set the personnel function into its organizational context, we next begin to see how human resource needs are planned for the future, and how those plans are implemented. In this part of the book, therefore, we explain how to recruit, select and induct people. As the various concepts are explained, we discuss what happens before the recruitment process begins and after it has ended.

8

Human Resource Planning

Introduction

If the organization is going to meet the objectives that are stated
in its future plans, then it will need to have the right kinds of
employees when it needs them. They have to be people who
possess skills that are appropriate to the necessary tasks, and
who are motivated to apply those skills towards the achievement
of the organization's goals and objectives. Before the advent of
HRM, 'manpower planning' was the term used to describe the
task of ensuring that this happens. It involves analysing the
corporate strategy, assessing its implications for future human
resource requirements, developing a strategy for ensuring that
the necessary human resources will be secured, and then developing and implementing the strategy itself.

Definition of Manpower Planning

. . . a strategy for the acquisition, utilization, improvement and retention of an enterprise's human resources.

Department of Employment, 1974

This is a definition that stood the test of time for almost two
decades. Most personnel professionals saw manpower planning
as: a conscious and rational attempt to ensure that the right
number of people is in the organization at the right time, appropriately skilled and motivated to contribute to the achievement

of the objectives of the enterprise. The term 'manpower planning' has virtually disappeared now, and has been replaced by Human Resource Planning (HRP) (see exhibit 8.1). Many personnel managers say that in relation to what actually happens, the definition given above is an adequate description. It is interesting to note that while HRM modifies the ways in which the organization regards its employees and communicates with them, HRP advocates claim that they do not reject the manpower planning perspective (McKenna and Beech, 1995). It should be emphasized that HRP is a *strategic* activity, which means that it is there to ensure that the medium- and longer-term human resource needs will be met.

Formulating the human resource strategy is a job for a highly skilled and experienced personnel professional, assisted by personnel specialists who understand and are skilled and experienced in such activities. Those who have been properly trained to work in the personnel function usually are able to assist in the

Exhibit 8.1

Drawing a distinction between 'manpower planning' and HRP raises the larger question that surrounds the distinction between personnel management and HRM. Such distinctions have been drawn but it is doubtful if their reiteration would assist the purposes of this book, which largely is about fundamental knowledge acquisition and operational techniques in the personnel field. Besides, while the tide around the HRM 'iceberg' is ebbing, explanations of the concept vary. Some say that it is a 'set of practices, activities and philosophies designed to manage the employment relationship' (Tyson, 1995), while others say that while HRM activities increase, those of the personnel function decline (Torrington, 1989). We sleepwalk through significant changes; HRM probably is the sixth generation in the history of management thought. Suffice to say here that HRM introduces particular differences in *what* is done, and significant differences in *why* and *how* it is done. These will emerge later in the book.

process. From what has been said above, we can see that HRP gives rise to the recruitment and selection, the training and development, the performance management and the severance of staff.

A human resource plan is formulated within the context of changing internal and external business environments. One cannot simply draw up human resource requirements on the basis of the overall corporate strategy and leave it at that. An organization's plans change in response to environmental changes, which means that the HR plan is not something that remains in its original form. It has to be monitored continuously, and modified to meet changing needs. This means that in turn, other strategies, such as those for recruitment and selection, also are under continuous review. In most organizations today, the human resource plan is computerized, which eases the task of monitoring and updating. Computerization has encouraged more organizations to formulate such strategies. Before computerization, the task of constructing and updating the human resource plan was likened to the never-ending task of painting the Forth Bridge.

All strategies are about the future, and the human resource strategy, therefore, is an assessment of the future human resource needs of the organization. It is an integral part of corporate strategy, which could cover, say, the forthcoming five or even ten years. Organizational plans are rolling programmes, which are divided into the short term, the medium term and the long term, indicating perhaps, two, five and ten years, respectively, so that as time passes, what was planned for the long-term becomes the medium-term; what was planned for the medium-term becomes the short-term. Fresh plans are made annually, and existing ones are modified continuously (see figure 8.1).

Few managers would try to predict the shape of the business environments of the long-term future. The organization itself, of course, with its products and services should have a significant influence on what happens in the market-place in the future, but many external factors are beyond the organization's control. Long-term plans, therefore, are comparatively vague in terms of content and direction. Medium-term plans, on the other hand, are slightly easier to specify, since, clearly, we can forecast what will happen in the forthcoming two to five years with more accuracy. Short-term plans, which might range from now to two

Present	2001	0	0	0	0	0	S	S	M	M	L→
	2000	0	0	0	0	S	S	M	M	L→	
	1999	0	0	0	S	S	M	M	L→		
	1998	0	0	S	S	M	M	L→			
	1997	0	S	S	M	M	L→				
	1996	S	S	M	M	L→					
		1997	1998	1999	2000	2001	2002	2003	2004	2005	2006

Future

Figure 8.1 Organizational plans as rolling programmes.

years hence, need to be precise and crystal clear; they contain demands for immediate action.

Human Resource Planning Activities

Every time an action or event takes place in terms of recruitment, selection, induction, training, or retirement or some other form of severance, the human resource plan has to be updated. This is a *skill-centred* activity that causes us to consider the influx of new employees, the type and number of employees needed in the future, current employees and those who are leaving. In this sense, HRP activities are akin to those of 'keeping the books balanced', in which the necessary skills are available to the organization when they are needed.

Organizational change, however, has become a significant influence on the shape and maintenance of the human resource strategy. The move towards flatter, leaner structures, for example, carries with it the need to remove layers of management, which in turn, often means redundancy, redeployment, re-training and a host of other associated activities.

Managing and maintaining the human resource strategy is an imprecise process. The human resource does not behave ideally as you would wish. People leave suddenly; they go sick, take maternity leave and, of course, they retire. Retirement is said to be a much more predictable feature of manpower behaviour, but it can give you some surprises, when, for example, a highly skilled operator suddenly decides that he or she would like to take early retirement. All of these comings and goings of people create what we call *staff turnover*. In most organizations, staff turnover can be predicted with a reasonable degree of accuracy. That is not to say that we know *who* is going to leave, or *when* they will leave. But if we look at the picture annually, we can see how many people, on average, leave every year. In other words, we use past trends to project probable future situations.

CALCULATING STAFF TURNOVER

Staff turnover can be affected by several factors. Low unemployment figures, for example, make it easier for people to move from one organization to another, while the reverse is true in times of high unemployment. Feelings of insecurity, perhaps brought about by news of a poor performance in terms of profitability, may cause people to move on. It is this latter factor, people leaving of their own accord, that makes planning difficult. Staff turnover rates are expressed as percentages and are calculated as follows:

$$\frac{\text{Number of leavers in a year}}{\text{Average number of employees}} \times 100 = \text{Staff turnover}$$

If, for example, the organization employs an average of 2,200 people, of whom about 95 leave every year, then the staff turnover is:

$$\frac{95}{2,200} \times 100 = 4.3\%$$

This calculation is fine, if the managers wish to compare the staff turnover to those of other organizations in the same industry, or against national trends across the whole of industry. But the figure is of little use to the human resource planners in a large organization, who wish to discover the proportional distribution of staff turnover across the various departments and functions. For that, you have to calculate staff turnover for every section and department. Most of the information needed for this exercise will be in the personnel records.

Applying this principle to the example given above, you may find that turnover in Department A is 2 per cent, in Department B it is 3 per cent and in Department C it is 7.9 per cent. This will produce an average of 4.3 per cent across the three departments, but clearly there is a more significant turnover problem in Department C. Rather than simply allowing for such a high figure when projecting HR requirements, you would investigate the possibility of reducing it, which means finding out why it compares so unfavourably with the figures for the other two departments. You would do this because staff turnover is a significant determinant of recruitment, which is costly. Not only is it costly in terms of the recruitment process *per se*, but in relation to the subsequent costs of inducting, training and generally servicing the requirements of new employees.

This kind of calculation will be helpful when you are projecting future HR needs. That is to say, if, as in the example given above, the past turnover trend of 4.3 per cent is likely to continue, then you can be reasonably sure that you are going to need to recruit at least 95 people in the forthcoming year; furthermore, having completed the second calculation (in the departments and functions), you will know roughly where the replacement staff will be needed and the kinds of skills and other qualities they should possess.

CALCULATING WORKFORCE STABILITY

Just as important as staff turnover is the workforce stability index (WSI). This is also expressed as a percentage and is calculated as follows:

$$\frac{\text{Number of employees with one year's service}}{\text{Number of employees taken on one year ago}} \times 100 = \text{Workforce stability}$$

It is known that people who are going to leave do so in their first year of employment and that those who stay for a year will probably stay for much longer. The WSI, therefore, is useful in that it provides an indication of the percentage of people who will be *unlikely* to leave in the forthcoming year. In the above form, however, it does not take account of the number of people joining the organization during the past year; nor does it account for exact length of service, although there are techniques that can be used to obtain such information.

Forecasting HR Demand

The main purpose of using the above techniques is to enable us to produce a plan that reflects the HR demand and supply situation that will be concurrent with the corporate strategy. The first task, therefore, is to estimate future demand and break that down into skill categories. This has to be carried out for every type of skill demand in the organization. For example, when examining the requirement for maintenance engineers, we may find that 27 will be needed in, say, 1997. At present 25 are employed, of whom 2 will go off sick (we have calculated the average sickness absence rate), 3 will leave (we know the average staff turnover rate among maintenance engineers), 2 will retire (we know their ages) and 1 will be away for training and development. The calculation for this situation might be:

Maintenance engineers currently in post	25	
Anticipated leavers (staff turnover)		3
Retiring		2
Off sick		2
Training and development		1
		8
Number required	27	
Number available	17	
Shortfall for 1996	10	

As we can see, the result of this particular calculation produces a shortfall in the human resource requirement. Another similar calculation carried out for, say, accounts clerks, might produce a surplus. If, for example, a work study showed that an accounts clerk can handle 100 accounts and there are 1000 accounts in the department, then it is reasonable to assume that the department needs 10 accounts clerks. It may be, however, that in the light of the forthcoming introduction of a new computerized accounting system, the work study team has revised its figures and now forecasts a 20 per cent increase in the clerks' productivity. In this new situation, it is reasonable to assume that the requirement for accounts clerks will be 8, rather than 10. Also, there may be other, more complex intervening factors, which means that such calculations are not always as simple as the one in the example given above. A total of the results of this kind of calculation throughout the organization will produce the HR demand figures for the forthcoming year.

There are a number of well-known techniques that provide a structured way of reaching this situation. Here, we will examine two of them: managerial judgement and ratio-trend analysis.

MANAGERIAL JUDGEMENT

This technique is not renowned for its accuracy, but it can be effective in small organizations and in those whose structure, technology and productivity remain relatively stable. What happens is that the organization's managers estimate their future productivity figures and the human resources that will be required to meet them. Attwood (1989) says that managers often do this under guidance provided by top managers, who are possibly acting on the advice of specialists, such as those in personnel. Attwood goes on to say that managers' deliberations should include:

- replacements for retirements, leavers, transfers and promotions;
- possible improvements in production;
- redeployment of existing manpower;
- planned changes in output levels;
- planned introduction of new methods and equipment;
- planned reorganization of work;
- the impact of changes in employment law or collective agreements.

Armstrong (1988) also refers to this 'top-down' approach and suggests an alternative 'bottom-up' approach, in which the line managers submit staffing proposals for agreement by senior management. He further suggests the use of both approaches, in which in addition to being given guidelines, line managers are encouraged to seek the help of the Personnel, Organization and Methods (O&M) or Work Study departments. Staffing targets usually are set, and while the line managers are producing their forecasts, Personnel, O&M and Work Study get together to produce an organization-wide human resource forecast. The two sets of forecasts may then be reviewed together by a human resource planning committee consisting of functional heads. This committee reconciles any discrepancies between the two forecasts and submits a final forecast to top management.

Considering what was said at the outset about the inaccuracy of this technique, one might be forgiven for thinking that what is described above seems like going to a lot of trouble to produce something that is inaccurate. The answer is that HR planning in any form is an imprecise process, and doing it is justified on the grounds that some information is better than no information. The integrity of any human resources forecast is eroded by external environmental changes, which are often outside of the control of those who compiled it, but its reliability also is significantly influenced by the accuracy of the records and the judgements from which the in-going information is derived. In any case, the HR plan is continuously updated; what will appear to be a reasonably accurate current forecast, may be run out of date by unforeseen changes.

Remember, too, that the framework of the HR plan is just as important as the information that is put into it, since the information is changing continuously, and the plan has to have a framework that is capable of handling the volume of the data, as well as being flexible enough to accommodate changes.

Changes within the organization, such as restructuring, introducing new technology, new work methods and so forth, will also be planned and will influence the profile of the first draft of the HR plan. It may be necessary, for example, to build in techniques for reducing or increasing the size of the workforce over a specified period of time. From time to time, however, unforeseeable events occur; new agreements are reached and legislation passed that may, for example, affect retirement ages, working hours, rates of pay and skill requirements. Not all of these factors can be considered when the HR plan is first being formulated.

Ratio-trend analysis

The effectiveness of this technique depends upon the future stability of the relationship between the volume of productivity and staff numbers. Those who use this technique in its crude form assume that the relationship will remain constant. Few organizations would survive without at least some element of growth or enrichment, and the technique, therefore, does allow for particular foreseeable changes. This implies that the efficiency with which the technique is managed relies upon the planner's ability to handle (juggle with) changing ratios, a task that is made somewhat easier if the changes are planned, or at least foreseen.

The basis of the technique is to identify trends in past productivity/staff ratios and use them, allowing for changes, to build up forecasts of future ratios.

The introduction of new technology probably has the most significant influence on the reliability of this kind of forecasting, since new technology is most frequently brought in to produce cost-efficiencies in the forms of increased productivity, greater versatility and improvements in product and process quality. Obviously, these are objectives that demand direct changes in the productivity/staff ratio.

There are more refined extensions to ratio-trend analysis, which include using the expertise of O&M and Work Study departments. These refinements tend to emphasize the organization's future requirements, in terms of the actual activities of employees, rather than to forecast future requirements on the basis of past trends. The cooperation and assistance of O&M and Work Study are sought because the application of the technique in this form requires the use of the further techniques of work measurement and task analysis. Firstly, the appropriate specialists assess the nature of the actual work that is to be done; secondly, they study the methods that are used, and thirdly, they review the results of what they have done and make suggestions for improving efficiency, usually by suggesting new work methods.

Human resource forecasts that are made on the basis of information that has arisen from this kind of exercise will be quite different from those that are made on the basis of ratio-trend analysis.

At this stage, we have gathered and collated information that enables us to estimate the HR demand in terms of the kinds of skills that employees should possess and where in the organization they will be required in the short, medium and long terms. Next, we discuss how and from where we are going to get the human resources, and examine techniques that will enable us to produce detailed and reasonably accurate estimates of the future HR supply situation.

Forecasting the Human Resources Supply

In estimating the future supply, there are two major sources to analyse and assess. The first is the current workforce, since most of the employees that will be required in the short and medium terms are already in the organization. We call this the *internal labour market*. The second source is the pool of potential employees in the community outside the organization: the *external labour market*.

THE INTERNAL LABOUR MARKET

When we assess the current workforce as a source of supply, we do so within the context of continuous movement and activity. It may be that a large proportion of employees will remain in their present positions, but there are always people leaving and entering, being promoted, transferring, retiring and so forth. From our records, for example, we know:

- how many people we employ;
- the nature of their skills and other qualities;
- their level or status in the organization;
- the standards of their performance;
- their attitudes and versatility;
- their potential for promotion or other movement;
- how many are likely to go sick, and when;
- how many are likely to resign or be dismissed;
- how many will retire, and when.

From what we know, we should be able to classify employees in terms of the departments or functions in which they are employed in the organization, and produce lists according to job title, status, nature and level of skill, sex, race and whatever other category is needed for the purposes of the organization. There are several ways of going about this. One approach is to produce lists of people and categorize them within their departments or functions. Alternatively, we can ignore departments and functions and list people simply in terms of their job titles and the nature of the skills they use in their jobs. The first approach is effective when particular skills are used exclusively in particular areas, but we often find that similar skills are used in different parts of the organization, in which case it would make more sense to group knowledge, skills and attitudes at the levels at which they are required, without necessarily also grouping them into their respective departments and functions. Bear in mind, however, that there are many examples of such 'choice' situations in supply forecasting and it is very easy to

Exhibit 8.2

> It is said that one of the differences between manpower planning and HRM is that, in the former, there was an emphasis on the *number* of people employed, while in the latter, the emphasis is upon people as a key resource. Here, however, we are saying that regardless of how one perceives the employees, there still have to be enough of them to do the job.

gather too much information, which, at best, produces large, unwieldy tracts of data and, at worst, causes confusion.

The next step is to match the qualities of the current workforce with those that will be demanded in the future. When we do this, we may discover discrepancies between, say, the current skills and attitudes of the workforce and those that will be required; and there is a very good chance that there will be a discrepancy between the current and future situations. New technology often reduces demand, while growth and expansion increase it. The positive or negative nature of the discrepancy, therefore, will be determined by the organization's strategy and objectives, as they are laid down in the corporate plan.

While training and development can be used to fill in many of the gaps in knowledge, skills and attitudes, a shortfall in terms of numbers may force us to look to the external labour market to fill in the gaps. Shortfalls can occur through such internal movements as those referred to in the last four items in the list above, but they can also occur as a result of the organization's plans to meet the demands of a rising market; strategic plans may give rise to new products and processes, producing the need for a larger workforce and the introduction of new knowledge and skills (see exhibit 8.2).

THE EXTERNAL LABOUR MARKET

If the results of our HR demand analysis produce a shortfall in skills or numbers of people, which sometimes means the same thing, we formulate a plan to recruit the additional staff we will require. This means analysing and assessing the external information we will have gathered about potential recruits in terms of NASKAT:

- **N**umber
- **A**vailability
- **S**kills
- **K**nowledge
- **A**ttitudes
- **T**raining amenability

We need to bear in mind that other organizations in the same region or industry may compete with us for the same recruits. In order to compete effectively with other organizations, HR planners maintain records of terms and conditions of employment that are offered at regional and industrial levels. This is often referred to as the 'going rate'.

For a variety of reasons, it is important to draw distinctions between different categories of employee. There is more about this in the next chapter, but for HR planning purposes, it is necessary to maintain a balance between the requirements of the law and the needs of the organization. In this respect, it is worth checking that the HR plan shows an acceptable distribution of the sexes and ethnic minorities at all levels and functions.

In another context, we need to distinguish between two further categories of potential employee, in terms of their availability and the exceptional nature of their knowledge, skills and special talents. Such people usually fall into professional categories, like engineering specialisms, linguistic talents, research chemists and so forth. These are people to whom their work is the most important aspect of their lives. They are prepared to relocate, sometimes globally, in order to pursue and advance their careers in terms of the work in which they feel deeply involved. If it needs such specialists, the organization has to be ready to offer a negotiated package of terms and conditions of employment that are favourable enough to attract and retain them.

At the opposite end of the dimension, there are people who work in a particular location because it is near to where they live, where they have family ties, friends and other external interests. If such people were to lose their jobs, they would look around in the same locality for a job with a similar salary and other terms and conditions, such as working hours, holiday entitlement, travel-to-work time etc.

Exhibit 8.3 A basic human resource planning system

> 1 From corporate plan and departmental information, establish and collate details for a **demand forecast**
> 2 From information gathered internally and externally, establish and collate details for a **supply forecast**
> 3 Combine and analyse information from 1 and 2, establish implications and draw up a **human resource plan**

Undoubtedly, there is a case for categorizing staff in this way in a chapter of a different title. On the other hand, when one is assessing the HR supply situation, it is important to build in such categories, so that when the plan is implemented, the recruitment specialists will know where to advertise for them.

In summary, the process we should have in mind is in two main stages, preparation and implementation. Preparation takes place as we are gathering information for the demand and supply forecasts. Implementation takes place when we formulate and activate the plan itself (see exhibit 8.3). From then on, it is a matter of maintaining and updating the plan in accordance with the changing requirements of the organization.

Human Resource Costs

The HR plan, then, is derived principally from the corporate strategy, and is moderated by realistic assessments of the supply situation. A further limitation, however, is one that prevails throughout the whole organization – cost. Finance, in common with all other resources, is scarce. In other words, we cannot autocratically produce an HR plan that ideally will meet every single organizational need, in terms of knowledge, skills, attitudes and timing. Costs have to be taken into account and the relevant budget in most organizations represents a significant proportion of total expenditure. The discussion on HRM shows that there are two ways in which we may regard the organization's people. Traditionally, personnel people talk about the 'wages and salary bill' and tend to regard the workforce as a cost.

Many senior managers see it in that way too and are continually on the look-out for ways of making cost savings on staff.

Unfortunately, their efforts often result in so-called 'redundancies'. While such savings may seem sensible in the short term, especially if salary and wage bills represent too large a proportion of total expenditure, the undeniable fact is that any human resource strategy that reduces the size of the workforce detaches valuable talents from the organization, talents that it might need in the medium or long term. One approach to redressing the human resources cost/total expenditure balance, is to review the ways in which managers maximize on the human resources at their disposal. Given the choice, most employees would rather change and develop further skills, than leave.

If, for example, we were to regard the workforce as a resource, rather than solely as a cost – and, in fact, the only resource a manager has that can increase in its value to the organization – we begin to see 'human resource planning' in a different light. The work that every person does in the organization makes a contribution towards its success and profitability. A more effective performance from people, which can be achieved through training and attitude change, produces greater success and higher profitability. There is a powerful link, therefore, between human performance and profitability, which means that when organizations are assessing future labour costs, they should do so in parallel with the arrangements they are making to improve human performance, thereby increasing productivity.

Employment Costs

While the calculation of the total annual wages and salary bill is a relatively simple task, the result does not represent the total cost of employment. Calculating the total figure includes . taking account of such things as National Insurance contributions, salary administration, administering 'check-off' systems through which trade union subscriptions are paid, and an accumulation of other factors. One way of demonstrating the relative significance of various employment cost factors is to present them in 'pie chart' form, as depicted in Figure 8.2. While an analysis of this kind may include or exclude any number of a wide variety of employment cost factors, the real value of the

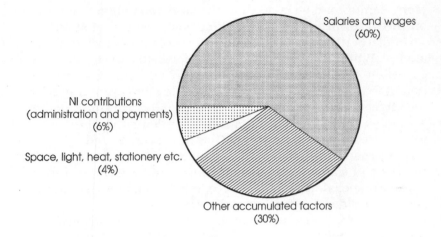

Figure 8.2 The relative significance of employment cost factors.

analysis is in the opportunity to see where savings can be made.

Summary

Planning for the future human resource needs of the organization involves us in a process which is in two major parts: preparation and implementation. The preparatory stage involves us in using techniques that provide a structured and systematic method of gathering information that enables us to assess *demand* and *supply*. The supply situation is matched against that of demand, and steps are taken to remove any discrepancies. These steps might take the form of training, to fill in any knowledge, skills and attitude gaps; recruitment, to replace a shortfall in the supply situation and/or to import new knowledge, skills and attitudes; and reduction, to address the problem of a future surfeit of supply, perhaps by putting a temporary stop on recruitment for certain areas of the organization and allowing 'natural wastage' (the normal staff turnover rate) to solve the problem. Implementation involves us in formulating and activating the plan, which leads us towards the further personnel specialisms of recruitment, selection, induction and training.

References

Armstrong, M. 1988: *A Handbook of Personnel Management Practice*, 3rd edn. London: Kogan Page.

Attwood, M. 1989: *Personnel Management*. London: Macmillan.

McKenna, E. and Beech, N. 1995: *The Essence of Human Resource Management*. London: Prentice Hall.

Torrington, D. 1989: Human resource management and the personnel function. In J. Storey (ed.), *New Perspectives on Human Resource Management*. London: Routledge.

Tyson, S. (ed.) 1995: *Strategic Prospects for HRM*. London: Institute of Personnel and Development.

9

Recruitment

While the main purpose of this chapter is to review recruitment processes, strategies and techniques, it is worth starting by making the point that, for several reasons, recruitment is regarded as one of the more important personnel functions. Firstly, it attracts people's attention to the organization and invites them to consider the possibility of employment. The image of the organization that is projected by recruitment advertisements and follow-up literature, therefore, has to be consistent with the self-image that the organization wishes to project publicly. Secondly, it brings people into the organization to be interviewed and sometimes to undergo occupational tests, which are steps that can lead to employment. Thirdly, it can be a costly process that sometimes results in failure.

The Range and Scope of Recruitment Practices

The recruitment process begins when a genuine vacancy is identified, and ends when a new employee is at work in the position that was vacant. This implies that recruitment embraces the broad range of activities that lead to the interview, the selection decision and the offer of employment, agreeing a start date, induction and deployment. Alternatively, it has been said that recruitment ends when the selectors are presented with a shortlist of candidates, at which point the *separate* processes of interviewing, selection and so forth take over. Although this is a discussion that crops up from time to time, the issue is really academic. In practice, the stages are handled consecutively, so that the whole process is continuous anyway. In some organizations, the personnel specialists who handle recruitment also handle interviewing and selection, whereas elsewhere these tasks are allocated to different people. Here, the chapters on recruitment and selection are separated, purely to ease understanding.

Identifying a Vacancy

So-called 'vacancies' appear when someone leaves, or when the organization expands and reorganizes internally or introduces new systems; recruitment seems to be the obvious way to fill such vacancies. Alternatives to recruitment emerged, however, when the assumption that such situations automatically created vacancies was challenged. The alternatives include:

- analysing the 'vacant' position, removing any redundant tasks and redistributing the remaining work across the department or function;
- redesigning the work system and computerizing or mechanizing the work. This may be favoured when several people leave, especially in an area where employees are doing similar work, but not if just one person leaves;
- offering overtime payments to cover the extra work created by the person leaving;
- subcontracting the work outside. The work may have to be above a certain quantity for the subcontractor to consider it worth while. Also, it may be difficult to move the work, especially if specialized equipment is needed;
- employing a temporary or part-time worker. This might be a suitable solution if changes are imminent anyway.

In most organizations today, there is a drive to reduce the size of the workforce, and the decision that results from these deliberations is usually preceded by a close examination of the cost of each alternative.

One fairly recent innovation in this respect is to devise company regulations through which the existence of a genuine vacancy may be confirmed and formal authority to fill it obtained. This involves the use of an Authority to Recruit (ATR) form. The ATR is one of the signs of the changes in management practice that have taken place in recent years. If the manager considers that none of the alternatives described above would be appropriate, he or she fills in an ATR showing why the recruitment of a replacement is essential.

On one side of the form, the line manager has to make a case in support of the need to fill a post and in doing so, justifies the appointment in terms of practicality, cost and productivity benefits. Next, the form is seen by a senior manager, who comments on the line manager's case and either gives or withholds the authority to make the appointment. Before making a decision, the senior manager may consult others, including the line manager concerned. Eventually, the form is returned to the line manager. If it is designed properly, the ATR will force the line manager, and at least one senior manager, to review the situation. These forms may be encountered under different names, such as the Appointment Authority Form (AAF), Appointment Justification Form (AJF). If authority is given, the line manager, in consultation with the recruitment specialist, makes out a *job requisition.*

THE JOB REQUISITION

This is a form on which the line manager describes his or her requirements in terms of: (1) the nature of the tasks that make up the job, (2) how the job has changed (if it has) since it was last reviewed, (3) the priorities of the job – key tasks, etc. and (4) the knowledge, skills, attitudes and other personal qualities needed for the job. It may be thought that this information can be found in the job description and specification, but those documents may be out of date, the job having changed since they were last reviewed. In practice, the line manager and the personnel specialist get together and agree on the information that will be included in the recruitment advertisement and any follow-up literature.

The Job Description

While job descriptions should be updated regularly, the personnel specialist should maintain contact with the line manager and gather information that will enable a further update to be carried out. In addition to their use in recruitment, job descriptions have a key role in other activities, such as identifying training needs, introducing a job evaluation scheme and devising other systems of payment; every opportunity should be taken, therefore, to bring job descriptions up to date.

At this early stage in recruitment, the personnel specialist should have access to two documents: the *job description* and the *job specification*. Both are produced from a job analysis (see Chapter 13). The job description contains details of the job, while the job specification describes the knowledge and skills

Organization	Farm-Fresh Foods Ltd, Wheatsheaf Lane, Penyard, Wiltshire.
Department	Accounts Department
Job title	Accounts Office Supervisor
Duties and responsibilities	**Main duties** 1 Keep the accounts of the company's largest customers, ensuring their accounts are kept up to date and that invoices and statements go out on time 2 Monitor credit limits, ensuring they are not exceeded without special permission 3 Arrange that all credit limits above £2500 are insured 4 Maintain liaison with credit reference agencies 5 Allocate work to clerical staff 6 Supervise the work of a team of eight accounts clerks, offering advice and guidance where necessary 7 Monitor the performance standards of accounts staff 8 Supervise the efficient and effective operation of the Accounts Office **Main responsibilities** 9 Maintain good customer relations when responding to their accounts queries 10 Report to the Accounts Manager on all of the above
Salary and other main terms and conditions	Salary £15,000 p.a. plus company car. Relocation allowance, well-appointed office, situated pleasant rural area. Option to join pension scheme after two years. Must participate in formal performance appraisal scheme after expiry of 6-month probationary period.
Performance and career prospects	Possible promotion to Assistant Manager after two years. The critical performance standards relate to the maintenance of good customer relations and the degree to which invoice and statement deadlines are met.

Figure 9.1 A typical job description.

necessary to do the job. Typically, a job description will be produced along the lines detailed in figure 9.1.

MAINTAINING JOB DESCRIPTIONS

The case for having job descriptions and keeping them up to date is not as strong as it once was. The rate at which organizations are changing and developing is increasing, and many managers feel that job descriptions inhibit flexibility: 'They are written on one day and the job changes on the next.' Inflexible definitions of jobs, they say, place limitations on change and development because they do not allow for changes in deployment, multi-skilling and a wide variety of other factors affecting the ways in which the talents of the human resource are maximized. The notion that job descriptions can and should be updated regularly is also losing credibility, since updating would have to keep pace with other developments in the organization and, at present, rates of advancement, time constraints and related costs would prohibit the exercise.

THE JOB SPECIFICATION

This is derived from the job description. The expectation that the main duties and responsibilities will be fulfilled at or above predetermined performance standards, and the nature of the duties and responsibilities themselves, will provide indications of the knowledge, skills and other qualities that are required. Since the job specification is a description of the knowledge and skills that are required for the job to be carried out effectively, it may be regarded as a reflection of the main features of the job description, but in the form of personal qualities. Typically, it will be produced as shown in figure 9.2.

THE 'PERSON SPECIFICATION'

The terminology surrounding the document that describes the ideal person has become somewhat confused, which has arisen primarily because of the importance that is attributed to the terminology related to sex discrimination. Before politically correct terminology invaded the language, we had a job description, a job specification and a man specification. Obviously, the word, 'man' had to go and it was replaced with the word 'person'. In the

	Job title: Accounts Office Supervisor	Farm-Fresh Foods Ltd, Wiltshire	Accounts Department
	Job requirements	Minimum attainment	Preferred attainment
1	Key skills	To meet minimum standards without exception	Able to exceed minimum standards, especially in key areas
2	Responsibilities	Capable of adopting responsibility	Enjoys responsibility, well organized personally
3	Experience required	At least two years in similar position	Three/four years in similar position
4	Special aptitudes	Good decision making and problem solving abilities; relates well to others	Good conceptual skills, able to assess situations and solve problems quickly; enjoys interpersonal contact
5	Personality	Emotionally stable, calm, at ease in crises	Outgoing, but stable, proven leadership skills
6	Availability	Within three months; prepared to relocate if necessary	Within 4/6 weeks
7	Health	Good for age	Very good

Figure 9.2 A typical job specification.

confusion, some people who had never heard of a 'job specification' began to think that it was the replacement term for man specification. Hence the confusion. For the purposes of clarification, the following might help:

1 *Job Description.* This is a detailed description of the job, typically containing the features shown in figure 9.1, although there are variations on this structure, which are determined by the nature of the job or the pattern preferred by the organization.

2 *Job Specification.* This document contains details of the knowledge, skills and experience that are needed to meet the demands of the job, as they are reflected in the nature of the duties and responsibilities (see figure 9.2).

3   *Person Specification.* This document contains a description of
    the qualities that the ideal person for the job should possess
    (see table 9.1).

When used together, as they are in recruitment, the set of the
three documents is often referred to collectively as the *personnel
specification.* One could be forgiven for assuming that it is
unnecessary to to have three documents that are so alike in
structure and content, but a closer look tells us that, in fact,
they are different, while experience tells us that they are used
individually for different purposes.

Table 9.1   A person specification structure (Rodger, 1952)

Quality	Description
1 Physical	This covers health, physique, age, appearance, hearing and speech. Physical attributes may be added or removed as necessary
2 Attainments	Including academic attainments, training received, knowledge, skills and experience already developed
3 Intelligence	The general intelligence, specific abilities and the methods for the assessment of these
4 Special aptitudes	Any special aptitudes, such as mechanical, manual, verbal, numerical, creativity, etc.
5 Interests	Personal interests as possible indicators of aptitudes, abilities or personality traits (e.g. intellectual, practical/ constructional, physically active, social, artistic)
6 Disposition	Personality characteristics needed (e.g. equability, dependability, self-reliance, assertiveness, drive, energy, perseverance, initiative, motivation)
7 Circumstances	Personal and domestic circumstances (e.g. mobility, commitments, family circumstances and occupations)

Figure 9.2 shows the minimum and preferred attainments demanded by the job in respect of the seven criteria shown. This should be regarded as a flexible document on which the line manager and the personnel specialist can build a person specification.

Considerable time and ingenuity has gone into the development of person specification structures. Each structure attempts to present a basic set of criteria, against which 'minimum/essential' and 'desirable' job requirements can be set. Table 9.1 shows one of the most well-known structures: Professor Alex Rodger's *Seven Point Plan* (1952).

If we examine the contents of the job description and job specification that relate to the post of Accounts Office Supervisor (see figures 9.1 and 9.2), we should be able to prepare a person specification, using the Seven Point Plan structure given above. The Seven Point Plan may be regarded as a 'checklist', but it is also a structure that many personnel specialists find gives them a systematic way of allocating the required personal qualities to their appropriate categories on the specification.

Equal Opportunities

It is important to exercise care over the provision of equal opportunities. The Seven Point Plan was published more than 20 years before the discrimination laws were passed, and was not, therefore, compiled with those laws in mind. The provisions of the relevant legislation require us not to discriminate against people on various grounds, including those of gender or ethnic origin. Also, there is legislation in respect of disabled people, which is currently under review. In this light, we need to be certain that the personal qualities we list, particularly under Points 1 and 7, do not conflict with the law.

Aside from the law, however, there are moral and practical issues to be considered when deliberating over personal qualities. When, for example, we say that a person should be physically fit, what do we mean? Do we mean that they should be physically fit in the general sense? This should be questioned. After all, the fact that a person is disabled does not mean that he or she is unhealthy; in fact, the person may be perfectly healthy, and physically fit to do the job, which surely is what counts. It is possible, on these grounds, to turn away people who possess

exceptional talents and who could have made significant contributions to the success of the organization. The fears and
prejudices that people have in these respects are largely socially
inherent, and the related behaviour is most frequently exercised
without conscious awareness. It is a matter of fact that organizations that wish to succeed in today's fiercely competitive markets
simply cannot afford to shun the potential of those who typically
are the subjects of discrimination.

On particular grounds, discrimination, whether it is deliberate
or inadvertant, is against the law, and, apart from the immoral-
ity of it, it is almost certainly unprofitable. On the other hand,
the next chapter will show that employment selection is, by its
very nature, a discriminatory process. The selector has to pick
'the best person for the job' and in doing so, is forced to decide
against those who are considered unsuitable. As we shall see
later, this is a tricky business.

Recruitment Advertising

Having gathered the necessary information and compiled or
reviewed (as necessary) the personnel specification, we are ready
for the next stage of the recruitment process, that of advertising
the position. Recruitment advertising is an extensive subject in
its own right, too complex and far-reaching to treat comprehen-
sively here. Nevertheless, we shall have achieved something
worthwhile if by discussing it we attain a reasonable understanding of the key factors in the process.

The Latin origin of the word advertise, *advertere*, translates
into 'to make known', although use of the word has developed it
into one that generally is used to refer to announcements in
newspapers and magazines, and on street hoardings and shop
fronts. And, as we know, 'advertisements' reach us through
television and other media.

Basically, there are three kinds of advertisement: corporate,
product and recruitment. Corporate advertisements are those
that inform us about the organization as a total entity, its
purposes, achievements, customer policy and so forth. 'ICI – the
pathfinders' and 'Philips – friend of the family' are typical corporate advertisements. 'Persil washes whiter' and 'Guinness is good
for you' are product advertisements.

Advertising is the organization's principal means of communicating with other organizations and individuals in its environment, and when it is done properly there is a consistent image projected by every advertisement. Corporate and product advertisements are created by the marketing department or the organization's advertising agents. Decisions are made about the most appropriate image, which usually includes the use of a logo. Normally, advertisers use the same agency for all three kinds of advertisement, so that problems of attaining the concept of the organization's image, the availability of artwork, and the form that the advertisements should take do not arise.

One approach to recruitment advertising is to create an advertisement framework that will accommodate the 'copy' relevant to any job. This can be used in any newspaper or magazine; less frequently, recruitment advertisements appear on television, in cinemas and on radio, but the same principle of using a common framework still may apply.

Going back to our Latin translation, however, 'to make known' can be interpreted in several ways. The purpose here is to capture the attention of individuals whom we regard as potential employees and there are several ways of doing that, which we can list as follows:

1   advertising internally on notice boards and in the company magazine;
2   interrogating the personnel records for suitable candidates;
3   using general and specialist selection consultants;
4   using employment agencies and job centres;
5   advertising externally in appropriate media (selected newspapers and professional or trade magazines, etc.);
6   scanning the files on people who have sent in curricula vitae on speculation;
7   taking up recommendations from current employees;
8   making direct contact with schools, colleges and universities, supporting their career conventions and maintaining good relations;
9   inviting applications from students who are doing their work experience with you.

Application Forms

Not all organizations use application forms. Some ask for a 'letter of application', while others prefer to see a neatly typed curriculum vitae (CV). The problem with letters and CVs is that they take so long to sift, especially if there is a large number of applicants. For most jobs, application forms are usually preferred; the layout of the form is the same for all applicants and sifting through them is made easier because each set of details is in the same part of every form. A typical layout of an application form is shown in figure 9.3.

A new kind of application form is growing in popularity, especially among recruitment agencies, and where large numbers of applications are received. Computer technology has made it possible to screen forms electronically, through a process called optical character recognition (OCR), or optical mark recognition (OMR). If, for example, it has been decided that only those who possess three A levels and a degree will be considered, the process will screen out all applicants who fail on this criterion. The application form is designed to lend itself to the process. Although OCR has been in use in other areas for more than 20 years, its use in recruitment is relatively new. Technologically, of course, the concept is brilliant, but one has doubts about its effectiveness in terms of the objectives of recruitment. For example, a candidate with three A levels at grades C and D might be screened in, while another with only two A levels, but at grades A and B, would be screened out, thus allowing potential talent to slip away. Certainly, the computer could be programmed to avoid this kind of thing, but that, in turn, may reduce the cost-effectiveness of the software.

Internal Appointments

Making an internal appointment can change the location of the vacancy, perhaps even from one department or function to another, since on taking up the position, the appointed person will leave a vacancy. This will take us back to square one, when we ask again: does a genuine vacancy exist?

Internal appointments should be handled sensitively. Before making an appointment that promotes an employee, we should examine his or her current status in the records on potential and those on employee development, otherwise we could cause one system to undermine the purposes of another (and displease at least one line manager in the process). A final point is that those

SOLENT TOYS LIMITED

APPLICATION FOR EMPLOYMENT

Surname:	Position applied for:
First name(s):	Date of birth:
Address:	Place of birth:
_____	Marital status:
_____	Number of children:
_____	Next of kin:

Present job title:

Present employer's name and address (this will not be used without permission):

EDUCATION			
Schools attended (name and town)	Examinations taken (including subjects and results)	Dates	
		From	To
College/University (name and town)			

1

Figure 9.3 A typical application form.

TRAINING

Please give details of any training you have undertaken

Training provider	Nature of the training (e.g. subject matter)	Date/s of training From To

Please indicate any academic and professional qualification you hold; e.g. BA (Hons), MIPD, etc.

Please indicate any specific knowledge and skills you possess, which are not indicated above and which you think will be useful in your future career; e.g. driving, using a computer, knowledge of a foreign language, etc.

EXTERNAL INTERESTS

Please state how your leisure time is spent; e.g. hobbies, sporting interests, etc.

2

Figure 9.3 *continued.*

EMPLOYMENT HISTORY

Please provide details of your employment since leaving full-time education. Include any periods of unemployment and military service.

Dates From To	Name and addresses of employers	Job title and duties	Salary on leaving	Reason for leaving

3

Figure 9.3 *continued.*

Do you have relatives working for Solent Toys Limited? If so, please say who and in what capacity.

Name _____ Job title _____

If offered employment, would you agree to a medical examination?   Yes [ ]   No [ ]

On what date would you be available to commence work: _____

Please give the names and addresses of two people of good standing, one of whom would be able to provide a personal reference, and one a professional reference.

Name: _____   Name: _____

Address: _____   Address: _____

_____   _____

_____   _____

Telephone: _____   Telephone: _____

This space is provided for you to make a statement in support of your application. Continue on a separate sheet if necessary.

I declare that the information I have given on this application form is true and correct.

Signature: _____   Date: _____

4

Figure 9.3 *concluded.*

who handle internal appointments seem too frequently to be insensitive to the need to provide equal opportunities. Women and minority groups often feel that they would not be considered for promotion or other favoured positions, and that making an application might put their current position in some kind of jeopardy. The straightforward way through this situation is positively to encourage them to apply. This is not a plug for positive discrimination – quite the reverse, since the objective still would be to appoint the best person for the job. The point I am making is that to some selectors, the concept of equal opportunity seems less relevant when internal appointments are being made.

Using Consultants and Specialists

External consultants and specialists are used when the organization lacks the necessary expertise to recruit for positions in the higher levels of management, and when vacancies occur in key specialisms, such as in certain aspects of engineering, information technology, medicine, chemicals – whatever the organization needs. A vacancy in such an area may have arisen because somebody has left, or it may be a forthcoming new position, created by plans to introduce new technology.

It is normal for a consultant to meet the senior managers of the organization, to reach agreement about the detailed person specification, when the appointment should be made and the terms and conditions of employment. The consultant then adopts responsibility for recruiting the right person for the job, a process which usually culminates in the consultant presenting the organization with a shortlist of candidates and offering to assist with the final selection. For these services, the consultants' fees are usually fairly high, but the probability that the right person will be selected is also high.

EMPLOYMENT AGENCIES

Employment agencies are often associated with temporary and part-time staff, but most of them are extremely good at finding people for positions in the main body of the workforce, especially for administrative, secretarial and clerical positions. There are, however, agencies that specialize in certain trades. One of the

UK's largest employment agencies started by specializing in placing people in the hotel and catering industry; another began by placing secretaries; yet another by placing labourers and general workers.

Agencies maintain files on people who seek to change their jobs, are prepared to work in temporary positions, or whose availability is limited and who can work only part-time. To use an employment agency, the personnel specialist simply telephones or writes to the firm, describes the job and gives the agency a profile of the kind of person required. The agency scans its files and recommends that certain people should be interviewed. Organizations tend to stick with the same agencies, they get to know each other and, in the process, a useful understanding of each other's needs and methods of operating develops, although there is evidence to suggest that, to some extent, organizations do not totally trust agencies.

Employment agents' fees for temporary workers are based upon hourly, daily, weekly and monthly rates. Their fee structure for full-time, permanent staff is based upon the appointed person's salary. The fierce competition in this field has produced a vastly improved service and competitive fees.

JOB CENTRES

People who register with Job Centres are usually unemployed, and some organizations may regard this as a disadvantage. Why someone is unemployed is an important question in recruitment. Also, seeing groups of people hanging around the Job Centres is a little reminiscent of the 1920s and 1930s, when men used to hang around factory gates hoping for casual work; the stigma associated with unemployment dies hard, and today's scene does nothing to assuage it. It is always more difficult for an unemployed person to find a job.

On a more positive note, however, Torrington and Hall (1987) point out that Job Centres are socially responsible and secure, that they can produce applicants very quickly and that the number of people who are finding employment through them has risen significantly.

A further advantage that the Job Centres have over other providers is that they can offer the facility of a locally situated national database, on which one may carry out a national 'trawl' for suitable candidates. Also, it is worth noting that they do not charge fees.

External Advertising

The copy for a recruitment advertisement is derived from the personnel specification. The tasks of creating a recruitment advertisement, selecting appropriate media in which it may be placed, monitoring response rates and administering the system are time consuming and, largely, technical. Most organizations delegate these tasks to their advertising agency. Advertising agencies are specifically structured to deal with the technical aspects of advertising and, indeed, some specialize exclusively in recruitment advertising. They have separate specialized departments for each function: copywriting, creativity, media selection, account servicing and so forth. If the business that you do with them justifies it, they will assign an 'accounts executive' specifically to ensure that your needs are being met. Plumbley (1985) points to some of the advantages of using an advertising agent:

> only one copy of the text need be supplied no matter how many publications are to be used; the agency will book space; prepare the layout and typography; read and correct proofs; verify that the right advertisement has appeared in the right publication at the right time; and only one cheque has to be raised to settle the agency's monthly account.

Another advantage is that competition for clients among advertising agents is very strong. Agencies, however, must compete with each other through the quality of the services they provide, rather than on price, since most of their income is earned through 'commission' paid to them by the media for placing the advertisements with them.

A further, major advantage is that they can provide anonymity, in which your advertisements appear under the name of the agency. Sometimes the advertisements are in *composite* form, in which the agency has taken a space in the newspaper to advertise positions on behalf of a number of its clients. This reduces the cost of an advertisement, while the anonymity can protect the confidentiality of the organization's marketing plans. The client organization, for example, may have plans to diversify into a new market, creating the need for new, specialized staff. Since the job title and other details about the job and the type of person can reveal the nature of the diversification, knowledge of who is advertising these positions would be useful information to competitors.

MEDIA SELECTION

Advertising agents are experts in this field, but it is as well to monitor the response rates of the media they choose, especially in the light of what is said above about their main source of income. 'Monitoring response rates' implies that we are inter- ested in *how many* replies the advertisement creates. What is more important, however, is the *amount of interest* in the job that is created by the advertisement, and *who* responds to it. After all, if there is only one vacancy to fill, then the *quality* of the responses is far more important than the quantity.

Thousands of newspapers and magazines are published every year, and they are all different from each other. There are national and regional daily newspapers, and the Sunday press, all of which appeal to different readership segments. Large towns and cities have their own weekly newspapers and there are local weekly freesheets. Magazines are classified as con- sumer, industrial, trade and professional, and the frequency of their publication varies. Consumer magazines do not carry recruitment advertisements, but industrial, trade and profes- sional journals live on them, with up to a third of the total space available occupied by them, usually in the form of a special section in the back of the magazine.

The choice of media is determined by the nature of the job and the date by which you wish to make the appointment. A monthly or quarterly journal, for example, will carry advertisements for positions in the industry, trade or profession that it represents, so if you wish to employ an engineer, it makes sense to place the advertisement in a professional journal that is read by engin- eers. However, because of the frequency of these publications, they are used to advertising positions that have been planned well in advance. Recruitment advertisers who are familiar with the media scene know that good quality responses from say, engineers, may also be obtained from certain Sunday and national daily newspapers.

The organizational level of the vacancy is another determinant of media selection. Typists, machine operators and other mem- bers of the main body of the workforce generally do not take the same newspapers and magazines as those at the top of the company. On the other hand, any member of the workforce, from any level, may read the local weekly newspaper.

The Recruitment Advertisement

People who boast about the number of replies they have received in response to an advertisement which they (of course) have written seldom boast about the amount of work they have created for themselves. Replies have to be studied, screened, acknowledged and categorized. Life is so much easier when you are dealing with a moderate number of good quality responses. But how do you do that?

The main factors influencing the quality and quantity of responses to job advertisements are (1) the state of the employment market, and (2) the style and content of the recruitment advertisement. There is little we can do about the state of the employment market, but the recruitment advertisement is entirely in our hands. As a rule, it is safe to say that the more generalized and vague the content, the more responses we will get, and the quality is usually mixed. Conversely, the more we tighten up the specification in the advertisement and narrow the description of the kind of person we are looking for, the fewer responses we will get, and the quality is usually high. Generalized advertisements that produce large responses are fine if we wish to fill several jobs, the specifications for which have many similarities, but beyond that, it is hard to make a case in support of them. A large number of responses increases administrative costs.

Without exception, the recruitment advertisement should contain four fundamental items: (1) the key features of the job, including the title and salary range, (2) the geographical location of the job, (3) the nature of the industry and, preferably, the name of the employing organization and (4) how and where to apply.

The job title and salary, together with details of the main duties and responsibilities, will give the reader a good indication of the type and 'ballpark' level of the job. Changing one's job is a very important event in a person's life and the geographical location is a strong influence on the decision to make an application. People like to know the name of the organization to which they are applying; in fact, not knowing can put them off. If the job is along the lines of what they are doing now, they might suspect that they could even be applying to their current employer. Readers need to know what kind of application is preferred. Should they send a letter of application, write in or telephone for an application form and further details, or is a curriculum vitae required? Whichever of these methods is to be used, the reader will need a name and address, or at the very least a telephone number.

In a sense, recruitment advertisements are a little like the goods on a supermarket shelf, screaming out to be noticed and selected in preference to their competitors. In most newspapers and magazines, they all appear together on the same pages, and to compel the readers' attention, your advertisement should have something special; it should contain an attraction that will draw the eye of the reader. If you study the total job situation objectively, you will usually find something: Is it a high salary? A pleasant location? Does the job carry unusual status? The job's most attractive feature should be a main feature of the advertisement, such as the caption.

Finally, the advertisement has to comply with the provisions of the legislation on equal opportunities and discrimination, and care should be taken to ensure that the advertisement is legal. Newspapers and magazines also 'vet' the advertisements for legality, but it is as well to provide them with legal copy in the first place. Beyond the strictly legal aspects is the *spirit* of encouragement, in which some organizations include a line or two in the advertisement, inviting members of minority groups to apply. Several organizations with which I am familiar have their advertisements translated and placed in local newspapers and magazines that are produced in the languages of ethnic groups, while others use the same media to advise ethnic minorities of when and where particular recruitment advertisements will be appearing shortly.

Summary

Recruitment begins when a genuine vacancy is identified. The line manager is involved from the outset, producing an Authority to Recruit (ATR) form, on which the need for the vacancy to be filled is justified. Authority is given by a senior manager, and the line manager then completes a job requisition, which is a form on which the key features of the job and the kind of person needed for it are described.

The next step is to produce (or review) the job description, the job specification and the person specification. These documents form the basis of the recruitment process, including the contents of the recruitment advertisement. Care should be taken at all stages to ensure conformity with the provisions of the legislation on discrimination and equal opportunity.

In a sense, recruitment specialists, like Janus, have two faces; one looking towards the inside of the organization, ensuring that policy, the law and the recruitment system are being followed, while the other faces outwards, to the environment, seeking the most effective means of attracting the right person for the job.

References

Plumbley, P.R. 1985: *Recruitment and Selection*, 4th edn. London: Institute of Personnel Management (now the Institute of Personnel and Development).

Rodger, A. 1952: *The Seven Point Plan*. London: National Institute of Industrial Psychology.

Torrington, D. and Hall, L. 1987: *Personnel Management: a New Approach*. London: Prentice Hall.

10

Selection

The purpose of employment selection is to choose the right person for the job, which includes predicting the in-job performance of candidates. In this chapter, we review the principal features of the selection process, which begin with screening and shortlisting applications, then corresponding with applicants, organizing and conducting interviews and making the selection decision.

Screening Applications

In some organizations, this is still done manually, but computerized systems have become quite widespread. Screening involves reading through the applications, comparing their contents with the demands of the person specification and sorting them into piles under the headings of *rejections*, *possibles* and *probables*. Rejection letters are sent to those whose applications have failed to reach the minimum requirements for the job. Sometimes this is not necessary. When a large number of replies is anticipated at the time of placing the recruitment advertisement, it is common practice to insert a line in the advertisement to the effect that only those applicants who reach the minimum standard will receive further correspondence. If a letter is sent, however, it should be worded courteously, thanking the person for their application and telling them why they have been rejected on this occasion.

Next, we re-screen the 'possibles' and 'probables', and it is normal to involve the line manager in this process. Firstly, we go through the possibles, to see if any of them should be moved into the probables pile. We then send a rejection letter to the remaining possibles, and an acknowledgement of the receipt of their applications to the probables.

Shortlisting

The next objective is to decide who should be interviewed. This is done, still with the line manager, by selecting from the applications those which most closely conform to the person specification. Eventually, a shortlist of what are considered to be the best applications emerges and the applicants are invited to attend for an interview. This time, a slightly longer letter is sent to those who have not quite made it, thanking them for their application, telling them that the competition for this particular post was high and, to particularly good applicants, saying that you hope that this outcome will not deter them from responding to your future advertisements.

Great care should be taken to ensure that the order and timing of these sequential steps is carried out correctly. Figure 10.1 is a checklist of the stages in the screening process.

Interview Administration

How we approach the organization and administration of interviews depends upon the kind of selection process that has been decided upon for the position in question. Interviews may be held in one- or two-to-one situations, panel interviews or selection boards, or a combination of some of these models. Also, the process may include the use of selection tests, such as occupational or psychological tests; the use of group selection processes and assessment centres is also well established. Arrangements, including the venues, timings and the people involved, need to be carefully coordinated.

The answers to the following questions make a standard administrative checklist:

Timing. Have all relevant dates been set and agreed by everyone involved?

Venues. Has all of the necessary accommodation been booked for the following purposes: waiting areas, medical examinations (if any), interviewing and selection testing?

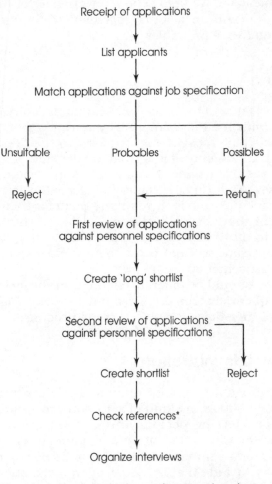

Figure 10.1 Stages in the screening process.

Reception. Have the people in reception been given a list of the candidates, the times and dates of their arrival and where they are to wait?
Personnel. (1) Has everyone who is involved in the interviewing and selection process been briefed on the timing and sequence of events? (2) If selection testing is involved, will a qualified test administrator be available?

Candidates. Have all shortlisted candidates been advised of the relevant times and dates and has their availability been confirmed?

Special needs. Have appropriate arrangements been made for people with special needs (not forgetting any members of your own organization's staff), such as the disabled people who may need special car-parking?

Medical examinations. Have arrangements been made for any medical examinations that the organization may require candidates to undergo?

SEQUENCE OF EVENTS

Figure 10.2 shows a recommended sequence of events from the arrival of candidates to the selection decision itself.

Arrival and waiting When candidates arrive, they should be shown to a waiting area and told approximately how long they will be waiting, which should not be so long as to give the impression of a poorly organized event. This stage can be handled by the receptionist, but some organizations, especially for particular jobs, have one of the selection team ready to go out

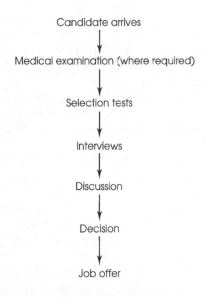

Figure 10.2 The interview process – sequence of events.

and greet the candidate and make him or her comfortable. Reasonably comfortable chairs, coffee tables, recent editions of the company magazine, perhaps a copy of the latest Annual Report and Accounts and any other relevant literature are usually found in the waiting areas. Candidates will be keen to learn as much as they can about the organization before the interview process starts, and they will be glad of the opportunity to read about it.

MEDICAL EXAMINATION

Where a company's own clinician carries out a medical, it may done on the premises shortly after the candidate arrives. Where this is the case, the candidate should be informed in advance that this will be a requirement.

Some organizations have a policy of getting a medical report on all new employees. Others obtain the regular use of an external consultant medical practitioner to carry out the examinations, in which case they may take place on the consultant's premises, in advance of the interview day. Yet others ask candidates to provide a medical history, which is obtainable from their own general practitioner, usually paid for by the organization.

SELECTION TESTS

These should always take place, and where possible the results should be known, *before* the interview. The information gathered in a selection test is usually very useful to the interviewer. Also, if from the start of each interview, candidates know that the interviewer is in possession of the results of the tests, they will be more inclined to be frank about their own strengths, weaknesses and any other qualities that the tests were designed to tease out.

Proper selection tests are not randomly designed by personnel people, or by anyone else in the organization. Ideally, they will have been designed by a firm of consultants and specialists, usually psychologists, who are experts in the field. Reputable consultants categorize their tests and train their customers in their application and administration, which includes the use of psychometric techniques, through which the test performance of the candidate is elicited. Ideally, tests will be valid and reliable, which means that they test what they are supposed to test and that their outcomes are consistent.

There has been a steady growth in the use of selection testing in recent years, partly because of the doubt that research evidence has thrown upon interviewing, and partly because the 'shrinking workforce' has highlighted the importance of selecting the right people. Also, the use of evidence from tests supports the organization's drive for fairness and equal opportunities, since all applicants for the same job undergo exactly the same test, and it is not a test that has been devised by the selectors.

Interviewing

The selection interview has been defined as, 'a conversation with a purpose'. This definition probably holds good for all organizational interviews, but it does suit our purposes here. The selection interview has been described as, 'The most used and least useful part of the selection process', and while research evidence tends to support this description, by casting doubt on its reliability and validity, its absence from the selection scenario would be regarded as highly unusual. Selection interviewing is as old as employment itself.

Despite what the researchers say, the interview does have some advantages. It can have good human relations value in that it provides an opportunity for a candidate and a member of the organization to sit down together and get to know something about each other.

There are some exceptional people who have a great deal of natural ability in interviewing and many of them make a good living from doing just that. However, there are also some people who should be kept as far away from the interview situation as possible!

Interviews should be structured, and when one is interviewing several people for the same job, it is advisable to ensure that all of the interviews have the same structure. In this way, one can be sure that all of the candidates have been treated equally. Some interviewers recommend using the structure of the application form as a basis for the interview, so that the form also acts as a kind of checklist.

Preparation

Every application should be studied carefully in advance of the interview day, and, as the personnel specialist involved, you should ensure that the line manager and other involved staff do the same. You are looking for several things. The details of the shortlisted applicants will, or should, closely match the requirements of the person specification. Scrutinize each application for inconsistencies, such as breaks in employment; claims of qualifications held; leisure and other spare-time interests; and the nature of positions held in the past. Make notes if you find anything important along these lines. As you examine each application, ideas for interview questions may occur to you; note these too.

Always prepare a separate sheet in respect of each candidate, on which you can record how well the questions were answered, any new information that came to light during the interview and, most importantly, jot something down that will enable you to remember which candidate is which – some distinctive feature or something they were wearing. When you have interviewed say, six in a row, it is difficult to recall who said what. Remember, you are going to have a discussion with your interviewing colleagues afterwards and you will want to make a sensible and meaningful contribution. The main part of the sheet, however, should be a record of how well the candidate performed. Figure 10.3 suggests a layout for the sheet. If all of those interviewing a candidate also have a copy, notes can be compared during the post-interview discussion.

THE INTERVIEW ITSELF

In many medium- and most large-sized organizations, interviews take place in custom-built interview rooms. Not all organizations can afford this luxury, however, and it will be satisfactory if the room has been properly prepared and sited in a quiet area. Candidates should be received in a pleasant, but businesslike way, introduced to the interviewer(s) and shown where to sit.

A certain amount of pseudo-psychological bunkum has been written and spoken about the way the furniture is arranged in the room, the relative heights of the chairs and strangely, which chair is chosen by the 'victim'. No useful information can be gained about the candidate's personality or anything else through this kind of gobbledegook. The selection interview is a business meeting. Everyone involved knows why they are there and it is best to get on with the conversation's purpose, which is to assess the person for the job.

Candidate name: _____ Position: _____ Grade: _____ Department: _____

CRITERIA	POOR	FAIR	ADEQUATE	GOOD	EXCELLENT	COMMENTS
Qualifications						
Experience						
Previous relevant training						
Education						
Knowledge and skills						
Appearance (where relevant)						
General rating						

Figure 10.3 Record of candidate's interview performance.

If there are several interviewers, it is as well if one of them takes the lead. This person should be a good interpersonal communicator, capable of controlling the track of the interviewing, of establishing a healthy rapport with the interviewee and maintaining it throughout the event.

At the outset, you will know more about the candidate than he or she knows about you or the company, and it is a good idea to redress this imbalance right away. Your manner when you are doing this should help to put the candidate at ease. A nervous interviewee will give you less information about himself than will one who is relaxed. From that point on, the interviewee should do most of the talking, 70:30 to 80:20 is the recommended balance. One of the aims of the interview is to supplement the information that you already have on the application form; the longer you talk, the more you will deprive the candidate of the opportunity to tell you things about him or herself.

QUESTIONING TECHNIQUES

How you ask a question is every bit as important as what you ask. Questions should be framed in a way that invites the candidate to reply in full. Questions may be 'closed' or 'open'. A closed question is one that invites a short, but informative answer: question: 'How old are you?', answer: 'Twenty-five'. Not exactly the beginning of a fruitful conversation. Some writers advise against the use of closed questions, but I always found them to be useful at the beginning of the interview when I was trying to put the candidate at ease and establish a rapport, the answers usually being easy, obvious and non-contentious. I have heard interviewers open with: 'Well, you found us then!' This is such a banal statement: obviously, the person found the place, otherwise they would not be sitting there.

Open questions are those that begin with 'Why . . .' or 'What do you think of . . .'. Such questions should not be too long or convoluted; and one should ensure that there is only one question in there. If you ask more than one question in a single statement, you will only get an answer to the last one. Let us explore two or three examples of open and closed versions of the same kind of question:

Open version: 'Why do you enjoy working in business development?'

Closed version:	'So, you enjoy working in business development?'
Comment:	The answer to the open version allows the candidate to explain the outcomes of the work and why they are enjoyable, while the answer to the closed version is, 'Yes'.
Open version:	'How do you see your career progressing from the point you have reached now?'
Closed version:	'Do you think your career will continue to progress well ?'
Comment:	Again, the open version invites a more detailed answer, while the closed version would probably produce, 'Yes'.
Open version:	'How does your present job differ from that of the business development manager?'
Closed version:	'Are your present tasks different from those of the business development manager?'
Comment:	None necessary!

The idea of asking open questions is to get the candidate to fill in more of the detail that has been given on the application form. The more relevant information you have about the candidates, the more able you will be to make a good quality selection decision.

RHETORICAL QUESTIONS

These are questions which, because of the way they are phrased, contain the answer. A rhetorical question to a potential shop-floor worker might be: 'Could you process a hundred of these a day?' When you mention a figure, the interviewee will take that as the standard and will, of course, say 'Yes'. The question should have been: 'How many of these could you process in a day?'

The job for which you are interviewing may be one that demands a special quality, which could be difficult to tease out at an interview. If we take leadership as an example, how do you assess an individual's leadership skills at an interview? One approach is to study the levels and responsibilities held previously and to question the person about them. If the questions are phrased appropriately, the answers could reveal incidents that required good leadership, in which the candidate was involved. Sometimes, clues can also be obtained from the section on the application form that contains details of leisure pursuits and other spare-time interests. The three most used entries in that section are reading, television and DIY, which could mean anything or nothing. On the other hand, you may notice that the candidate holds office on the committee of a sports club, a charitable organization or some other group. Finally, if some special quality is required, it is a good idea to put the person through an appropriate test; at least then you will have some corroborative evidence. You should never make an employment decision on the basis of test results alone, but *some* evidence is better than *no* evidence, especially if it supports what you already know about the candidate.

CLOSING THE INTERVIEW

When you have got all of the information you intended to get, the interview is almost at its end. It is then that you should give the interviewee the opportunity to make any points or ask questions. People often have studied the job requirements and come to the interview hoping to put across four or five major points which they feel are in their favour. During the course of the interview, they will have taken any opportunities that arose to express these points, but there may be something they wish to say that they feel would complete their case for being appointed.

Some people are insensitive to the non-verbal signals that indicate that the interview is drawing to a close, even after you have given them a final opportunity to speak. There are several courteous approaches to dealing with this situation. One is to gather your papers together and put them to one side, thanking the person for attending. If they do not stand at that point, then you stand and walk towards the door. If, in the unlikely event that none of that works, you just have to open the door and tell the person plainly that the interview is over. Thankfully, such occasions are rare and most people will respond to the first signs.

Making the Decision

Selection decisions are seldom made by just one person sitting alone, and while personnel people do contribute with information and guidance, they should make such decisions only if the position is in the personnel department.

The objective is to select the best person for the job and the decision has to be made fairly and legally. To achieve this, you have to be sure that all of the candidates received exactly the same treatment, that the selection process (including any selection tests) was structured in the same way for everyone and that they all received an equal opportunity to make a case.

The decision making process itself also has to be fair, and seen to be fair. The form that is shown in figure 10.3 will be a useful reference document in this respect. Notes can be compared and agreements reached between and among the decision makers about the performance of each individual. One suggestion is to structure a form on the basis of the personnel specification, on which each candidate may be graded according to his or her performance in the interview and on any tests that were carried out (see figure 10.4).

In the figure, the left-hand column indicates the seven most important criteria for selection. The criteria are taken from the personnel specification and entered on the form in their order of importance. During the interview, pre-arranged questions that relate to the criteria are asked and the interviewee is scored according to his or her responses. Obviously, we would be looking for people who scored well in the top right-hand area; that is to say, people who score highly against the most important criteria.

Candidate name:	Interviewed for (job title):				
Criteria	Assessment				
	1	2	3	4	5
1.					
2.					
3.					
4.					
5.					
6.					
7.					

Figure 10.4 Candidate ranking form.

A structured decision making process that focuses upon how highly the individuals rated throughout the selection process, in which evidence from tests and interviews is seriously considered, has the hallmarks of a fair system.

Having borne in mind the demands of fairness, legality and the provision of equal opportunities, it is up to the decision makers to select the person whom they think is the best one for the job, bearing in mind that the superior considerations are the requirements of the organization. This is a difficult decision to make, not least because the very idea of selecting just one person makes the whole process discriminatory by nature. This kind of problem can be surmounted by deciding *in advance* that your sole objective is to act in the best interests of the organization, without considering any other factors.

Making an Offer of Employment

The timing of making offers is handled differently by different organizations. In the public sector, where so-called 'panel' interviews were at the centre of the selection process, all of the candidates were assembled in a waiting room and called into the interview one by one. At the end of this process, the panel members would make a decision, call the candidate they had selected back into the interview room and ask the remaining candidates to wait. The panel would then make the job offer and ask the candidate if he or she would accept. If the answer was 'Yes', then the waiting candidates would be told of the decision, and they would leave. The selectors may have made first and second choices and if their first choice declined then the offer would be made to the second choice. Several public-sector organizations still use this rather crude and outdated system, even when selecting for fairly senior positions, although most have converted to more modern methods of selection.

In the private sector, the shortlisted candidates are usually interviewed across a number of days. It really depends upon the level and importance of the job. A method that is commonly used is to create a 'long' shortlist of, say, 10 or 12 applicants and invite them to a 'first' interview with the personnel specialist. The 'short' shortlist is then derived from the results of those interviews, and the applicants who are on it are invited to a second interview. The line manager may be involved in both series of interviews, and certainly in the second series. Some practitioners refer to the first interviews as 'screening' interviews. Such interviews tend to be arranged when it is clear from the application forms that the competition to be shortlisted is close. Shortlisted interviewees are normally notified of the result by post.

An offer of employment is usually made 'subject to satisfactory references'. The candidate's permission to take up references should be obtained, especially since one will be from the current employer. If, as in the 'panel' method, there is more than one possible choice, it is wise to wait until the offer has been accepted in writing, before communicating the final decision to the rest of the candidates.

Summary

Applications are screened and categorized as *probables*, *possibles* and *rejections*. Rejection letters are sent to the unsuccessful applicants, and the probables and possibles are re-screened, a process which involves the line manager. From the remaining applicants a shortlist is compiled and the candidates are invited to attend for interview. Interviews should be well planned in terms of timing, venues and accommodation. If selection tests are to be used, additional appropriate arrangements should be made. Decisions have to be made about the approach to interviewing; should they be one-to-one, panel, series, etc.?

The selection process should be structured to produce fair, non-discriminatory treatment of candidates and there should be a systematic decision making process that takes account of the need to provide equal opportunities and meets the requirements of the organization.

Offers of employment should always be made 'subject to satisfactory references' and you should always have at least one 'second choice' in reserve, in case your first choice declines the offer.

Further Reading

The titles of the most recent texts on this subject are HRM-related and most are aimed at practising managers and students who have reached an advanced level of knowledge and skills. Nevertheless, it is a good idea to examine the chapters in these texts which cover the selection process. Examples of such texts are:

McKenna, E.F. and Beech, N. 1995: *The Essence of Human Resource Management*. London: Prentice Hall.
Molander, C. and Winterton, J. 1994: *Managing Human Resources*. London: Routledge.

11

Induction

Introduction

In this chapter we discuss the process of induction, which is the term used to describe the introduction of the new employee to the organization. We explain how the individual and the organization can benefit from induction and examine a number of systems.

The primary purpose of induction is to make the new employee effective in the job as soon as possible after joining. An individual's best performance will not emerge until he or she has attained a sense of direction and identity in the place. This will only come with familiarization, in which a process of socialization takes place. Socialization is the process in which people become familiar with their environment and learn about the kind of behaviour that is expected of them. We all go through this process in our developmental years, and then, when we enter an organization, we go through it all again; it is a kind of micro-socialization, which involves learning a culture which is different from that of the outside world and different from that in any other organization. Some people find the process traumatic, and, if it is incorrectly handled, they may leave.

Effective Induction

Indications that an induction system is effective include: (1) a reduction in staff turnover, (2) an increase in the staff retention rate, and (3) good interpersonal relations between new and longer-serving employees. An effective induction system helps people to survive the socialization trauma and, as a result, they do not leave the organization, thus reducing turnover and increasing retention rates. Good interpersonal relations are the result of the speed with which new employees gain an understanding of the work environment. Once this is done, they no longer feel like 'intruders', are accepted by the group and attain a perception of the role they are expected to adopt.

The Induction Crisis

The phenomenon that I have called the 'socialization trauma' is frequently referred to as the *induction crisis*. As the individual begins to get to know the job and the organization, there may be 'second thoughts' about the decision to join, and at this stage he or she may decide to leave. The severity with which the new employee experiences these feelings depends on the degree to which the job and the organization fails to match up to the individual's expectations. Also, the decision to leave or stay will be determined by additional factors, such as the likelihood of getting another job. If the crisis is not felt severely enough to justify leaving, the person may decide to 'put up with it for now', and hope that things will improve. If the person stays, a period of *accommodation* will follow, in which he or she begins to adjust to the new environment. During this period, people modify their perceptions of each other and begin to have expectations that are more in keeping, on the one hand, with the needs of the organization and on the other, with the character and skills of the new employee. Their mutual expectations alter as they get used to each other. Inside the first year or two, there may be further crises, but if the person stays for more than one year, he or she will usually stay for more than two. If the individual has replaced someone in the job, the expectations of others are often influenced by their expectations of the previous incumbent, with whom they were familiar. This can increase the severity of a crisis, since the conflicting expectations are verbally and/or non-verbally communicated. If the individual has taken up a newly created position, the trauma is more likely to be with the relevant managers and specialists.

Staff turnover that is attributable to such causes provides a yardstick by which the efficiency and effectiveness of the recruitment and selection system can be measured. Obviously, if there is a wide discrepancy between what the individual was told about a job and the actual job situation, then there is something amiss with the job requisition, description or specification. Alternatively, there could be something about the individual that the selection process has missed.

Systematic Induction

Individuals' initial thoughts about the organization occur when they first see the recruitment advertisement, and, in a sense, this is when induction really begins. A properly designed recruitment advertisement will give people clues about the organization's style and make them consider employment there. With such thoughts in mind, they will begin to notice other items of the organization's publicity. Eventually, they get the job and find themselves inside the place, relating to its people and learning more about the nature of the organization's industry, its size and, above all, its culture.

I remember, several years ago, asking a personnel manager if I could see the arrangements he had for induction. He took me to a room in which dozens of cardboard packages were stacked on a shelf. He lifted one down and proudly presented it to me. It contained several pieces of literature, including a map on how to get to the site, directions to the various parts of the organization, such as the car parks, works canteen, personnel offices and the various departments. There was a copy of the most recent Annual Report and Accounts and a copy of the current edition of the company magazine. And that was it. Hardly the beginnings of a long and mutually beneficial relationship.

Induction may be visualized as two parallel processes: formal and informal. Formally, the new employee has to acquire a perception of his or her *role* in the place, and this begins with the job description. From this, new employees can see what they should be doing in order to perform effectively in the job. This means that the individual has to attain a perception of the job in terms of its status in the department, the normal performance standards, how the job affects others in the department and their expectations of his or her behaviour. Informally, however, the role is bigger than the job; role is a term that relates to the the individual's total behaviour, in and out of the formal job. For example, there is a 'jargon' to learn; all organizations have their own expressions and abbreviations and there is a technical vocabulary related to the industry and the skills within it. Longer-serving people have deep-rooted, underlying assumptions about 'the way things are' and 'the way things should be done around here'. The place has its own distinctive climate and managerial style. All of these aspects of the employees' life are unique in each organization, and they combine to make the *culture* of the organization.

People may be inducted at two levels. Firstly, there is *corporate induction*, which includes the kind of information that was in the pack to which I referred above, although that was totally inadequate. What people need is an understanding of the history of the place, its current situation and its plans for the future. A complete corporate picture will include photographs and 'thumbnail' biographies of the members of the Board and other senior managers, along with hierarchical charts, showing the organizational, management and workforce structures. Secondly, there is *departmental induction*, which is more directly concerned with the new employee's role in his or her immediate work area. Of the two, departmental induction is the more informal, and it is usually the longer process, since it is concerned with the technicalities and other details of the job itself.

INDUCTION DOCUMENTATION

All organizations have rules of behaviour which are written down in the form of procedures and regulations. In most organizations, these are presented in the 'Company Handbook' along with the Terms and Conditions of Employment, and in many cases the structure of the system of payment. A copy of the Company Handbook and any other documents that are relevant to the organization's regulations should be given to all new employees as part of their induction. Health and Safety at Work should be seen as an important item on the induction agenda, and all induction programmes should contain relevant information on the subject. Where there are gaps in people's knowledge, skills and attitudes towards health and safety, full training should be given.

Induction Training

Induction is best handled through training. It is possible to overload people with information, and if you send them home at the end of their first day carrying an armful of documents, they may 'get down to reading them one day' and some of the information is critical. On the other hand, if the information is put across in a training environment, clearly and in a controlled way, the person will absorb and internalize it more easily, and it is more likely to 'stick'.

Induction programmes vary in their complexity and duration. I know of programmes that last no more than two or three days, and yet are very effective. Others last up to two years and have formal examinations at the end of each year. There is no set pattern or 'blueprint' of an induction programme; the content and process of it is determined by the varying needs and complexity of different organizations.

Summary

The purpose of induction is to make the new employee effective in the job as soon as possible. New employees are in a learning situation as soon as they join, and need to attain a perception of their role in the place, and understand its culture and the expectations that others have of them. Some employees experience an 'induction crisis', which occurs shortly after joining, and which happens as a result of the job failing to match up to expectations; an induction crisis may make someone decide to leave. An effective induction system is handled through training, and contains 'corporate' and 'departmental' induction processes.

Part III

Developing Employees

The development of employees has always been an important part of personnel work. It has to be ensured that people are properly trained to carry out their jobs, and developed further with coaching, counselling and planned experience, so that in the future they may take on positions of greater responsibility. Here, we include the learning process, the role of training in the organization, and the techniques and evaluation of training.

12

Aspects of Learning

Introduction

This chapter is included because an understanding of the major theories of learning is essential to your understanding of employee development. Employees are developed through *education*, *training* and the modification of their *attitudes* towards particular attitude objects, with a view to changing their behaviour. Employees, therefore, are developed in *knowledge*, *skills* and *attitudes*. This chapter describes early theories of learning and goes on to show how the application of modern theories attempts to create ideal learning situations, and evaluate the effectiveness of learning. You will also come to understand why learning is also a natural process.

The study of how learning takes place probably began before the Middle Ages; certainly it goes back to the times of the very early philosophers. It is still going on today and a vast bank of information has accumulated as a result. Most of this information is the result of research carried out by psychologists and/or those associated with, or working with, psychologists, studying human behaviour and the behaviour of other living creatures.

Definition

Learning can be defined as 'A process of developing new knowledge, skills, attitudes and values through participation in formally organized learning situations and natural social interaction.' The descriptions of the early theories are included to provide you with a background to the subject, which will enhance your perception of modern approaches. Most of this chapter, therefore, is concerned with examining the theories that influence modern training and employee development practices in organizations. The principal characteristic of learning is that it relates to how knowledge, skills, attitudes and values are *acquired.*

Natural Learning

In one context, learning is a natural process in that it is a feature of our personal development. We learn to conform to societal norms by observing others and through a system of reward and punishment. If, for example, in the early stages of our development, we behave in a way that invokes the disapproval of our parents or teachers, they express that disapproval with more or less strength, depending on how seriously they view what we have done. On the other hand, they will reward us with expressions of approval when we behave in accordance with their expectations (conformity). As time goes by, we develop patterns of behaviour based around societal norms, many of which we internalize as habits, so that much of what we do is done without conscious thought. What is described in this paragraph is part of the process known as *socialization.*

Organized Learning

In another context, learning is organized; laid on for us, mostly by the education system and those responsible for staff development, training and instruction in organizations. In well-run organizations, the managers are responsible for the development of their staff, supported by the expert advice and assistance of personnel specialists. The personnel department organizes training courses and brings in specialist trainers; the department also liaises with external bodies when highly specialized or longer-term award-bearing courses are needed. The managers identify their staff's training needs and advise the personnel department accordingly; but that is only one way in which the training needs of the organization are identified. In most cases, the employee ultimately finds him or herself in a formal training situation, such as a classroom, training room or some other situation, such as 'on-the-job' training, being developed in particular aspects of knowledge, skills and attitudes that are needed in the job.

The Learning Process

We saw above that the principal characteristic of learning is that it is acquired. *How* it is acquired has been the focus of theorists' attention for at least a hundred years. Research has shown that learning is determined by (1) the personal characteristics of the learner, such as motivation and intelligence, (2) the effectiveness of the 'agent' and (3) the nature of the learning situation. So far as the individual's characteristics are concerned, it is clear that motivation plays a significant role, but the learner also has to be *able* to learn. If, for example, the learner's intelligence is such that he or she is unable to grasp the ideas or achieve the necessary skill standards, then the likelihood is that *sufficient* learning will not occur. In this respect, people will differ in that they will be *more* or *less* able, so that the amount of learning that actually takes place will vary from one individual to the next. Furthermore, some people are able to pick up only some aspects of the training. One example of this is in the field of leadership training. Such training will be totally ineffective if the trainee does not possess any natural leadership ability at all, when the underlying objective is to turn people into effective leaders. On the other hand, some may acquire the knowledge, but not the skills, which is why at present, there is a large number of people in industry who can tell you all you need to know about leadership, but can not actually lead people, since they lack the essential elements of natural leadership ability.

When we refer to the 'effectiveness of the agent', we are talking about the teacher, trainer or whoever is responsible for developing the trainees. In this context, effectiveness means how good the trainer is at developing people, but it also relates to the credibility of the person selected to do the training. The level of the agent's credibility will be an important factor in determining how much learning takes place.

Finally, we come to the learning situation. This refers to the physical environment, the ambience of the location and the methods and media that the agent had decided to use. All of these factors have to be appropriate in the light of the subject to be learned. Considerable amounts of time and ingenuity have been invested in the creation of effective learning situations, particularly in the field of employee development.

Early Approaches to Learning

The study of learning includes an understanding of *classical conditioning*, *operant conditioning* and *cognitive learning*. This section explains the early and modern theories that underpin these three divisions of learning theory, along with the main techniques that are available for their application. We can then examine how the theories and techniques can be applied in the workplace.

CLASSICAL CONDITIONING

We have seen that human beings develop patterns of behaviour. In terms of 'natural' learning, these are related to the routines that we adopt and the sets of habits we develop in order to make our lives easier. For example, when we get up in the morning, we go through a routine of behavioural acts that lead to us being ready for work. We have bathed, dressed and eaten without having to make detailed conscious decisions about how we are going to carry out these tasks. The concept is similar to that of our driving habits. After we have learned the routines of driving a car and we become accustomed to the vehicle itself, we operate the car's instruments and adopt particular positions on the road almost as naturally as we walk or breathe. Through learning, we have 'conditioned' ourselves to react to recurring and familiar situations in consistent ways.

Psychologically, regularly occurring, familiar situations trigger off our patterned responses. The regularity with which situations occur can be very significant. If we eat at regular intervals and always at the same time of day, for example, then we know when a meal time is nearing. Behaviourally, we tend to get ready to leave what we are doing and prepare ourselves for the meal. Since we know that it is natural for human beings to develop behavioural patterns and sets of habits, it follows that we should be able to create situations that produce particular responses.

In other words, it should be possible to cause people to behave as we would like them to. But we can take this idea a little further. Patterned responses not only develop around our external overt behaviour; there are physical, internal responses too.

The results of the first studies into internal physical responses were published in 1927 by the Russian physiologist, Ivan Pavlov. Classical conditioning is the term used to describe the association of a number of events that leads to a pattern of behaviour in the way that we have described above. In his experiments, Pavlov was interested in, among other things, internal reactions to external stimuli. The internal function he studied was the digestive system and the external stimulus was food; the subjects of his first experiments were dogs. The objective was to determine whether the dogs would associate the external stimulus with another event, such as the ringing of a bell. Pavlov started to feed the dogs according to a regular regime. On seeing the food, the dogs began to salivate, indicating that their digestive systems were prepared to receive food. After several days of feeding, Pavlov introduced the bell, which he rang every time he served the food. After several further feeding sessions in which the serving of the food was accompanied by the ringing of the bell, Pavlov rang the bell without serving any food and the dogs salivated.

Natural learning was already in place when the dogs salivated in response to the sight of the food, the readiness of the digestive system being an innate response; but actual learning, that is to say, 'organized' learning that was new to the dogs, did not take place until the dogs had associated the ringing of the bell with the sight of the food. This is because the dogs had always salivated at the sight of food, whereas their salivating in response to the bell was a change in their behaviour.

The terminology that is used to describe the various factors of classical conditioning includes the unconditioned stimulus (US), which was the appearance of the food, the conditioned stimulus (CS), which was the ringing of the bell, and the conditioned response (CR), which in this case was the dogs' salivating in response to the ringing of the bell. The dogs' salivating in response to the sight of the food is called an unconditioned response (UR). It is worth noting that the CS had *replaced* the US as the stimulus that produced the response. Later research showed that in a somewhat more complex way, the principles of classical conditioning are just as effective when applied in the human situation.

OPERANT CONDITIONING

The American, E.L. Thorndike, a contemporary of Pavlov, was the founder of operant conditioning; the subjects of his experiments were cats. Operant conditioning differs from classical conditioning in that the subject's response occurs *before* the reward for the behaviour is given. Operant conditioning is also referred to as instrumental conditioning.

In Thorndike's experiments (1913), a hungry animal was placed in a cage or box from which it needed to escape in order to get food. The animal, therefore, had to 'learn' how to escape, usually by pulling on a wire or by pressing a lever. This differed from Pavlov's studies in that the animals played an active role in the experiments.

The animals eventually did escape, but only after 'accidentally' discovering how to get out, whereupon they were rewarded with food; as we said above, in operant conditioning the reward comes after the required behaviour. After several repeat sessions, the animals remembered what they had done last time they escaped and thus had learned how to get out. Eventually, they pulled the wire or pressed the lever as soon as they were put into the cage. Thorndike maintained that when the required response is followed by the reward, the behaviour is more likely to occur again, provided the circumstances are similar, and he called this the 'Law of Effect'.

Today, the researcher mainly associated with operant conditioning is the American B.F. Skinner, whose work (1953) is really an extension of the work of Thorndike. Experiments in which animals were the subjects typified the work of both researchers, although Skinner, after researching mainly with rats and pigeons, went on to research into human learning, to produce what he called stimulus–response psychology, which has come to be known for short as S–R psychology. The study of S–R psychology focuses upon positive and negative *reinforcers* of behaviour and Skinner developed a complex terminology to describe his central theory, much of which has made its way into the language of other psychological approaches. As in classical conditioning, the behaviour that is achieved through operant conditioning techniques will extinguish if the reward ceases.

BEHAVIOURISM

The works of Pavlov, Thorndike and Skinner classify them as *behaviourists*. This is an approach to the study of human behaviour that was introduced by John B. Watson in 1913, and it is an approach that is not universally accepted by psychologists. Behaviourists work within more limited parameters and their approach to the study of animal and human behaviour excludes factors that many psychologists regard as basic requirements (Watson and Rayner, 1920). In their approach to learning, for example, they exclude such significant components of human consciousness as insight and creativity.

THE COGNITIVE APPROACH

Cognitive theorists are among those who regard behaviourism as narrow in its approach to the study of learning. Change in behaviour is the criterion by which the amount of learning is measured. Cognitive theorists, however, are mainly interested in changes in individuals' knowledge, since they regard this as more important than changes in what the learner does. Cognitive learning includes all of the elements of human consciousness that the behaviourists ignore: imagination, creativity, problem solving, human intuition and perception. The cognitive approach has two components: *insight learning* and *latent learning*.

Insight learning Having an understanding of what is being learned is an important feature of cognitive theory. if we take a problem solving exercise as an example. Experience of working with children has shown that when a person is given a problem to solve, he or she sometimes studies it, analyses and thinks about it and then, after a period in which an onlooker might think that the person was stumped, the solution is suddenly produced. Wolfgang Koehler (1959) claimed that such insight was not an exclusively human ability. In his experiments, he placed a hungry chimpanzee in a cage. Food was placed outside the cage, where it could be seen but not reached by the chimpanzee. Inside the cage was a stick that was long enough to use as a tool with which the food could be dragged to the cage. Would the chimp crack the problem? After several attempts at reaching the food with his hands, the chimp suddenly seized the stick and used it to pull in the food. Insight? In another experiment, both the stick and the food were outside the cage, not within the chimpanzee's reach. The stick was nearer than the food. There was a slightly shorter stick inside the cage and this was long enough to reach the stick that could be used to get the food. The chimpanzee paced and rolled around the cage for a while and then suddenly grabbed the shorter stick and used it to pull in the longer stick, with which he then brought in the food. The point was that the actions that led to getting the food appeared to start after a sudden flash of inspiration, of realization that there was a way to get the food. Undoubtedly, insight had been used. In repeat sessions, the chimpanzee, when presented with the same problem, solved it immediately. It has also been shown that when animals use insight to solve problems, they can transfer the ability to problems that are similar in structure but set in a different context.

Latent learning   Cognitive theorists also maintain that learning can be 'latent'; in other words, it can be added to one's knowledge and then used only as and when needed. An interesting feature of latent learning is that the learner does not always appreciate that he or she has gathered something new. Students and trainees, for example, sometimes come away from a course believing that they have learned nothing. It is not until a later date, perhaps at work, that they find that they can solve particular problems or carry out tasks that were directly related to the training they had received.

In another example, a person may develop a number of items of knowledge and skills that he or she has developed at different times and in different places. Later, when presented with a problem, the person is able to put the items together and use them in his or her quest for a solution to the problem.

Learning in the Work Environment

All of what is said about learning in this chapter applies to human beings in the workplace. To work effectively, people need knowledge and skills, not only so that they can do their jobs, but so that they can relate effectively to working colleagues, the boss and subordinates. They need to be able to manage themselves, their time, their careers and their health, and skills and know-ledge for these purposes have to be learned. Sometimes they are learned in the workplace and sometimes they are learned exter-nally in training establishments and educational institutions, and then returned to the workplace, where the person applies what he or she has learned. An understanding of the various approaches to learning and how learning takes place, therefore, is crucial to the development of an efficient and effective work-force.

Modern Theories of Learning

Most of the modern approaches to learning have their roots in the theories we have examined in the previous sections of this chapter and, indeed, some of the older theories still exercise an important degree of influence over current practice. It is notice-able, however, that modern theorists are not so keen on develop-ing hard and fast 'rules of learning' and are more inclined to empower individuals over the means through which they are developed. Learning is no longer seen as the preserve of the researcher, experimenting with subjects in isolated areas, detached from the environment in which the learning is to be applied. In this final section of the chapter, we examine several of the major contributions to modern theory and discuss the con-text in which today's approaches are set.

KOLB'S LEARNING CYCLE

The *experiential learning cycle*, developed by David Kolb in 1979 probably is the most well-known model in modern theory (Kolb, 1985). If we look at what happens in learning areas today, it is not difficult to challenge Kolb's perception of the approaches of teachers and trainers to developing people. He claimed that students and trainees in the classrooms of training establish-ments and educational institutions were being 'processed' under the authority of the teacher or trainer, while the learner played a passive role. This situation, he said, detaches the learner from reality. The implication here is that the learner is taught some-thing, but does not actually have to demonstrate the ability to do it. It separated learning and doing, as if they were different activities. Kolb contrasted this kind of learning with that of problem solving, in which the responsibility for producing solutions rests with the learner. In other words, he distinguished between 'teacher-centred' and 'student-centred' learning. Kolb, however, regarded the classroom situation as a necessary function, his main criticism being that insufficient attention was being paid to other forms of learning, such as problem solving. When he developed his *experiential learning cycle* (figure 12.1) he incorporated the features of both the classroom and problem solving situations.

Looking at the model, we begin with 'concrete experience', the first point in the cycle (top centre in figure 12.1), in which the learner practises a skill for the first time, such as using a machine. This is followed by a process of familiarization, in which the learner makes observations and reflects upon the experience, the second point in the cycle, from which he or she begins to makes sense of the structure of the machine. In other words, he or she attains the concept of how the machine functions – what it is for, the third point in the cycle. Going back to the machine, the fourth point in the cycle, produces a new situation because it includes prior learning. This is then tested in a new situation, which includes using the machine, which bring us back to the first point in the cycle, the use of the machine providing a new experience. The cycle continues and learning improves. Kolb emphasizes that this whole process is driven by the individual learner, thus empowering the individual

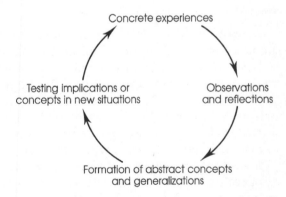

Figure 12.1 The Kolb experiential learning cycle.

to strive towards his or her own internally motivated needs and goals.

SOCIAL LEARNING

This is the kind of learning that hitherto I have described as 'natural' learning. I used the term 'natural', firstly because what is learned is instinctive and spontaneous, rather than specified and planned, and secondly because the learning most often takes place in the learner's natural, informal situations. The most obvious form of social learning occurs during our early developmental years, when we are learning to adapt to the social and cultural environment into which we were born; this part of our development is called *socialization*.

In this context, our infancy can be a testing time. We are aware of other people around us and the need to communicate drives us to learn the language very quickly. Eventually, we gain an understanding of the values and expectations of our immediate family, and as we learn we tend to adopt those values as a first step; also, we learn very quickly about those items of our behaviour that meet with their approval and those other items that do not.

It should be remembered that when we use the term 'behaviour', we are referring not only to what we do physically, but to what we think and say about things. We learn that some of our behaviour is rewarded and some of it is punished. Rewards and punishments mean gifts and smacks, but they also mean feelings of pleasure or feelings of misery. Frederick Herzberg (1966) says that through 'hedonism', which is the seeking of pleasure and the avoidance of pain, we are motivated to learn to conform, and that this is an innate human characteristic; it is part of our inherent 'survival kit', but we have extended it into our social behaviour.

SOCIAL AND ORGANIZATIONAL CULTURE

The long-term survival of groups and societies has produced many factors that are unique to the culture that has developed in every specific society. The result of this is that every society has its own complex set of norms and values that are shared by every one of its members. As we develop, we learn to conform to the norms and values of our own culture. The culture itself, however, is something that is far more deep-rooted that the sharing of norms and values. It is based upon sets of long-held assumptions about how things are and how things should be, how we should do things in our society and how things should look. Eventually, we internalize the culture until we have an intuitive feeling about what it is. Somehow, we know what we can and cannot get away with and we notice the anti-cultural behaviour of others. Mostly, these deep-rooted assumptions about how things are and how things should be are held unconsciously; events, rituals and concepts that result are simply taken for granted.

When we go into an industrial or business organization for the first time, we find that a micro-society with its own peculiar culture has developed within it. If we are going to work in the organization, we have to learn new sets of norms and values, new concepts and rituals, and we have to learn to behave in ways that are acceptable to our working colleagues. The culture within an organization is never a microcosm of the external culture. The culture of an organization is influenced by technical and social factors that do not exist in the external environment; we go through a process of re-socialization. One very significant aspect of this process is that we have a role in the organization and we have to learn how to carry out that role effectively, in social as well as technical terms. Naturally, we have our own perceptions of what is required. Usually, we are given a job description and presumably we have the knowledge and skills to meet its demands. But what do others in the workplace expect of us? We find that the *role* is broader than the *job*.

Finally, our *ability* to conform is just as important as our *willingness* to do so. This means that as we move in and out of the organization in the mornings and evenings, we have to change. Cultural boundaries are defined by *time*, *place* and *language*, and as we move across those boundaries we automatically suspend our conformity to one culture and adopt the demands of another. In other words, we go to work and come home at set times (*time*); in doing so we have moved from one *place* to another; in the organization we learn its technical and social terminology, which are parts of a *language* that would be meaningless elsewhere. All of this is not to imply that organizational and social cultures are mutually exclusive, discrete entities. They interact with and influence each other in very marked ways.

GAGNE'S 'HIERARCHY OF LEARNING'

One important question to be answered in our approaches to learning is the relationship between simple and complex forms of learning. In his attempt to explain this relationship, Gagne (1977) maintained that there are eight hierarchically ordered forms of learning, ranging from primitive learning to complex learning. Although different from each other, many of these forms of learning are interdependent. From the hierarchy, we can see that each form of learning is a little more complex than its predecessor: the third (chaining), for example, having been built upon the first and second, is more complex than signal learning and S–R learning (see table 12.1).

When, in the hierarchy, we say that one form of learning is 'based on' another, the implication is that it is necessary to acquire one form of learning before one becomes able to acquire the next; hence, it is a *hierarchy* and not just a set of discrete forms of learning.

TRANSFER OF LEARNING

The idea that learning is a sequential process is very important in this area of study. For example, the 'transfer of learning' refers to the process in which previously acquired learning influences current learning. This is believed to be an innate feature of learning. The transfer of learning carries significant implications for training, in that transfer may be either *positive* or *negative*. When the transfer is positive, the previous learning has a beneficial effect upon the subsequent learning, but when the transfer is negative, it has an inhibiting or even a harmful effect on the new learning. This affects many areas of industry and business, especially when they wish to redesign jobs, introduce new technology or make other kinds of change.

As we have seen, individuals develop patterns of behaviour around their work, and having learned how to do a job, they become accustomed to doing it in a particular way. This previously acquired learning may stand well in their stead (*positive transfer*). If, for example, an individual who is a skilled and experienced typist is asked to learn to use a computer for word processing purposes, the skills that he or she possesses as a typist will assist the learning process. On the other hand, when a lecturer who has been 'teaching at' people for many years is

Table 12.1 Hierarchy of learning (Gagne, 1977)

Type of learning	Description
1 Signal learning	Involving the response to something that is taken as a signal. This is typified by the bell in Pavlov's studies with dogs.
2 Stimulus–response learning	Based on operant conditioning, in which a *learned* response as opposed to an *instinctive* response is made. Also, the response is made in pursuit of the satisfaction of some need or goal.
3 Chaining (based on 1 and 2)	Involving the connection of a number of previously learned sets of stimuli and their associated responses. For example, when we do two things at once, such as guiding cloth under the needle of a sewing maching, while turning the handle or operating the treadle.
4 Verbal association	Learning and using a language, involving connections between words and the ability to speak them in a meaningful sequence.
5 Discrimination learning (based on 3 and 4)	Involves responding differently to stimuli which are related to but different from each other. This is more sophisticated than simply associating a single stimulus with a response, since it calls upon us to separate the meanings of stimuli.
6 Concept learning (based on 5 and 7)	This includes 'discrimination' and 'rule learning'. It is a form of learning in which we make a common response to concrete or abstract stimuli which are of the same category, but different in their physical characteristics. This higher form of learning requires internal information processing to classify and reorganize concepts.
7 Rule learning (based on 6)	Acquiring a chain of several concepts; e.g. 'if X then Y'.
8 Problem solving (based on 7)	This involves the use of 'insight' in developing new rules from previously learned rules, giving the ability to solve problems, especially in new situations involving human beings.

asked to change to a 'student-centred' approach, most of the lecturing skills that he or she acquired will be of little use and, indeed, could inhibit the development of new skills (*negative transfer*). In such a case, great difficulty is experienced when preparing for classes and handling students. To adopt the new system of development, he or she has to learn new skills and somehow 'unlearn' all of the lecturing skills which became redundant when the new system came in.

References

Gagne, R.M. 1977: *The Conditions of Learning*. New York: Rinehart and Winston.

Herzberg, F.W. 1966: *Work and the Nature of Man*. New York: Stagles.

Koehler, W. 1959: *The Mentality of Apes*. New York: Vintage Books, 1959.

Kolb, D.A. 1985: *Experiential Learning: Experience as the Source of Learning and Development*. London: Prentice Hall.

Pavlov, I. 1927: *Conditioned Reflexes*. Oxford: Oxford University Press.

Skinner, B.F. 1953: *Science and Human Behaviour*. New York: Macmillan.

Thorndike, E.L. 1913: *The Psychology of Learning*. Columbia University: Teachers College Press.

Watson, J.B. and Rayner, R. 1920: Conditioned emotional reactions. *Journal of Experimental Psychology*, 3, 1–14.

13

Training

Training is for now, development is for the future.

Introduction

In this chapter, we define training and examine its role in the organization. We review the variety of senior managers' attitudes towards training, and the roles of the government, employers and individual employees in the provision of training. We explain the relationship between training and development; the systematic training cycle; the main activities related to training, and training at different organizational levels and functions.

Definition

> Training is the systematic development of the knowledge, skills and attitudes required by an individual to perform adequately a given task or job.
>
> Michael Armstrong,
> *A Handbook of Personnel Management Practice*

The main purposes of training are to improve the performance of the organization by improving the performance of its employees and, thereby, improve the economic performance of the country. Also, training's purpose is to reduce learning time while developing best practice within people.

The effectiveness of training may be measured by the degree to which it has caused a change of in-job behaviour on the part of the trainee.

Training and Performance

From what is said above, it is clear that training is concerned with influencing employees' performance and, having discussed learning theories in chapter 12, it is important at this stage to draw a distinction between learning and performance. We know that the degree to which learning has taken place is measured by observing the extent to which resultant changes in behaviour occur. On the other hand, performance is evaluated by measuring the degree to which an employee has met or surpassed standards of work in terms of quality and quantity, and the degree to which he or she has achieved agreed objectives; for example, the monthly figures of sales representatives, and the nature of the relationships they have fostered between the customers and the firms they represent.

It is clear, of course, that training can improve the quality of such outcomes, but learning can limit an outcome because all we can do is what we have learned. It is true that in a conducive situation, an individual can raise his or her game and perform better, owing perhaps, to added motivational factors, but this cannot raise an employee's performance beyond the level of his or her actual ability. This means, therefore, that when we regard performance as a feature of an individual's behaviour, the level of that performance depends upon two factors: *ability*, which is developed through learning, and *motivation*, which is a function of the individual's perception of the reward, thus:

$$\text{Performance} = \text{Ability} \times \text{Motivation} \ (P = A \times M)$$

No part of the above statement is interchangeable with any other. As we have said, a person's ability is directly and exclusively related to the variety and level of his or her learning. In the context of the above statement, the 'ability' factor may be regarded as a constant, while the 'motivation' factor influences the degree to which a person maximizes on his or her ability. Clearly then, if motivation is at its optimal level and it is still necessary to improve performance, then the employee's ability has to be increased, which means further learning. In this way we can see how training, which of course involves learning, increases performance.

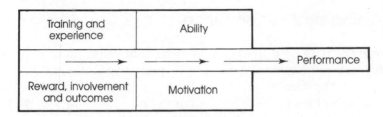

Figure 13.1 Factors influencing performance.

In figure 13.1 we can see that 'reward', 'involvement' and 'outcomes' influence motivation, whereas 'training' and 'experience' influence both motivation and ability. Our perception of what is implied by the figure, however, should be tempered by the fact that we know that ability is the result of learning and if the aim is to improve performance by using training techniques to broaden or deepen an individual's ability, consideration should be given to the individual's trainability. In chapter 12, for example, we saw that among other things, learning is determined by the individual's personal characteristics, some of which, such as intelligence, might limit his or her capacity to learn.

Let us suppose, for example, that the performance of an individual is below standard, even though the person is highly motivated. We may decide that his or her level of performance is due to a shortfall in the ability factor and that this can be addressed through training. In such a case, the amount of improvement that can be achieved will be determined by the individual's capacity to learn. This means, of course, that even though some marginal improvement may be achieved, it could still be insufficient to enable the individual to reach acceptable performance standards.

In this context, the amenability of an individual to training is very important. In such a case, it may be that the individual is in the wrong job, or that the job needs to be redesigned. Training can be expensive and to incur the cost of attempting to train someone who will not benefit as a result is an obvious waste of resources. It may be more cost effective to transfer the person to a job in which he or she is capable of meeting the required standards. One way of approaching this problem is through the use of occupational testing. The results of a relatively inexpensive trainability test will help when such decisions need to be made.

The ultimate purpose of training is to improve the overall performance of the organization. The individual employees, however, may regard training as the means of improving their own performance to enhance their career prospects. Training, therefore, may be driven by the organization and its employees. Ideally, training is driven by the organization when it is part of a larger scheme. The organization has plans for the future, plans that could involve change, as when new technology is introduced, when the need for new products is identified or when the internal structure of the organization needs to be altered. In this context, training is seen as one of the means through which the demands of the human resource strategy might be met. The identification of particular training needs originates in the corporate strategy, since the human resource strategy is formulated on the basis of the corporate strategy. Training is also driven by individual employees when, for instance, they detect a shortfall in their own repertoire of skills and wish to fill the gap.

Training and Development

Sometimes there is confusion between what is training and what is development. Training was defined at the beginning of this chapter. Development, however, is a term that refers to the bigger picture of human resource development (HRD), in which training is one of three broad concerns, the other two being management development and career management. From this, it should be seen that HRD is concerned with the longer-term, continuous development of people and the regular assessment of their performance. HRD is also concerned with the relationship between the individual and the organization in terms of the extent to which the individual's career aspirations match the organization's expectations of that individual. Training, therefore, is a major contributory factor in the long-term development of employees and, as such, can be regarded as a component of development.

Systematic Training

The responsibility for the provision of training lies in general with the personnel department and in particular with a personnel specialist, who usually carries the title, Training Manager or Training and Development Manager. Today, we also may see the alternative, Human Resource Development Manager. While personnel people organize training and develop the training system, the line managers decide who is to be trained in what.

Developing a systematic training programme involves the HRD specialist in a well-known sequence of activities: (1) devise the training policy and have it accepted at top level, (2) identify training needs, (3) plan the training, (4) carry out the training, and (5) evaluate the training. The process is often referred to as the 'systematic training cycle' (STC) as depicted in figure 13.2

To implement each of the components of the STC, the HRD specialist has to specify the kinds of training that will meet the

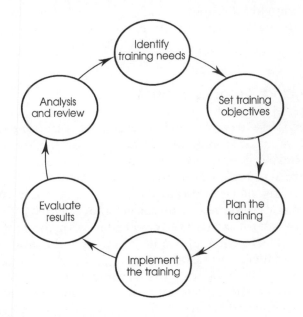

Figure 13.2 The systematic training cycle.

needs, earmark appropriately qualified and experienced trainers, organize the dates and venues for the training, and ensure
that the administration is carried out correctly and efficiently;
for example, that the prospective trainees and their managers
receive sufficient notice of the times and dates of the training
events.

Identifying Training Needs

A training programme consists of a number of training courses,
each of which has been designed to meet predetermined objectives, the whole programme having been designed to meet corporate training needs in the overall context. The subject matter
of each training course, the methods to be used and the level at
which it is pitched are based upon the nature of the training
needs and the level in the organization where they have been
identified. There are numerous situations in an organization in
which training needs are identified:

- Managers identify training needs in their staff in their day-to-
  day monitoring of performance and during formal performance appraisal sessions.
- Individuals identify training needs within themselves and ask
  to be included in particular courses.
- Training needs are identified during the recruitment process,
  in which it can be seen that there are gaps in candidates'
  knowledge, skills and attitudes.
- Training needs may also be identified when things change,
  such as when new technology is introduced or when restructuring brings about a redistribution of duties and responsibilities.

The most objective and effective approach to the identification of
training needs starts at job level. Central to most job descriptions are the lists of the job-holder's duties and responsibilities.
Clearly, then, for a person to be able to do the job, he or she has
to possess the relevant knowledge, skills and attitudes. The
'training gap' is the term commonly used to express the difference between what the job-holder *is able* to do and what he or
she *should be able* to do. There are also training gaps between
what the job-holder *actually does* and what he or she *should do*,
and, indeed, between how the whole company should be performing and how it is *actually performing*. Where there is a 'gap'

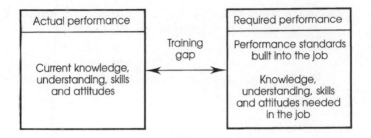

Figure 13.3 The training gap.

between *actual* and *required* performance, it needs to be filled by training (see figure 13.3).

Job Analysis

Training plans are implemented on the assumption that *all* training needs have been identified. Job analysis is a structured technique that is used in the planning and implementation of many personnel systems, including *training needs analysis* (see later). Meanwhile, for our purposes, it may be regarded as a means of identifying the training gap.

Job analysis entails the process of breaking a job down into its constituent parts and examining the situation in which the job is carried out. From this information, we can list the job's tasks, duties and responsibilities, along with its location and status in the organization, the performance standards that are required and any specific or unusual problems associated with that particular job.

At this stage in the analysis, we can develop a job description, which includes, among other things, describing the tasks, duties and responsibilities in their orders of importance. This brings us to the point where we can also develop the job specification, or person specification, as some call it; whatever you call it, it is a prioritized list of the qualities that the job-holder should possess, in terms of knowledge, skills and attitudes that will enable the person to perform in the job at or above the required standards.

An examination of the job-holder's actual performance will help to identify any problems that the individual is having in carrying out the job. If problems are identified in the job-holder's performance, the analysis can be taken to yet a further stage, that of *task analysis*, which is a technique that breaks down the job's specific tasks to identify those with which the individual is experiencing difficulty. Analysis in this kind of detail can take time and increase costs, but the fruits of an improved performance will usually justify the process in terms of cost. Having said all that, however, it should be remembered that a performance that fails to meet the required standards could be due to one or more of several causes, such as faulty equipment, under-resourcing, motivational problems or shortfalls in the performance of others. A shop-floor worker, for example, who is responsible for completing 250 widgets a day will not reach his or her targets if there is a shortfall on the part of those who are supposed to supply the widget's components. This last kind of problem may come to light if a thorough job analysis is being carried out on the whole department.

Finally, having analysed the job, created the job specification and examined the job-holder's performance, we are in a position to compare the requirements of the job with the input of the job-holder and identify the training gap for that particular job. This is done throughout the department on a job-by-job basis and, if necessary, throughout the whole organization. For training purposes, the products of job analysis are, (1) a job description, (2) a job specification and (3) a training specification.

Going through the organization on a job-by-job basis can be a time-consuming and costly process, but when it has been completed and all of the information is on the computer, it begins to pay for itself; when, for example, particular systems are being modified or new ones introduced, such as job evaluation, performance related pay, recruitment and selection and performance appraisal, all of which, if they are to be carried out properly, demand a thorough analysis of the job affected. It is advisable to monitor and review job descriptions and specifications at regular intervals as well as when new job-holders are being recruited.

Training Needs Analysis

The technique for identifying training needs at individual, group and corporate levels is known as a training needs analysis (TNA). This involves carrying out surveys on the particular areas of the organization: its departments, sections, functions and individuals. If the survey is being carried out for the first time, all of these areas should be covered. We will refer to this aspect as the 'scope' of the survey.

Bearing in mind that the purpose of a TNA is to identify problems in a general sense and then tease out those that can be solved through training, the personnel specialist can approach it in one of two ways. He or she can get the managers and supervisors involved firstly by asking them what their problems are and building up a picture from their responses, or secondly, by conducting a structured survey. The first approach is a rather informal method of collecting data, but it can be very effective, especially if it is conducted as a series of face-to-face interviews. In these situations, managers will tell you things about their problems that they would never commit to paper. People do like to chat, however, and the method can take more time than the second approach, the training needs survey. This is a more formalized approach that is often based on information derived from the personnel records, backed up by further information gathered on the basis of a questionnaire. Some organizations use both approaches to gain maximum information.

PREPARATION

The need for a training survey might have arisen because such surveys are conducted in the organization regularly. On the other hand, a particular area of the organization might be seen to be having problems – failing, perhaps, to meet quality or quantity targets – and the decision is made to carry out a training survey on that specific area. This kind of decision determines the scope and size of the survey. Usually, we think we know in advance what the problems are likely to be and we can set our survey objectives accordingly: these will consist of the items to be included in the questionnaire and where to look in the personnel records. Finally, surveys, like almost everything else, incur a cost and you only get what you are prepared to pay for. If it is thought that an organization-wide survey should be done, decisions have to be made about the extent and depth of the survey, what resources will be necessary and the period of time over which it is to be carried out.

INFORMATION GATHERING

Let us say that we have completed our preparation and the scene is set for the first ever full-blown, organization-wide training survey. Firstly, we need to gather the necessary information. Having decided on a time frame for the project, we distribute the questionnaire to the managers, supervisors and other key people, making sure that we give them an attainable deadline for the return of the completed forms. Concurrently, we set about interrogating the personnel records. So what are we looking for? The basic informational requirements are as follows:

1 To assist our decisions during the preparation process, we will have looked at staff numbers, to assess the volume of data to be processed. Knowing how many employees there are is important, of course, but the numbers have to be broken down into departmental, sectional and functional group numbers.

2 From the human resource plan, we obtain information about future requirements in terms of knowledge, skills and attitudes.

3 Also, from the human resource plan, we will have information about the degree to which this requirement is likely to be met. Will our present staff be able to cope? Can they be trained in any necessary new knowledge and skills? Is there a recruitment implication and, if so, can the external environment provide the people?

4 To what extent is the organization achieving its objectives? Are there shortfalls? If so, what are the likely causes?

5 To what extent are the various groups and functions effective in meeting their objectives? Can we identify specific problem areas?

6 Are there individuals who are falling short of minimum standards of work performance or failing to meet their objectives?

7 Have any of the jobs run out of date? Do jobs need to be redesigned in the light of the effects of an accumulation of minor organizational changes?

8 What is the staff turnover rate and what does this indicate? Are there particular areas of the organization where staff turnover is higher than it is in other areas?

INFORMATION ANALYSIS

All of this information has to be analysed and inferences drawn from what has been discovered. To some, this may seem to be a daunting task, but the speed, accuracy and versatility of today's personnel software packages has dispensed with most of the difficulties that, before computerization, meant that this kind of work either was a continuous, arduous process or it did not get done at all. Mind you, you still have to ask the right questions. Essentially, we are looking for two sets of answers: firstly, the accumulative size of the areas of the organization in which training needs have been identified – in other words, *how much* training is needed, where and at what levels – and second, what is the *nature* of the needs that have been established?

The identification of training needs that are brought about by a significant change in the organization, such as the introduction of new technology, is, to some extent, a separate issue. In these circumstances it may be necessary to set up new performance standards. Whereas training plans are usually concerned with raising standards of performance from what they are to what they should be, the installation of new technology may bring with it the need to develop new knowledge, skills and attitudes so that new performance standards can be met.

Information that has been derived from the personnel records should be checked in detail before it is used for purposes such as these. Sometimes, the information gathered directly from managers and supervisors conflicts with what is on the official record, and this should be investigated. It has been known, for example, for employees to 'cover' for each other; that is to say, where an employee lacks the skill necessary to carry out a particular task, a more skilled colleague will carry out the task instead. This is happening today in areas where managers are overly authoritarian, which results in employees fearing that such shortcomings may cause them to be seen as 'problem children', a designation that could earn them a place on the redundancy list. Obviously, in most organizations such fears are groundless, but the point that is being made is that poor management can conceal genuine training needs which, had they been identified and met, could have improved 'motivation' as well as the 'ability' factor.

Once all of the facts have been established and the training needs are known, we have to use our findings as the basis for a set of recommendations. The findings and the recommendations should be contained in a report, along with estimates of the costs and benefits. The decision to implement the recommendations is made by senior managers. This is where training managers encounter difficulties and frustrations. When, in many organizations, senior managers give the 'go-ahead' to a project, the decision carries with it the implication that the resulting recommendations will be implemented. Alas, this is not the case in all organizations. In some companies the directors will agree to implementation, while in others the directors will 'postpone' things or find the results 'interesting'. Yet others will direct that *some* of the recommendations should be implemented, while others should not. This last kind of decision can also be frustrating, especially when the recommendations relate to an integrated training system in which the various component courses are interdependent. Such a decision may lead to the reformulation of the plan, which may reduce its effectiveness.

There are signs that senior managers' attitudes towards training and developing their staff are changing, but it is a slow process. Britain still languishes around the bottom of the employee training and development league among the major trading nations of the world, most of whom, unlike us, understand the positive relationship between work performance and profitability. Still, let us imagine that we are in an enlightened organization and the decision to implement the recommendations has been made. What is our next step?

Preparing a Training Programme

Having completed all of the tasks related to the activities that are described above, we are now in a position to produce a draft training programme. At this stage it is a good idea to sit back and take a long and dispassionate look at what you have got and what you wish to do with it. By now, you know the size and scope of the training task you have in front of you and you know the nature of the training that is required. What you have to do is turn what you have into a meaningful and integrated whole. One approach to the design of a training programme might contain the following stages:

1   *Framework.* Rough out a provisional framework set within a time frame.

2   *Programming.* The timing of each course within the programme is a critically important factor. Obviously, it is more effective, for example, to train someone in the knowledge and skills required *before* new technology is installed, rather than afterwards; similarly, an employee who is earmarked for a supervisory position should be trained in the skills of supervision before being promoted. This may sound like simple common sense and indeed, it is, but in fact many organizations in Britain deploy people first and train them afterwards. From the information you have gathered, you should be able to see what the requirements are in terms of timing. The task then is to range the courses loosely across the time frame to see how they fit in. This normally will involve you in a little juggling, and depending upon the number of courses, their timing and their duration, you may find that you have to schedule some of them concurrently.

3   *Course development.* This is the most complex stage. Each course has to be studied and you need to be very clear about several issues relative to the individual courses:

(a)   The objectives of the course. What are its actual purposes?

(b)   The objectives of the trainees. What are they supposed to achieve in terms of knowledge, skills and attitudes? In other words, what should the trainees know and be able to do after the course, that they did not know and could not do beforehand?

(c)   Course content. What should the course contain if the objectives outlined at (a) and (b) are to be achieved?

(d)   Methods and media. What training methods are most likely to assist the achievement of objectives? Lectures? Seminars? The use of training videos? Group work? Using case studies and role-play techniques? A combination of several of these alternatives? Most experienced trainers will say that the nature of the subject matter and the type of trainee will be the main considerations when making decisions about the selection of methods. The choice of media is implicit in some of what is said above. Media equipment includes the use of flip charts, whiteboards, overhead and slide projectors, hand-outs and so forth. Decisions have to be made about how the equipment might best be employed, again in the light of the subject matter and the type of trainee.

(e)   Course process. How will the course be structured in terms of the sequence in which the contents are put across? The importance and complexity of each item of content will attract a particular allocation of time. This factor determines the duration of the whole course. What is needed here is a logical sequence of events that allows the trainees to move progressively through the items, developing knowledge and skills as they go. The sequence should include measures to sustain the interest and attention of the trainees, perhaps by varying the methods and media employed.

4   *Course delivery.* This is the stage in which we consider where the course is to be carried out, what kind of approach should be adopted and who should deliver the training.

(a)   Course location. Where is the training to be carried out? This is when we have to consider if the objectives will be best achieved through the use of an external course provider or by running it internally. If it is to be run internally, where will it be located? Training varies considerably in terms of the kind of venue to which it lends itself. Internal courses can be run in training centres, simulated workshops and, if it is decided that 'on-the-job' training would be most effective, in the office or on the shop floor itself. External courses are carried out in the custom-built facilities of private training centres, and longer-term, external award-bearing programmes are delivered in further and higher education establishments. These last two types of location are usually related more to the long-term development of employees, rather than short-term training requirements.

(b)   Who will deliver the course? This is another important factor that will be determined by the course duration, con-tent, location, level of expertise required and cost. A course of two days or more normally is delivered by several different experts; even a course that is dedicated to a single subject will benefit from having more than one expert's point of view and delivery style; the change from one trainer to another helps to sustain trainees' interest. If the course content is diverse, you may need to engage disparately qualified experts. The venue may influence the choice of trainer. 'On-the-job' coaching and training is often carried out by line managers and/or key departmental specialists. The location will also be an influence if the expert you need lives a long way from the training venue, and this will also affect costs. The credibility of the trainer is another important factor affecting choice. Possession of appropriate knowledge and skill does not carry with it the guarantee that the person is able to transfer that knowledge and skill to someone else in an interesting and effective way; that is an entirely different skill. The reputation of the trainer as an authority on the subject *and* as an effective and interesting communicator are factors that will influence his or her credibility to the trainees.

THE EVALUATION OF TRAINING

When stages 1 to 4 above have been completed satisfactorily, the final version of the programme can be published and the training can 'go live'. Each course in the programme should be monitored in terms of the quality of its administration and the attendance of trainees, while the effectiveness of the training itself should be evaluated.

1   Administration. Is all of the equipment in place and does it all work satisfactorily? This should be checked in advance of the training sessions, right down to details such as ensuring that there is a spare bulb for the overhead projector, 'marker' pens for the flip chart and 'dry-wipe' pens for the whiteboard. Certain items can be monitored in retrospect, such as the quality of the catering, the travel arrangements (if any), and the suitability of the venue in terms of physical adequacy and ambience. It is usual to obtain information about these items by issuing trainees with a questionnaire at the end of the course. This kind of questionnaire has been nicknamed the 'happiness sheet', a title that gives a good indication of its purpose. When the responses on the sheet are collated, any problems will become visible and action can be taken where necessary.

2   Attendance. It is vital to obtain a list of the names of all of the trainees who attend the course. The fact that they have

experienced training in particular items of knowledge, skill and attitudes will be entered on their respective personnel records. It is not safe to assume that they all attended just because they had been nominated to do so.

3   Evaluation. The purpose of evaluation is to assess the effectiveness of a training course by establishing the degree to which it has achieved its objectives. If the results of a formal evaluation are unsatisfactory, the problem must be identified and treated. This can range from minor problems that require just a corrective tweak here and there through to problems that are large and complex enough to justify rewriting the whole course. It is worth mentioning that satisfactory results may also lead to modifying the course, since the evaluation process is designed to provide information. This enables us to see the 'good' and 'moderate' areas of a satisfactory course and make adjustments accordingly, on the grounds that a 'satisfactory' rather than an 'excellent' assessment demonstrates scope for improvement.

So how do we evaluate a course? What is the actual process? As we develop a course and plan its delivery (see stages 3 and 4, Course development and Course delivery above), we are identifying the features that lend themselves to formal evaluation. Bearing in mind that through evaluation, we are trying to establish control over the degree to which the course achieves it objectives, it makes sense to assess the effectiveness of the content and processes that we have devised. If, therefore, we can discover the value of what we have put into it, we will be in a position to change our inputs with a view to modifying (improving) the outputs.

One of the most frequently cited writers in this rather complex area of thought is Hamblin. He defined evaluation as 'Any attempt to obtain information (feedback) on the effects of a training programme, and to assess the value of the training in the light of that information' (Hamblin, 1974).

In 1974, he proposed that evaluation should take place at five levels:

1   Reactions. How did the trainees react to the course in terms of their perceptions of the content (what should and should not be included), its relevance to their work, what they thought of the person(s) delivering the course and the 'happiness' factor? Was it enjoyable?

2   *Learning.* To measure how much learning has taken place as a direct outcome of the training. To what extent have attitudes changed? Is there a change in behaviour that indicates the development of new knowledge and skills?

3   *Job behaviour.* To what extent do the trainees apply the new learning in their jobs? This will tell us the extent to which the individual has carried the learning from the course to the job. This level is about evaluating the 'transfer' of learning.

4   *Organization.* At this and the next level, the focus switches from the individual to the group and the organization as a whole, and this involves the measurement of changes in performance, not necessarily of the individual but of the area in which he or she works. How, for example, has the training affected the performance of the section or department? What is measured here is the degree to which performance has (hopefully) improved.

5   *Ultimate value.* At this level we measure the extent to which the benefits of the training extend to the organization as a whole, in terms of improvements in the company-wide performance. Has profitability improved? Has the training enhanced the likelihood that the organization will achieve its main purposes of survival and development? The difficulty of measuring these outcomes is far greater than that of measuring individual outcomes.

Hamblin suggests that the five levels are interrelated and that they are linked in a 'cause-and-effect' way, in the order given above. By this, he means that training causes a reaction, which in turn leads to learning, which, as we know, causes changes in behaviour. If, therefore, the training was job-related, then the change in behaviour would also be job-related. Eventually, this leads to an increase in the performance of the whole organization. Obviously, for the whole organization to benefit in the way that Hamblin suggests, it needs to have a wide-ranging training policy that is designed to produce improvements in the performance of a large number of its employees, since it is obvious that the 'chain reaction' that commenced with the training of a small group of employees would take a long time to percolate upwards and have its organization-wide effect. Whether or not senior managers would attribute an improved corporate performance to the effects of training is doubtful, but the training manager who carries out the evaluation at all five levels will have his or her finger on the 'effectiveness' pulse from the level of the individual, right through to the company-wide perspective.

Summary

If the organization's human resource is going to meet the demands of the corporate strategy, it needs to be appropriately skilled and motivated to do so. The human resource strategy, therefore, will define the types and levels of the knowledge, skills and attitudes that will be required and, on the basis of these prescriptions, the personnel specialist will have drawn up training and development strategies. He or she will also have developed a system through which the strategy will be implemented. A surprisingly large number of organizations do not formulate such strategies and tend to carry out these functions in a random, ad hoc fashion, in which courses are hastily thrown together on an 'as and when required' basis. As we said earlier, if training and development programmes are to be effective, they have to be systematic.

References

Armstrong, M. 1993: *A Handbook of Personnel Management Practice*, 4th edn. London: Kogan Page.
Hamblin, A.C. 1974: *Evaluation and Control of Training*. Maidenhead: McGraw-Hill.

14

The Techniques of Training

Introduction

This chapter, although training-related, is separated from the previous one to emphasize how important it is for personnel staff to understand and be skilled in the techniques of training. The chapter's main purpose is to take you through a variety of techniques that are suitable for particular kinds of training. We have seen that organizing, providing and administering training is the responsibility of the personnel specialist, while the training itself is carried out by experts who are engaged for that specific purpose. The trainers may be specialist employees of the organization, or they may be external people from consultancies, training agencies, educational establishments or professional bodies. But you as a personnel specialist need to understand and be skilled in the techniques of training, firstly so that you will be able to make a better job of monitoring and evaluating courses, since you will know what to look for, and secondly, because there will be times when you will need to organize and conduct training courses yourself.

In many organizations, initial induction training sessions are conducted by personnel staff, before handing the new employees over to their line managers. Yet again, when personnel policies and systems are changed, those who implement them have to be given a fresh understanding and be trained in the new methods of implementation. Changes could be made to the performance-related pay scheme or to the recruitment and selection system, which, among several others, are personnel systems in which the line managers are very much involved and in which they will need to develop a clear understanding of any changes and acquire the skills necessary to carry them through.

Skill Classification

Since we are going to explain training techniques in terms of their suitability for developing particular kinds of skill, it is a good idea firstly to classify the skills themselves, so that when we understand the techniques, we will see the types of skill to which they relate.

Skills can be placed into two broad categories: *Manual* and *Cerebral* (see table 14.1). Those that fall into the manual skills category involve the individual in skills that require predominantly eye–hand coordination, whereas the exercise of those that fall into the cerebral category involve the individual in skills that require thinking and reasoning. In terms of their degree of complexity, the specific skills in each category may be regarded as incremental, that is to say, skill number 2 is more complex than skill number 1, number 3 is more complex than number 2 and so on. Within each category, the development of each type of skill may require its own training technique.

From the table we can see that skills can range from elementary manual skills through complex manual skills to the more cerebral skills of numeracy, analysis, problem solving and decision making. Social, interpersonal skills are regarded as somewhat different, in that while they are often very relevant to the demands of the job, their development is just as dependent upon particular aspects of an individual's personality as it is upon specific training techniques.

Training Techniques

When a trainer is employing particular techniques, it is essential for him or her to understand exactly what is happening and what should be happening within the individual in the training situation. That is to say, the trainer needs an understanding of the learning process, the purposes of training and the role of the trainer. Since these topics are addressed in earlier chapters, we

Table 14.1 Examples from a range of skill categories

Example of skill	Example of task behaviour
Manual	Eye–hand coordinated behaviour
1 Typewriting	Hitting correct keys, ensuring layout conforms to required style, details of addressee in correct position, etc.
2 Using a camcorder	Checking it is switched on, lens cover removed, subject is in frame and in focus
3 Bricklaying	Reading the plans, checking shape and dimensions, ensuring bricks are flush and even
4 Using an IT package	Accessing package on computer, input and retrieval, processing and manipulating data
Cerebral	Thinking and reasoning behaviour
5 Composing a letter	Deciding what to say, mentally organizing the sequence of what is said, adopting a particular tone, etc.
6 Producing a video tape	Deciding on the subject matter, analysing any foreseeable difficulties and producing possible solutions, mentally establishing logical sequence of events, assessing impact of end product
7 Designing a house	Identifying site, deciding on size and style, number of rooms, etc., designing interior, producing layout and drawings, etc.
8 Developing an IT package	Analysing user's needs in terms of capacity, versatility, ease of use, designing functions and their access, etc.

will assume that the reader has developed such understanding. It is important, however, when deciding which training techniques to use, to have an understanding of the relationships between the various conditions of learning (see table 12.1), those of skill acquisition in the workplace, and the purposes of specific training techniques.

The objectives of training programmes are to develop within people those items of knowledge, skills and attitudes that have been identified as training needs. The techniques to be employed should be related appropriately to those needs. The objectives of training vary, depending upon the nature and variety of the training needs that have been identified. Managers and supervisors, for example, may need to be trained in interpersonal communication (social skills), operators in practical, manual skills (psychomotor skills) and specialists in problem solving (cognitive skills). Different outcome requirements demand different training techniques. Decisions about which techniques to employ, therefore, cannot be made until *after* the objectives have been identified and agreed upon, the aim being to select techniques that are most likely to achieve the objectives.

It is reasonable to classify training techniques under two broad headings: firstly, those that relate to the training location, and secondly, those that relate to the means through which the training is transferred to the trainee. The former can be related to 'on-the-job', 'off-the-job' and 'on-and-off-the-job' training, and the latter to coaching, counselling, lectures, seminars, workshops, case studies, films, role-play, training videos and so forth. Also, it should be borne in mind that particular training techniques lend themselves to particular training situations. The techniques, for example, that are employed in 'on-the-job' training may be totally inappropriate in other training situations.

While it is helpful, in terms of deciding upon the techniques to be used, to distinguish between training locations, the focus here is upon how the desired outcomes (the training objectives) determine the techniques to be used. The following two sections, therefore, describe two broad categories of technique. Section 1 addresses those that are employed in the development of knowledge and understanding, while section 2 examines those that are applied in the development of skills. It should be emphasized, however, that some of the techniques that are used for the development of knowledge and understanding may also be applied in the development of skills. The categories of technique, therefore, are both broad and flexible; hopefully, the appropriateness of their use will become apparent to the reader.

Section 1: Developing Knowledge and Understanding

LECTURES, DISCUSSIONS AND SEMINARS

Lectures, discussions and *seminars* may be used effectively for these purposes and it is normal to utilize all three methods in the same session. The objective, for example, may be to communicate information about a change in the system of performance-related pay, in which case the trainer would explain the change and any effects it might have on the other parts of the system or, indeed, on other systems. The group could then have a discussion about the change, thereby exchanging their perceptions of it (and usually their views!). Finally, to check that the delegates' understanding of the change is correct, the trainer could lead a seminar, interjecting now and then with a 'what if . . .' type of question.

It is important to note that people generally absorb information more readily in an informal, rather than a formal atmosphere. It is helpful if the trainer knows the delegates, can address them by their first names and passes a few informal remarks before introducing the subject matter. Also, account should be taken of the fact that people do not all assimilate information at the same rate and they vary in terms of how much information they actually take in and are able to recall. An experienced trainer will know intuitively who's who in these respects, and during the seminar will elicit answers from the group at large to questions about the items he or she suspects have not been fully digested by everyone.

The number of people in the group is an important factor. Large numbers can be addressed if the information to be communicated is clear and fairly straightforward, but it is widely accepted that an attempt to put a complex or delicate matter across to a large audience is usually ineffective. Too large a group can also be difficult to manage in a discussion or seminar. If it is necessary to put something complex across at a large conference, the delegates are normally divided into 'syndicate' groups. The syndicates depart into separate rooms and work alone for a predetermined period of time. When the time has expired, the delegates reconvene and each syndicate's spokesperson delivers a short presentation on his or her syndicate's perceptions. However, 'the more intricate the subject matter, the smaller the audience' is a broad rule for effectively passing on complicated information.

Case studies

Some of the case studies that are available describe hypothetical situations, while others are based on reality. They are a useful means of exposing trainees to organizational events and situations that are relevant to what the trainer wishes to communicate. Case studies can be used for a variety of purposes and in various situations.

An *informational* case study describes a situation, the factors influencing it, the decisions and actions that were taken and the consequences that followed. This, of course, is the simple passing on of information and is useful when trainees would benefit from an example. This may also be referred to as a case history.

A *reflective* case study is one which presents the trainee with a problem or a set of interrelated problems, but stops short of revealing the decisions that were made and their consequences. Instead, the trainee is asked to identify the cause(s) of the problem and provide a set of alternative solutions. The trainee decides on the most appropriate solution, takes action, and justifies this by indicating what he or she thinks would be the outcome and why it would be the preferred outcome. The case may be accompanied by sets of model alternative solutions, which are revealed to the trainees at the end of the case study session. This allows them to analyse and discuss the model solutions and compare them to their own.

The reflective case study is the type most frequently used. It puts the learner in a safe situation, in which he or she can make decisions and take actions without the jeopardy of having to face the consequences if things go wrong, as they would in the real situation. It is good practice for trainees to explore possible solutions; they can do it alone or in groups and they can keep trying until they reach a satisfactory solution.

Role-play exercises

These are presented as organizational case studies, in which the employees involved are identified by their names and job titles. A significant difference between case studies and role-play exercises is that in the former, the trainees are objective and analytic observers, who make judgements about what might or might not be advisable in determining solutions to problems, while in the latter, the trainees become active participants by adopting the roles of those named in the script. Role-play exercises depict typical organizational situations, such as a selection interview, a negotiation, a meeting, an encounter with a customer, a selling situation and so forth. The script includes personality profiles of the 'employees' and the trainees are expected to react accordingly. The 'interviewee', for example, might be shy and reticent, the 'other side' in the negotiation might adopt a tough, confrontational style, the 'customer' might be irate and hard to handle, and the sales 'target' might offer considerable resistance. The learning opportunities are built in to the exercises, the trainee learning from doing, rather than from listening passively.

Many people feel self-conscious when they take part in role-play exercises for the first time, especially if the event is being recorded on CCTV, but they soon become involved in the action and adopt their roles. Trainers should beware of trainees who become personally involved in the situation, to the extent that heated arguments develop. While this can be hard to control, there is no doubt that learning is taking place. Participants usually enjoy role-play exercises and have vivid recollections of the training events in which they occurred. It is often said that in terms of learning, there is no substitute for experience, but in that respect, a well-managed role-play exercise is the nearest one can get to the real thing.

GROUP DISCUSSIONS

In this kind of situation, it is not advisable to have more than eight people in the group. They can be led by the trainer or take place with the trainer as a group member. A group discussion presents an ideal opportunity for learning through problem solving and is frequently used for that purpose. The format is to present the group with a problem, which they analyse and try to solve through discussion within a limited period. Where the trainer is leading the group, he or she will control the discussion by dealing with digressions, and putting in the occasional guide word or phrase if it looks as if the group members are on the wrong track. The trainer as a group member should strive to do the same thing, but in a more subtle manner. In both cases the group members must themselves solve the problem and *feel* as if they have done so.

Group discussions are also used in non-training situations. All organizations have problems of one kind or another and it is normal to appoint a group of appropriate specialists to attempt to find solutions. Groups are used in quality circles, planning sessions, the implementation of tasks and for many other purposes.

COUNSELLING

The purpose of this method is to develop the trainee's knowledge, skills and attitudes through individual tuition. Typically, counselling takes place because the need has been identified in a 'potential review' or a performance appraisal session, so the counsellor will have relevant information about the 'client'. The counsellor, who may have the alternative role of tutor, plans one-to-one developmental sessions and uses direct methods in which the trainee participates. In this way, the counsellor can monitor the progress of the individual as he or she is developing, provide guidance and use his or her influence on the spot. Ideally, the two will agree about the nature of the problem and jointly set about the task of arriving at a solution. If the client is not amenable to this approach, the counsellor may decide to try to 'sell' ideas to the client, or use persuasive information.

COACHING

Coaching and counselling have similar purposes, to improve performance and change attitudes, but their approaches differ in their emphasis. While counselling addresses the input of knowledge and attempts to influence attitudes, coaching is a teaching technique through which skills are developed. Coaching and counselling are often used together, depending on the nature of the needs that have been identified, and sessions are sometimes conducted alternately by different specialists, with the same employee.

It should be stressed that coaching and counselling are not techniques that were invented for dealing with an organization's 'problem children'. In fact, they are most frequently used when developmental needs have been identified in employees who have been earmarked for promotion or further education and training, and it has been decided that coaching and/or counselling would be the most appropriate methods of filling in the gaps in their understanding.

Section 2: Developing Skills

The techniques we examine in this section were designed to 'fill in', where there are gaps in an individual's ability to carry out practical or manual tasks. The gaps may have appeared when the nature of the employee's job changed, when new technology was introduced or simply because the employee has been moved to a different job. Also, new employees rarely possess *all* of the skills that are demanded in the job description. Usually, they are selected because they possess *most* of the skills. We address the question of selection decision making later; suffice to say at this point that it is virtually impossible to recruit candidates who possess every single quality that is asked for in the person specification.

'SITTING-BY-NELLIE'

This is not a technique that has arisen from research-based knowledge of learning and training. Rather, it has evolved over the years on a 'let me show you how' basis and, gradually, it has acquired status as an effective means of developing skills within people. Typically, Nellie is highly proficient in the skill(s) that the trainee needs. The trainee sits next to her (or him!) and observes her as she carries out her tasks. The trainee has a workstation that is the same as Nellie's and, from observations of the way she operates, and after several attempts at carrying out the tasks, begins to pick up her skills, eventually attaining the minimum required standard and, from there, progressing to greater proficiency.

Clearly, sitting-by-Nellie is 'on-the-job' training, and it has long been thought that observing and copying an experienced and proficient worker is the best way to develop manual skills within people. The technique is usually associated with training semi-skilled factory workers and office workers who carry out standardized administrative tasks, although there are also strong elements of it in the training of craft and technician apprentices. It is a natural teaching technique that is used in many countries. In Russian factories, for example, a

Stakhanovite is a high-performing skilled worker who receives awards in recognition of his or her performance.

'Sitting-by-Ivan'

If productivity falls in a factory, the Stakhanovites are asked to do their work 'sitting-by-Ivan'. In this situation, the low-performing worker sits next to a Stakhanovite and observes and copies his or her style of task performance, until the low performer's standards rise to the required levels of quality and quantity. During the process, the Stakhanovite observes and guides the trainee and recognizes when the minimum required standard has been achieved, whereupon he or she then moves on to sit next to another low performer and repeats the process. Stakhanovites who are asked to do this regard the event as a reward for their performance.

Delegation

Delegating tasks, assignments and projects to subordinates is a technique that is often used by managers who wish to provide their staff with relevant experience. The technique is open to abuse, in so far as it can be used as a work-shedding tactic, but when it is carried out correctly, it is an extremely effective form of employee development. It involves employees in acquiring knowledge, skills and attitudes that will stand them in good stead in their careers. The successful completion of an important project justifiably attracts considerable attention when it is included in an individual's curriculum vitae.

Developing numeracy skills

Further and higher education establishments have much to offer in this respect, although their core business is that of developing people in career-related or academically orientated subjects. Within this context, numeracy is one of the items on a course syllabus, rather than a subject that is treated in a discrete fashion. Internally, organizations develop short courses in certain aspects of numeracy, which are run in-house and either on- or off-the job: budgetry control, the use of particular accounting systems and the use of IT packages that include the need to be numerate are just a few examples. Similar courses are offered externally by commercial training establishments and some further education institutions. In the highly skilled, professional areas of the organization in which numeracy is an integral part of the job, such as in accountancy and most aspects of engineering, the employees usually are long-term experienced or professionally qualified people by whom numeracy is exercised as a matter of course; whereas training in numeracy is most frequently organized for those who are new, perhaps, to budgeting and certain aspects of quality assurance.

DEVELOPING ANALYTIC AND PROBLEM SOLVING SKILLS

It is widely accepted that the use of case studies and role-play exercises is effective and cost-efficient in developing these skills. The keys to learning, confidence-building and the internalization of the results of these experiences are built into the process itself, especially that of role-playing. The main advantages of employing these techniques are explained earlier, so there is no need to reiterate them here. It is worth pointing out, however, that case studies and role-play exercises are effective methods, not only for developing knowledge and changing employees' attitudes, but also in the development of skills.

DEVELOPING INTERPERSONAL SKILLS

Interpersonal skills are alternatively referred to as interpersonal communication, interpersonal interaction and 'social' skills. I have even seen them referred to in a higher education course document as 'Relating to and influencing people'! Whatever euphemism one decides to use, 'interpersonal skills' is a reference to how we behave when we are in the company of others. The all-embracing term that is used colloquially is 'people skills', and I will go along with that. It is simple and everyone knows what is meant.

People skills are important in most aspects of organizational life. The ability to relate to people effectively is known to be essential to successful leadership, interviewing, working as a member of a team, representing the organization externally in a sales or technical capacity, coaching and counselling people, carrying out performance appraisal reviews, making project presentations, participating in meetings, handling grievances and matters of discipline: the list is virtually endless.

Not everyone is amenable to training in interpersonal skills. Indeed, some trainers maintain that if their efforts are to be effective, the trainees have to have some degree of natural ability in handling relationships. 'If there is just a trace of know-how,' they say, 'then it is possible to train them from that point on. But if there is nothing there, there never will be.' Similar comments are heard about leadership training. It is probably true to say that everyone knows someone who is totally lacking in interpersonal skills and who seems to be trying to make a profession out of being abrasive, obstructive or simply 'bloody-minded'. On the other hand, there are those who are poor at developing and maintaining relationships because they are shy or naturally uncommunicative. On the other hand, such people are not generally those who aspire to positions in which such skills are essential. People who become leaders, representatives, interviewers, etc. usually do so because they enjoy meeting people, talking to them and generally communicating with their fellow human beings.

Interpersonal skill development is usually delivered in short courses, either as 'one-off' events or as a series, depending upon the developmental distance that the trainees need to travel. The selection of people for this kind of training event is an issue that should be addressed carefully. Where it is possible and practicable, in terms of their availability, it is advisable to bring together people who are roughly equally skilled and in need of a similar degree of development, bearing in mind that 'equally skilled' means anything from 'poor' at one end of the spectrum to 'good' at the other. In this way, the objectives of an interpersonal skills course, in which, say, the trainees are thought to be poorly skilled, would be to develop them up to the 'fair-to-good' mark, whereas the objectives where the trainees are considered to be 'good' would be to develop them towards 'very-good' to 'excellent' standards.

It is essential for the trainer to be well-versed in human behaviour, good at developing skills in others and, in particular, experienced in running courses of this nature. Courses in inter-personal skills should contain reasonable inputs of knowledge of human behaviour, emphasizing the importance of verbal and non-verbal communication. Ideally, each knowledge input session will alternate with sessions in which the trainees prac-tise what they have just learned. In this way, the trainees will experience using the skills, will discover the difference that their use can make to a relationship and will internalize the know-ledge, thereby reinforcing the truth of the concepts that the trainer is putting across to them. Role-play exercises that simulate the types of organizational situation in which interpersonal skills are important have been found to be very effective. Courses may last from one to five days, depending upon the amount and type of development needed and the learning capacity of the participants.

The Learning Curve

When decisions are being made about which training techniques to employ in a training event, consideration should be given to the learning curve. The learning curve is something that we often hear referred to in passing conversation, but it is an important human phenomenon. Not everyone learns at the same rate; as we saw in chapter 12, the amount of learning that takes place depends upon (1) the effectiveness of the trainer, (2) the situation in which the training is taking place and (3) the individual's capacity to learn. While the nature of the first two of these three factors is the same for everyone, the third factor, the individual's capacity to learn, is different for everyone, since it depends upon individually different levels of intelligence and motivation to learn. A standard learning curve shows the degree to which learning takes place within an individual inside a particular period of time, as shown in figure 14.1.

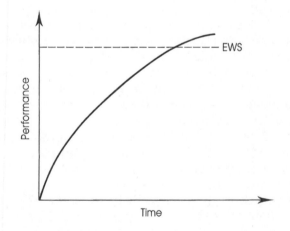

Figure 14.1 A standard learning curve.

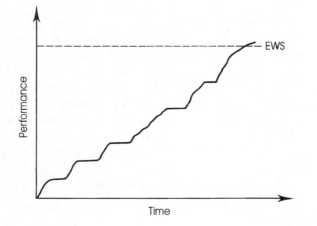

Figure 14.2 A 'plateau' learning curve.

The curve shows how much learning (the vertical axis) has taken place across a set amount of time (the lateral axis). The horizontal, dotted rule shows the level of performance that is expected from the training and, as we can see, the curve has just about surpassed it. The expected level is referred to as the experienced worker's standard (EWS) or the minimum required standard (MRS). These standards do not exist at the same level. For example, someone who has reached the MRS may not yet

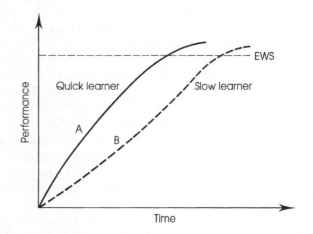

Figure 14.3 A comparative learning curve.

have reached the EWS, the implication being that the standard of an experienced worker is higher than the minimum requirement. Not all learning takes place in an even and unbroken way, as depicted by the curve. Learning is often interspersed with interruptions, and some aspects of the subject matter might be more difficult than others, for the learner. If this is the case, the learning may plateau, as shown in figure 14.2.

A learning curve can be used to plot an individual's learning, but it may also be used to compare learning rates between several individuals. Figure 14.3 demonstrates how this can be done. In this figure, the learning progress of each of the individuals A and B is shown on the appropriate curves.

Summary

Skills are categorized under two headings, manual and cerebral. Skill development can be regarded as 'incremental' in the sense that 'how-to' skills, such as operating a machine, using a filing system or loading a lorry, involve the coordinated use of the eyes and hands. From this we can progress to other skills, the practice of which is less likely to form an overt behavioural pattern, such as composing letters and memoranda, in which there is a uniform pattern for all of them, but the contents are different, which implies that an element of thinking and reasoning is required for the completion of each task. From this level, we progress from skills in which eye–hand coordination is predominant to those in which the use of the brain predominates: analysis. numeracy, problem solving and decision making.

Training techniques are classified under two broad headings: (1) those that are appropriate for the development of knowledge and understanding and (2) those that are appropriate for the development of skills. Some techniques are suitable for both categories and, indeed, knowledge, skills and attitudes are often developed through the use of the same technique.

Decisions about the selection of training techniques can not be made until after the objectives of the training have been identified and agreed upon; in fact, the selection of training techniques is *dependent upon* the nature of the training objectives.

The main techniques that are in use today are: lectures, discussions and seminars, case studies, role-play exercises, group discussions, coaching and counselling, and 'sitting-by-Nellie'.

Part IV

Performance Management

This part of the book aims, firstly, at providing an understanding of why individuals and groups behave as they do at work, and secondly, in the light of that understanding, at determining what steps might be taken to manage their performance. There are, therefore, chapters on personality, perception and intelligence, and attitudes and group development, after which we examine and discuss systems of appraisal, objective-setting and motivational techniques. Finally, reward management, including systems of payment, is described and discussed.

15

Personality, Perception and Intelligence

Introduction

In this chapter we will examine personality and perception in terms of individual differences – how, for example, individuals all develop different personalities and how those differences play their part in causing people to perceive things as they do. It is essential for personnel practitioners to understand individual differences if they are going to advise others on matters such as leading and motivating people, making decisions about the use of occupational tests, and generally understanding differences in people's motivations and perceptions.

Individual Differences

All individuals are different from each other. They are different physically, mentally and behaviourally. In these respects, the chance that two individuals will be exactly the same as each other may be likened to the possibility that their fingerprints will have the same patterns. Of course, we all know this. We know that people have different physical *looks* different *voices*, use the language in their own particular way, have sets of habits that are recognizable as uniquely theirs, and so forth. But if we are going to study individual differences, it is not enough to rely on what we call our experience and our 'common sense'. We have to have some kind of organized framework through which we can approach the subject – we have to study it scientifically. Firstly, however, we need to know *why*, and in what ways, all individuals are different and we need to be able to measure those differences by using structured observational methods and techniques.

We study individual differences by observing people's behaviour. It is in this way that we are able to measure the degree to which they differ from each other in their personalities, perceptions, attitudes, motivations and intelligence. Psychologists vary in their approaches to such measurement. Some, for example, maintain that it is primarily the make-up of the individual's personality characteristics that causes people to behave differently from one another, while others have said that situational factors cause us to behave in the way we do.

These differences in approach *emphasize* the importance of the situation or the person; they do not say that it is exclusively one or the other. More recent theories say that it is a combination of the two. '*Interactionists*', for example, say that it is the interaction between the individual and the situation that causes behaviour (Bandura, 1977).

Why We Are Unique

Here, we will examine how people differ in their personalities and how those differences are reflected in personal styles and patterns of behaviour that characterize them as unique individuals. Once we understand all of that, we will be in a better position to understand how differences in personalities cause people to behave as they do in the work situation.

Historically, psychologists have produced a variety of explanations of individual differences. When psychologists talk about individual differences they are referring mainly to personality. They may refer to the classical theories of personality such as *type* and *trait* theories and the *psychoanalytic approach* of Sigmund Freud; and to such modern approaches as *behaviourism*, *social learning*, *phenomenological (humanistic) theories* and *cognitive* and *interactionist* theories.

While our purpose here is to make you aware of the importance of personality in the workplace, rather than educate you in the various approaches to psychology, your route to a clear understanding will be eased by, firstly, some definitions of personality, secondly, a synopsis of the early approaches to personality theory, and thirdly, a more detailed account of modern theories.

Definitions

(Note that definitions of personality vary with the psychologists' approach to the subject.)

the total pattern of characteristic ways of thinking, feeling and behaving that constitute the individual's distinctive method of relating to the environment. (Kagan and Havemann, 1980)

the characteristic patterns of behaviour and modes of thinking that determine a person's adjustment to the environment. (Atkinson et al., 1983)

an individual's characteristic patterns of thoughts, emotions and behaviours. (Huffman et al., 1987)

Classical Theories of Personality

While by today's standards, some of the early theories may not seem to be totally acceptable, others have had a serious and long-lasting influence over the ways in which psychologists study personality. Undoubtedly, the central assumptions around which we base our studies of personality first arose with *type theories*, *trait theories* and the *psychoanalytic approach*.

TYPE THEORIES

Type theorists studied people's most obvious, broad characteristics and categorized them according to a *typology*, which was the system they used to classify people. In this way, individuals were classified or coded as one type or another, depending upon their most obvious characteristic. Type theorists are still around today, although they work according to a much more sophisticated system than did the earlier theorists; for example, two American theorists developed a dimension on which people could be classified as *Type A* or *Type B*, depending upon how they behaved and in particular, how they behaved at work (Holmes and Rahe, 1967). Type As are ambitious and drive themselves hard, while Type Bs are more relaxed and tend to take things easy. While this theory was developed in 1959, further similar research was carried out in the 1960s and 1970s, and the Types A and B dimension is frequently used, among other studies, in research into causes of occupational stress.[1]

Constitutional theories   In the 1930s and 1940s, constitutional theorists attributed personality characteristics to people's body types. Theorists such as William Sheldon associated each of the three main types with a particular set of personality character-istics. Thin people were intellectuals, sensitive and inhibited; podgy, overweight people were happy, relaxed, fond of their food, and easy to get on with; while muscular, athletic people were aggressive and independent. Not surprisingly, this theory was heavily and frequently criticized, principally for its inaccuracies and lack of scientific validity. Personality 'type theories' of this kind (like Sheldon's) were based on the 'mind–body rela-tionship'.

TRAIT THEORY

For the trait theorist, personality is inherited genetically; it is made up of identifiable factors that are present at birth, can not be modified and can be assessed through the use of objective tests. When they are describing personality, trait theorists do so in terms of individuals' possession of 'traits'. A *trait* is one of the vast array of mental or behavioural characteristics that a person may have. Trait theorists assume that people differ according to a variety of personality 'scales', each scale or 'dimension' repre-senting a trait. The scales were devised so that traits could be assessed and to enable us to measure an individual on, for example, an aggressiveness scale, a sociability scale, an intelli-gence scale, an impulsiveness scale and so forth. Such theorists claim to have identified some 40,000 traits.

Probably the most well-known trait theorists are Gordon All-port, Raymond B. Cattell and Hans Eysenck. Eysenck found that the ways in which people interact socially can be related to individuals' arousal level in *physiological* terms. People were measured on an 'introversion–extroversion' dimension, which was used as a personality test. Those who had high scores at the introversion end of the dimension had a higher level of arousal than those who scored high at the Extroversion end. High 'introversion' scorers responded with a greater level of arousal to such stimuli as sudden loud noises and 'thrilling' experiences. Eysenck said that introverts tend to keep their levels of stimula-tion more under control in order to avoid stress in social inter-action. Extroverts, on the other hand, are not so sensitive as introverts and need a great degree of social interactive stimula-tion in order to sustain a normal physiological balance.

It is well known that from the genes of our forebears we inherit externally visible features, such as our height, weight, eye colour and shape, hair colour and texture and facial features. We also inherit internal organic features, some of which are unfortunate, such as heart, digestive and other organic problems. All genetic decisions that cause such inherent factors are made at the moment of conception; but there are strong differences of opinion among psychologists about the degree to which we inherit individual psychological differences, such as personality characteristics.

Gordon Allport drew distinctions between what he called *common traits* and *unique traits*. Common traits were those such as aggressiveness and sociability, while unique traits were those that were more related to a particular individual, such as a brilliant command of the language or quick-wittedness. Allport also said that some traits were *cardinal traits*, which were the characteristics that determined an individual's life, such as personal power, career-mindedness and self-sacrifice. He also identified what he referred to as *central traits*, which were significant beliefs or personal qualities, such as integrity, intellectual or artistic interests, sensitivity and independence.

Raymond B. Cattell developed the *Sixteen Personality Factor Inventory* (16 PFI). This is an objective, self-report questionnaire that produces a personality profile based on 16 traits. The 16 PFI is still widely used in industry today, particularly as part of an organization's selection processes. Cattell identified around 18,000 personality traits and grouped them together using a statistical technique: *factor analysis*, which is based on the concept of correlation, the degree to which things go together, or co-vary, without cause and effect. To those who are unfamiliar with statistical analysis, correlation may seem complex, but in crude terms and for our purposes here, it means that where one trait was found in a person it was frequently accompanied by another. Impulsiveness and aggression, for example, are frequently found in the same individual. Cattell grouped together large numbers of traits into clusters and then, via the same process (factor analysis), grouped the clusters together, finishing up with 16 clusters of clusters. He identified the main characteristic associated with each cluster and letter-labelled them A to Q, breaking the consecutive order of the alphabet to indicate the distance in relationship between the nature of the clusters. Against each named cluster, Cattell placed an opposite characteristic and subjects were measured on a 10-point scale between each of the two traits, as shown in figure 15.1.

A	Reserved	1 2 3 4 5 6 7 8 9 10	Outgoing
B	Less intelligent	1 2 3 4 5 6 7 8 9 10	More intelligent
C	Affected by feelings	1 2 3 4 5 6 7 8 9 10	Emotionally stable
E	Submissive	1 2 3 4 5 6 7 8 9 10	Dominant
F	Serious	1 2 3 4 5 6 7 8 9 10	Happy-go-lucky
G	Expedient	1 2 3 4 5 6 7 8 9 10	Conscientious
H	Timid	1 2 3 4 5 6 7 8 9 10	Venturesome
I	Tough-minded	1 2 3 4 5 6 7 8 9 10	Sensitive
L	Trusting	1 2 3 4 5 6 7 8 9 10	Suspicious
M	Practical	1 2 3 4 5 6 7 8 9 10	Imaginative
N	Forthright	1 2 3 4 5 6 7 8 9 10	Shrewd
O	Self-assured	1 2 3 4 5 6 7 8 9 10	Apprehensive
Q_1	Conservative	1 2 3 4 5 6 7 8 9 10	Experimenting
Q_2	Group-dependent	1 2 3 4 5 6 7 8 9 10	Self-sufficient
Q_3	Uncontrolled	1 2 3 4 5 6 7 8 9 10	Controlled
Q_4	Relaxed	1 2 3 4 5 6 7 8 9 10	Tense

Figure 15.1 Cattell's 16 personality factor inventory.

PSYCHOANALYSIS

Psychoanalysis is a *developmental* approach to personality. Unlike type and trait theories, which either pigeonholed people into categories or attempted to identify particular personality traits, psychoanalytic theorists believe that unique personalities develop as a result of individuals' experiences and interpretations of encounters with the environment throughout childhood and adolescence, and into adulthood. For such theorists it is difficult to accept that one's personality can be present at birth and not subject to change. Whereas trait theorists talk about 'laws that govern human behaviour' and classify individuals into particular personality categories, psychoanalytic theorists emphasize the depth and abundant complexity of the unique individual. This implies that while the trait theorist sets out to classify an individual's personality as if it is made up of a selection from a predetermined matrix of traits, the psychoanalyst embarks upon a psychological voyage of discovery by investigating the distinctive characteristics of one particular individual. For the non-psychologist, Freud's *psychoanalytic theory of personality* will seem rather complicated; indeed, much of what he did say is still being unravelled. Suffice to say that Freud had a significant influence on nineteenth and early twentieth century studies of psychology.

Individual Differences Revisited

At this stage, it is probably a good idea to explain the main elements in which, as individuals, we are different from each other. I said earlier that when psychologists are talking about individual differences they are usually concerned with personality. Indeed, some psychologists say that the whole of psychology is a study of why and in which ways individuals are different from each other. Personality is a broad and all-embracing concept, which includes how we perceive, what motivates us, our levels of intelligence, how we learn, and our attitudes towards things, ideas and people, most of which is based on our beliefs and values.

Perception

Even as we pass people in the street, a fleeting assessment of them floats through our minds; first impressions account significantly for our subsequent perceptions of people. We see what we *need* to see, what we *expect* to see and what we *wish* to see.

To the psychologist, human perception is an extremely important area of study that is rich in past and current theories and in grounds for further investigation. Human beings have five main organs of sensory perception (the senses): the eyes, ears, nose, mouth and skin. The world is full of stimuli that continually bombard us with sensations (sights, sounds, smells, tastes and textures), which are conveyed to the brain by our senses, through the organs mentioned above. Our experiences of these sensations, however, do not necessarily amount to perception. Perception, it is said, occurs when the sensations we experience have meaning for us: *Perception = Sensation + Meaning.*

Perception is a mental *process*. It is the process that gives us the ability to make sense of the world around us through the variety of sensations that we experience; it enables us to inter-pret and organize them in a manageable way. In fact, the organs of sensory perception are our personal media, carriers of mes-sages made up of sensations, whereas perception itself is some-thing that takes place in the brain.

SELECTIVE PERCEPTION

Environmental stimuli are not presented to us in a piecemeal or isolated, one-at-a-time way. There are literally millions of them; they are around us all of the time, and, mostly, they occur in patterns. As we develop from childhood, we become accustomed to them; we take them for granted, and, in perceptual terms, we select from them. What we select is determined by what we *need*, *expect* and *wish* to perceive. Also, we have built-in value systems which cause us to assess what we perceive, and from this, we develop preferences and prejudices.

What we need *to perceive*   If I am driving home from the office, I will select the information I need in order to proceed safely home. I see the colour of the traffic lights and take action accordingly. Perception occurs when I attach meaning to the sensations I am receiving and that enables me to make decisions about what I should do. I am, therefore, selecting only the information I need for my current purposes. I am conscious of many stimuli: road signs, pedestrians, speed limit signs, one-way arrows, the speeds and positions of other vehicles and so forth, and I drive accordingly. But there are other stimuli around; stimuli that I do not need in order to achieve my present objective. For example, I am aware of shop window displays, people on the pavements, advertisement hoardings, and so forth. While on the one hand I ignore the presence of these objects and people because I do not need them for my specific purpose, I am somehow aware of the total scene, so that I can select from it the information that I need.

What we expect *to perceive*   We remember our perceptual experiences and as we develop, we construct an internal record of how things look, sound, taste, smell and feel. In a slightly more complex way, our experience gives us the ability to anti-cipate sensations. If we look at a piece of cloth or the surface of a piece of furniture, we think we know how it would feel if we touched it. We even build up mental pictures of people we have never seen, whose voices we hear on the radio or telephone, and sometimes we are surprised when their appearance fails to match up to our expectations. Similarly, when we see people, we are surprised if the pitch of their voices fail to match up to our expectations.

Also, our experience can fool us. In time, we learn the shapes, sounds, colours and sizes of the things and people we encounter frequently. In one experiment, for example, an incomplete triangle was presented to subjects for a fraction of a second. Most of the subjects 'saw' a complete triangle (see figure 15.2). The experiment was repeated using a variety of geometric shapes and consistent results were obtained, in that most subjects saw complete shapes.

Conversely, our perceptual expectations can cause us not to see certain things, especially things that have changed. While having a meal with a friend of some 20 years' acquaintance, we had been at the table for at least an hour before I noticed that he had shaved off his moustache, which he'd had for all of the time I had known him.

What we wish to perceive   If we receive a letter containing an ambiguous sentence in that it could be taken in one way as a compliment and in another way as a criticism, we choose the interpretation that suits our relationship with, and consequently our perception of, the sender. If it is from someone we like, we might take the complimentary meaning and if it is from someone we dislike, we might regard it as a criticism. Further than this, we focus our attention on the pleasing features of our loved ones while bypassing, moderating, or often not even seeing their less attractive features. We do, however, notice them in others. 'I

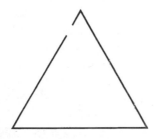

Figure 15.2 The incomplete triangle.

can't imagine what she sees in him' (or, of course, vice versa) is a comment we often hear.

THE PERCEPTUAL PROCESS

Perception is a very complex process. The organs of sensory perception do not act in isolation; they are capable of combining to give us the most accurate perception possible, not only of objects and people, but of all living creatures, ideas and concepts. Also, our beliefs about all of these things and our personal values give us our attitudes towards them.

As we develop, our unique way of interpreting our experiences causes us to internalize sets of beliefs and values about people, objects, concepts and events; we see things in a way that nobody else sees them. It is this *value system* that gives us our preferences and prejudices, expectations and perceived needs, and our own evaluations of what is right and what is wrong, what is good and what is bad. Our value systems give us our attitudes and it is our attitudes that cause us to behave in the way we do.

PERCEPTION IN THE WORKPLACE

One of the most important aspects of this area of thinking is our perception of other people. In the workplace, we have feelings and beliefs (attitudes) towards the work we do, towards the organization we work for and its policies and so forth and, perhaps, towards the industry in which we are employed. But we also have perceptions of the people around us at work: working colleagues, the boss, subordinates, customers and suppliers (see figure 15.3).

An understanding of the process we call *interpersonal perception* is useful in our attempts to understand people's behaviour at work. Ineffective communication, for example, is often attributed to weaknesses on the parts of the sender and/or the recipient. Critics of such weaknesses seldom identify insufficient understanding of interpersonal perception as the problem. Usually they attribute poor communication to lack of clarity in the message or a general lack of understanding of the mechanistic principles of communicating. But no matter how well 'tuned in' people try to be when they are sending or receiving messages, there is no escape from the fact that the recipient's

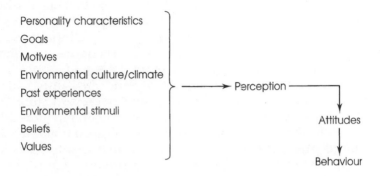

Personality characteristics
Goals
Motives
Environmental culture/climate
Past experiences
Environmental stimuli
Beliefs
Values

Perception

Attitudes

Behaviour

Figure 15.3 Factors that influence the way we see the world.

perception of the importance or credibility of the message is strongly influenced by his or her perception of the sender.

Perceptions of the work of others   So far, we have seen that everyone lives in his or her own perceptual world. We all have our own orders of priority and unique value systems. In the workplace, we often fail to have sufficient regard for other people's priorities and value systems. The company accountant, for example, may appear irritated, or even downright furious, when the production manager has failed to produce his monthly figures on time. To the accountant, getting the figures in from the various managers is at the top of his priorities towards the end of the month, whereas the priorities of the production manager are quite different. Similar altercations occur in the National Health Service, when a business manager's priorities are different from those of the senior consultant, who is principally interested in the well-being of the patients.

The influence of perception on motivation   In chapter 5, we saw the differences between 'content' and 'process' theories of motivation. It is worth noting, however, that an individual's perception of his or her job has by far the strongest influence over the degree to which that individual is motivated to work. In Maslow's terms, for example, we know that one person's 'lower order and higher order needs' will be different from those of another person who may be doing exactly the same kind of job (Maslow, 1987). In Vroom's framework, we know that individuals' 'expectancies'

214 PERFORMANCE MANAGEMENT

will also vary from one to another (Vroom, 1964). This is simply because different people see the same things in different ways.

The development of different individuals' personalities also causes them to have their own personal perceptions of different kinds of work and, indeed, of different jobs and professions. Think about your own job for a moment. How much of the content of your job was planned by someone else? More than half of it? Less? As an example, if the work you do includes filling in forms, who designed the forms? If you operate a machine, who determines the settings? If you use systems, who designed them? And what kind of job would you prefer? One in which, largely, you perform tasks that someone else designed? Or would you rather have a job that allows you to express yourself through your work? All jobs are divisible in this way: part *coping* and part *expression*. When you are carrying out work that was designed by someone else, you are said to be *coping*, and when you are imposing your own personal style on your work, you are said to be *expressing* yourself.

To illustrate this *coping–expression* concept further: when an actor is on a stage playing say, Hamlet, to some extent he is coping because he has adopted a role that was planned by someone else; in fact, by William Shakespeare. He has to exercise his stagecraft and carry the role through in exactly the way that Shakespeare intended. On the other hand, you develop your own assessment of the actor's interpretation of the role and of his acting ability, but in particular of his personal style. To this latter extent, he is expressing himself. Also, regardless of which part of the theatre you are in, you recognize the actor. This is because he has stamped his own unique personal style on the role. Similarly, composers, when they write music, set it down on paper according to a universally understood set of rules. His or her manuscript can be bought by someone on the other side of the world and from it, the music can be played; composers have to cope too. On the other hand, you can tell the difference between the work of Chopin and that of Beethoven. When they wrote their music, they were both coping by following the same rules as each other, but their personal styles were unique unto themselves. How much of your job is 'coping' and how much is 'expression'? The division in quantitative terms is important because you have a preference. Some people prefer more expression than coping, while others are the reverse. It depends on your perception of work. It also depends on your perception of the actual job itself because what one person might regard as a coping element could present to another person an opportunity for expression. Our perception of the degree to which this coping–expression balance meets our personal needs is an important determinant of motivation.

The 'halo-and-horns' effect   Many refer to this concept simply as 'the halo effect', which is an effect that becomes apparent when our perception of someone is benign to the extent that we fail to see, or mentally bypass, any adverse qualities the person may have. It is a concept that is most frequently related to the selection interview situation, in which the interviewer may perceive in the interviewee a quality that the interviewer also perceives in him or herself and, as a result, will favour that particular interviewee over the others. The 'horns' element becomes effective when the reverse of what is said above occurs.

Attribution theory   This was developed to explain the bases upon which we perceive the *causes* of behaviour. We tend to try to attribute people's behaviour to *individual* causes or to *situational* causes; generally, we are looking for reasons for the behaviour. This is probably explained best by example: if a person completes a project two weeks later than the previously agreed date, we might attribute the lateness to the nature of the person, since we know from experience that this person is usually behind time with things. On the other hand, we might attribute the delay to a known fault in the computer network, especially if everyone working on that network is also late with work. The former explanation attributes the behaviour to an individual character-istic, while the latter attributes it to the situation.

Stereotyping   When people behave in particular ways, we have a tendency to seek explanations for their actions. Also, through experience, we have in-built expectations of the behaviour of others. Sometimes, we attribute the likelihood that people will behave in certain ways to something we already know about them, such as their nationality, profession, age or appearance. If we hear that a person is Welsh, for example, we expect them to be able to sing. We expect accountants and engineers to be precise, older people to have outdated ideas and so forth. When we stereotype people, we do so on the basis of few known facts and we attribute to them traits that are generally associated with nationalities or social groups. This is another concept that is important in the job interview situation. An interviewer, for example, will observe that the interviewee is in 'punk' attire and has a hairstyle to match and may, therefore, consider the possibility that this person is violent or is on drugs. Stereotyping is a form of biased perception, but it can have a positive side. Research has shown that when people were asked to describe someone they had only just met and then asked to describe them again after becoming acquainted, the initial descriptions were quite accurate and in fact, some of them were more accurate than the second descriptions!

In the 1930s and 1940s, a very popular series of American films appeared featuring a Chinese detective named Charlie Chan. Much of the screenplay depicted Chinese people in criminal roles. Other films copied this image of the Chinese as sinister people whom one should not trust. As a result, Chinese people became stereotyped in that image.

Several theories have been developed to describe the way we perceive others. Many of them are based on the notion that first impressions account significantly for our subsequent perceptions of people. When you first meet someone, there is an initial 'like–dislike' effect between you. These initial assessments that we make at the time of 'first contact' influence the rest of the relationship.

SUMMARY OF PERCEPTION

Sensation occurs when we use our senses (eyes, nose, ears, mouth and skin) to detect the raw stimuli in the world around us. *Perception* is the mental process of selecting and organizing the stimuli, and then interpreting them into meaningful representations of the world: *Perception = Sensation + Meaning*. We perceive what we *need*, *expect* and *wish* to perceive. Through experience, we develop expectancies of what things will look, smell, sound, taste or feel like, but sometimes we are surprised when our expectancies are not fulfilled. We build up experience of perceiving complete images and our brain, as it organizes what we perceive, tends to 'fill in' any missing portions of images, that we would normally expect to be complete. In the workplace, our understanding of interpersonal perception is of primary importance when we are communicating with others, although how we, and others, perceive our work and the importance of what we do is also important.

Intelligence

> I would not answer for the integrity of my intellect for a single year.

> Michael Faraday[2]

Some writers include intelligence as a personality factor, while others treat it separately. Huffman, Vernoy and Williams (1987) say that intelligence is 'the capacity to solve problems and readily adapt to a changing environment'. There have been other definitions and descriptions of this very elusive and abstract concept, but if anyone ever does succeed in encapsulating the meaning of intelligence in two or three crisp and succint sentences, then one would wonder about how it would be used. Researchers are continuously studying intelligence and they would probably rather work freely, than within the confines of a definition. Many things have never been defined, yet seem to work well enough. So far as intelligence is concerned, the quest for a definition is driven by the need to measure it. 'You can not measure anything that you can not define' is what some writers say.

On the other hand, Binet and Simon devised a method for measuring intelligence, and that was 100 years ago, long before it was ever defined. Furthermore, the method they devised still provides the broad basis for many of today's measures of intelligence.

When we use the term 'intelligence', most people know what we mean – there is a kind of shared, common understanding of what is meant by the word, particularly when those using it are seeing it in the same context. As someone once said, 'I cannot define an elephant, but I know one when I see one.'

One has to distinguish between definitions and descriptions. Sometimes, when we read what theorists say in their descriptions of intelligence theories, and of the means they have devised for measuring it, we can obtain, from their writing, an insight into their perceptions of intelligence. Charles Spearman (1904), for example, proposed that intelligence is made up of two main factors. The first is a general cognitive ability with which people think and reason, enabling them to solve problems in the day-to-day context and do well in generally understanding common

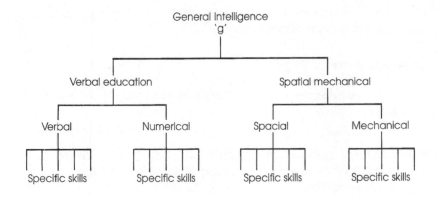

Figure 15.4 Spearman's hierarchical intelligence chart.

concepts and situations. Spearman referred to this general cognitive ability as the 'g' factor and said that this was the factor through which people did well on tests of mental ability. He referred to his second factor as the 's' factor, which he saw as a number of specific abilities. Spearman produced a hierarchical chart to describe the way he saw intelligence (see figure 15.4).

Other theorists, however, have contested Spearman's concept and said that there are several major mental abilities. Researchers in the twentieth century have pursued intelligence theories; among the most prominent are Thurstone (1938) and Weschler (1939).

L.L. Thurstone (1938) was the first to challenge Spearman's model, saying that there were seven primary mental abilities, which he divided into categories: verbal ability, word fluency, numerical ability, spatial ability, memory, perceptual speed and reasoning. Both Spearman and Thurstone were interested in identifying mental abilities that produced performance on intelligence tests, and both used factor analysis as the method of arriving at a representation of the breadth and scope of these abilities.

Most intelligence tests today are based on a number of mental abilities. It would be wrong, however, to assume in broad terms that you can identify the level of someone's intelligence through the use of a test such as, for example, a well-known IQ test. You cannot. To be scientifically acceptable, tests have to be valid, which means that the creator of a test has to show that it measures what it is supposed to measure. Tests are normally made up of batteries of measures of different mental qualities, such as verbal reasoning, numerical ability, spatial awareness, mechanical ability and so forth. But there is more to intelligence than the specific factors that the tests measure. Test results, therefore, should not be used as predictors of success in life, nor even as predictors of specific behaviours. On the other hand, tests are all that we have come up with so far, in terms of measuring intelligence, and they are, therefore, often used by practitioners, such as those involved in employee selection processes. From the results of tests, experienced psychologists can sometimes arrive at a reasonable estimate of an individual's intelligence.

IQ TESTS

The first IQ test was devised by Alfred Binet in Paris towards the end of the nineteenth century. He was working on the problem of measuring intelligence in children. He subjected children from the age of three up to the mid-teens to tests from which he was able to establish their average mental abilities. For example, most children of, say, 11 years, were able to perform tasks involving a certain degree of difficulty. On the other hand, most children of, say, 13 years old were able to carry out more difficult tasks, and so on. Having established these 'norms' among the population's children, he was then able to discover the degree to which children who were thought to be below average were different from the norm for their age. To arrive at his conclusions, he subjected the suspect children to tests that were typical of particular ages, thereby identifying their mental age. He then produced the children's 'IQ', which would identify the degree to which they were different, by placing the mental age over the chronological age (the real age) and multiplying by 100 (100 being the norm). Thus, if a child of 12 years could at best only perform the tasks that were typically performed by 9-year-olds, then the formula would produce an IQ of 75:

$$\frac{\text{Mental age}}{\text{Real age}} \times 100 = \text{IQ} \qquad \frac{9}{12} \times 100 = 75$$

Conversely, a 9-year-old with a mental age of 12 would have an IQ of 125. Since Binet developed it, this test has been regularly revised at Stanford University in the USA, and has become known as the 'Stanford–Binet Intelligence Test'. Predictably, when Binet tested children to discover the norm for the age, they did not all produce precisely the same scores. In statistical terms, intelligence is normally distributed in a population, which means that most people are at, or close to, the established norm, which we identify as 100. Others fall to varying degrees below and above. This is depicted in figure 15.5, which is known as a 'normal' curve, often referred to as the 'curve of normal distribution'. In the figure, we can see that the highest percentage of those tested are just above or just below the 100 mark; as intelligence measures fall, the percentages reduce to the left, indicating the numbers of lower intelligence levels; and as measures increase, the percentages reduce to the right, indicating the numbers of higher intelligence levels. In the Stanford–Binet test, descriptive labels are related to IQ scores, as in table 15.1

Binet, as we know, was principally interested in the intelligence levels of children and developed his scales accordingly. But the mental abilities of children are not comparable with

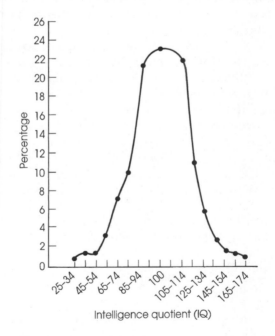

Figure 15.5 The curve of normal distribution.

Table 15.1 IQ scores and descriptive labels

IQ	Description	Percentage
Above 139	Very superior	1
120–139	Superior	11
110–119	High average	18
90–109	Average	46
80–89	Low average	15
70–79	Borderline	6
Below 70	Mentally retarded	3
		100

those of adults, and the formula given above cannot be used when measuring adult intelligence levels. Lewis Terman (1916), working at Stanford University developed the Stanford–Binet Intelligence Test, but he too was mainly interested in measuring the intelligence of children. But once people are out of their 'teens', their intelligence settles at individually different levels, which are identified through the use of standardized tests.

One of the most widely used of such tests is the Wechsler Adult Intelligence Scales (WAIS). Writing in 1939, when he was a clinical psychologist at the Belle Vue Hospital in New York, David Wechsler developed the WAIS. There are two sets of items on the Wechsler Scales, one is listed under the heading of *Verbal* and the other under *Performance*. While Wechsler certainly measured intelligence on the basis that there is a number of mental abilities, his approach was different from that of any of his predecessors. He attempted to cover the total range of ages. To this end, he generated three tests: The Wechsler Pre-School and Primary Scale of Intelligence (WPPSI), which was administered to very young infants, The Wechsler Intelligence Scale for Children – Revised (WISC–R), which was administered to children from the age of 5 to 15 years, and the Wechsler Adult Intelligence Scales – Revised (WAIS–R), which was administered to adults.

What was different about Wechsler's scales was the two sets of items on the scales. Rather than produce a single IQ score, he was able to identify separate scores for the Verbal and Performance items, in addition to an overall score. In examining the WAIS, for example, we can see the two sections and the types of item in each (see table 15.2).

Table 15.2 The Wechsler Adult Intelligence Scale

Item	Description
Verbal scale	
Information	Questions tap a general range of information, e.g. 'How many nickels make a dime?'
Comprehension	Tests practical information and ability to evaluate past experience, e.g. 'What is the advantage of keeping money in a bank?'
Arithmetic	Verbal problems testing arithmetic reasoning.
Similarities	Asks in what way certain objects or concepts (e.g. Egg and Seed) are similar; measures abstract thinking.
Digit span	A series of digits presented auditorily (e.g. 7 5 6 3 8) is repeated in a forward or backward direction.
Vocabulary	Tests word knowledge.
Performance scale	
Digit symbol	A timed coding task in which numbers must be associated with marks of various shapes; tests speed of learning and writing.
Picture completion	The missing part of an incompletely drawn picture must be discovered and named; tests visual alertness and memory.
Block design	Pictured designs must be copied with blocks; tests ability to perceive and analyse patterns.
Picture arrangement	A series of comic-strip pictures must be arranged in the right sequence to tell a story; tests understanding of social situations.
Object assembly	Puzzle pieces must be assembled to form a complete object; tests ability to deal with part–whole relationships.

Source: Reproduced by permission of the Psychological Corporation.

There are many examples of intelligence theories and their associated assessment techniques. The twentieth century has seen considerable progress in this field and research still continues, not only into the nature of intelligence itself, but into developing more valid and reliable techniques of measurement.

Notes

1 Clearly, it would be extremely difficult to obtain a copy of this reference. It is, however, referred to in several more easily obtainable texts, including David Fontana, *Managing Stress*, published by the British Psychological Society with Routledge (1993).
2 This was Faraday's response to being offered the Presidency of the Royal Society; quoted in Tyndall (1868).

References

Allport, G.W. 1935: Attitudes. In C.M. Murchison (ed.), *A Handbook of Social Psychology*. Clark University Press.

Atkinson, R.L., Atkinson, R.C. and Hilgard, E.R. 1983: *Introduction to Psychology*, 8th edn. New York: Harcourt Brace Jovanovich.

Bandura, A. 1977: *Social Learning Theory*. New York: Prentice Hall.

Holmes, T.H. and Rahe, R.H. 1967: The Social Readjustment Rating Scale. *Journal of Psychosomatic Research*, 11.

Huffman, K., Vernoy, M. and Williams, B. 1987: *Psychology in Action*. New York: Wiley.

Kagan, J. and Havemann, E. 1980: *Psychology: An Introduction*, 4th edn. New York: Harper Brace Jovanovich.

Maslow, A.H. 1987: *Motivation and Personality*. New York: Harper & Row.

Spearman, C. 1904: General intelligence, objectively determined and measured. *Journal of Psychology*, 15.

Terman, L.M. 1916: *The Measurement of Intelligence*. Boston, MA: Houghton-Mifflin.

Thurstone, L.L. 1938: *Primary Mental Abilities*. Chicago, IL: University of Chicago Press.

Tyndall, J. 1868: *Faraday as a Discoverer*. London.

Vroom, V.H. 1964: *Work and Motivation*. Chichester: Wiley.

Wechsler, D. 1939: *The Measurement of Adult Intelligence*. Baltimore, MD: Williams and Wilkins.

16

Attitudes

Introduction

An understanding of attitudes is extremely important to our study of workplace behaviour. Employees' attitudes determine how they will behave, and we need, therefore, to understand how they are formed and the various techniques that are available for changing them. The study of attitudes intensified in the 1930s, since when there has been a variety of definitions:

> An attitude is a mental disposition of the human individual to act for or against a definite object. (Droba, 1973)

> An attitude is a learned predisposition to respond consistently in a positive or negative way to some person, object or situation. (Petty et al., 1981)

The Attitude Object

People, situations, events and concepts towards which people have attitudes are referred to as *attitude objects*. Thus, when considering my attitude towards, say, 'Yuppies', then Yuppies are the attitude object. This means that I have *feelings* and *beliefs* about Yuppies which may be positive or negative, and which will determine my behaviour towards them.

Components of an Attitude

The main concept of attitudes is that they are the products of an individual's *feelings*, *beliefs* and *behaviour* towards other people, situations, events and concepts, and that attitudes may be positive or negative. Feelings, beliefs and behaviour generally are referred to as the components of attitudes.

Feelings, beliefs and behaviour can be positive or negative, and people like all three to be consistent. If a person has positive feelings about an attitude object, then his or her beliefs about the object will also be positive and, consequently, so will his or her behaviour towards it. It is thought that the 'feelings' component is of major importance in that it can have a significant effect upon the two other components, but that is not to say that it is always the 'feelings' component that influences the other two. If a person receives information about an attitude object that he or she has never previously encountered, that information may cause the person to develop positive beliefs about the attitude object and, thereby, generate positive feelings within the person and, again, his or her behaviour towards the attitude object will also be positive. The process that leads to consistent or 'balanced' attitude components can start with any one of them.

If a discrepancy arises between the three components, we take steps to redress the balance. The theorist, Leon Festinger (1957), proposed a *cognitive dissonance theory*, in which he demonstrates that when we notice dissonance (inconsistency) between two or more components, we are motivated to change our attitudes by taking steps designed to restore consistency. Festinger said that we experience anxiety when, for example, our behaviour does not match our beliefs. Dissonance can be attributed to several causes:

- *Situational changes*: positive feelings and beliefs about the job we do may become negative when its nature or structure have to change for organizational reasons, but we still carry on doing it, justifying our behaviour on other grounds.
- *Unfulfilled expectations*: Festinger's famous research into this cause of dissonance studied a group, the leader of which predicted that the world would end on a particular date, but that her followers would be rescued by a vessel from outer space. The followers had surrendered their original lifestyles, spouses, jobs, homes etc. to join the group and when the predicted date came and went and nothing happened, dissonance was high. They reduced their dissonance, however, by claiming that their prayers had saved the world.

- *Making a decision*: after making a decision, we are motivated to justify it, even if we suspect it may not have been as good a decision as we first thought, by avoiding information that might produce negative feelings and beliefs. For example, if we decide to buy a particular car, we feel commited to the decision. Afterwards, we avoid receiving information that conflicts with the decision and we seek out information that supports it.

In these ways our attitudes change naturally; we change them ourselves by behaving in ways that restore any imbalance we detect between our feelings, beliefs and behaviour.

How Do We Develop Our Attitudes?

> You have to be taught before it's too late, before you are six or seven or eight, to hate all the people your relatives hate, you have to be carefully taught. You have to be taught to be afraid of people whose eyes are oddly made, of people whose skin is a different shade.
>
> Oscar Hammerstein II, *South Pacific*

Attitudes are formed as a result of our encounters with the environment as our personality develops and as we are socialized. When we are very young, we adopt the attitudes of our parents and then, slightly later, of other reference groups, such as the school teachers and our pupil colleagues. In other words, we learn. We learn to prefer steak to fish, one football club rather than another, one kind of music rather than another. We also learn negative attitudes towards social groups that are different from ours. We learn these attitudes because they are held by the groups and individuals to whom we are exposed in our formative years. Also, these attitudes are reinforced when we are rewarded for demonstrating them through our behaviour. From what is said above, it appears that our attitudes are formed developmentally, as environmental forces exert their influence.

Another approach, however, indicates that human beings are not just sponges, blandly absorbing the mores of the society into which they happened to be born. We are capable of thinking for ourselves. As we experience environmental factors, we exercise our powers of thinking and reasoning and we place interpretations on them, hence we all have different attitudes towards things. *Self-perception theory* (Bem, 1972) says that people are not always aware of their own beliefs and feelings about particular things. As a result, they take note of their own behaviour and it is from this that they identify their attitudes. Indeed, it is also true that many people never think about their attitude towards an issue until they are asked, perhaps in a survey.

Measuring Attitudes

There are many reasons why one group of people may wish to understand the attitude of another group towards a particular person, issue, situation or concept. The media, for example, may wish to make predictions about the outcome of a forthcoming general election, so they conduct a survey to find out how people feel about the present political party in government.

Television companies monitor people's viewing preferences by conducting surveys, not only on the channels they use, but on specific programmes, to test their popularity. The results of these surveys, or the 'TV ratings' as they are known, help them to organize their programme policies and contents.

The personnel director of an organization may need to establish the attitude of the workforce towards the service that his or her department offers, towards the system of payment, the

Statement 1: Dogs are very dangerous and should not be kept as pets

−1	−2	−3	0	+1	+2	+3
Strongly disagree	Disagree	Mildly disagree	Don't know	Mildly agree	Agree	Strongly agree

Statement 2: Dogs should only be kept by those who keep them clean and in safety

−1	−2	−3	0	+1	+2	+3
SD	D	MD	DK	MA	A	SA

Statement 11: People should be encouraged to keep dogs

−1	−2	−3	0	+1	+2	+3
SD	D	MD	DK	MA	A	SA

Figure 16.1 Examples of three questionnaire statements.

pension scheme and many other issues that affect their lives at work.

Normally, attitudes are measured through the use of questionnaires. They are 'set pieces', which contain statements about an attitude object, and people are asked to respond to the statements. Measurement is on a scale, which is made up of strings of numbers with graded responses attached to them, ranging from negative to positive, as shown in figure 16.1.

The respondent is asked to circle the number that most accurately reflects his or her *feelings* about the statement that is made about the attitude object. Every statement on the questionnaire appears alongside or immediately above the scale and the statements themselves are graded from negative at one end to positive at the other. A questionnaire may contain say, 11 statements ranging from highly favourable to highly unfavourable (examples of three statements are shown in the figure), with a scale attached to each of them on which the respondent can register his or her feelings.

Attitudes, therefore, are measured on the basis of what people *say* are their feelings and beliefs about, and their behaviour towards, a particular attitude object. But the statements are very carefully constructed and should never be compiled by just one person. Usually, psychologists compile questionnaires and they put them together so that they obtain valid measures of what they are supposed to measure.

There are several well-known approaches to measuring attitudes; here we will examine two of the most frequently used: the *Thurstone* method and the *Likert* method.

THE THURSTONE METHOD

L.L. Thurstone developed one of the earliest approaches to attitude measurement. Working with E.J. Chave in the 1920s, he devised a system in which a large number of statements were produced about a particular attitude object (Thurstone and Chave, 1933). Each statement expressed a particular opinion or judgement about the object, and collectively, all of the statements covered all possible views, ranging from extremely positive to extremely negative. Often, to achieve total coverage, hundreds of statements had to be produced. Thurstone's ultimate objective was to produce a questionnaire containing no more than 11 statements about an attitude object.

The numerical value that is allocated to each statement may not necessarily be a whole number. This is because the numerical distance between the statements has to equal the semantic distance between them; otherwise it would have to be assumed that the relative difference in meaning between any two adjacent statements was equal all the way through the range of the scale. This is best clarified by giving an example: see table 16.1.

To understand how the figures in the right-hand column are reached, you have to look for the *perceived difference* between the meanings within the statements that are next to each other. For example, if we look at the ninth and tenth statements, the perceived difference in meaning – that is to say, the implication in each statement – is less than that between the tenth and eleventh statements; these differences in meaning are reflected in the numerical scale values allocated to them.

Table 16.1 An example of a Thurstone scale to measure employee attitudes towards the quality of the personnel service

Statements	Numerical value
1 The organization's personnel service is excellent	11.00
2 All aspects of the personnel service are very good	10.80
3 Most of what personnel does is very well done	9.30
4 Most of the time our personnel service is good	8.90
5 I like the way our personnel services operates	8.50
6 Our personnel service is probably as good as any other	7.00
7 Our personnel service is not too bad	6.50
8 Our personnel service could be better organized	5.10
9 Our personnel service is somewhat disorganized	3.90
10 Our personnel service could be considerably improved	2.30
11 Our personnel service is a mess	0.50

When the questionnaire is issued, the numerical values in the right-hand column do not appear. They appear only on the master copy, which is held by the surveyor. Instead, the respondent is asked to use that column to tick all of the statements with which he or she agrees. The survey form should be designed to preserve anonymity.

To measure the attitude demonstrated, the surveyor may calculate an average, simply by totalling the numerical values of each statement that has been ticked and dividing the results by the number of ticked statements.

For example, if a respondent had ticked statements 5, 6 and 8, the numerical value of the respondent's attitude would be 6.87, which would have been calculated thus:

$$\frac{8.50 + 7.00 + 5.10}{3} = 6.87$$

The Likert method

This attitude measurement technique was devised by Rensis Likert in 1932. It is much quicker and easier than the Thurstone technique and of the two, is probably the more frequently used. In style, it is a little like the examples given in figure 16.2, except for the numbering, which is on a 1 to 5 or a 1 to 7 scale, rather than placing 0 between the positive and negative responses. Likert's scale simply asks the respondent to agree or disagree to some extent with the statement, or to express no feelings about it at all. On a five-point scale, for example, the 3 (the central point) might demand the response, 'neither agree nor disagree'. There are disadvantages to this kind of scale. A respondent may circle the '3' because he or she neither agrees nor disagrees with the statement, which could imply indifference to the object of the statement.

A statement is presented to the respondent, who is asked to express his or her response to it by using the scale depicted in figure 16.2.

1	2	3	4	5
Strongly disagree	Disagree	Neither agree nor disagree	Agree	Strongly agree

Figure 16.2 An example of a five-point Likert scale.

Changing Attitudes

Measuring attitudes in the workplace enables us to assess the degree to which the results of that measurement indicate a need for change. It is said that if we know where we are going, we are more likely to get there, but of course, knowing where we are starting from is equally important when we wish to change an attitude from say, negative to positive. Measurement tells us not only whether attitudes are positive or negative, but the degree to which they are one or the other.

Changing attitudes can be a very complex business. People set out to change the attitudes of others because they want their behaviour to change. Most attitude surveys in organizations are carried out precisely because it has been perceived that a change is necessary. Sometimes addressing, say, a negative attitude involves making a change in the nature of the attitude object. This, however, does not effectively change someone's attitude; it gives them a new attitude, because if you have changed the attitude object, you have given them something different to perceive. For example, employees' attitudes towards the company's pension scheme may be unfavourable. If we change the scheme for a better one, then employees' attitudes towards the pension scheme may be positive, but their attitude towards the old scheme remains the same.

To change people's attitudes towards an unchanged attitude object is quite a different – and more difficult – job. In many professions, the ability to change people's attitudes is vital to success. Salespeople do it when they are trying to sell their product or service; politicians do it when canvassing for votes; and managers and trade unionists do it when they are negotiating terms and conditions of employment.

Sometimes changes in attitudes occur naturally. When, for example, a person is exposed to environmental stimuli that are new to him or her, such as the input of previously unknown information about someone or something, attitudes towards that object may change. The degree to which such change will take place will depend upon several factors: firstly, the credibility of the source of the information; secondly, the nature of any reward factor that the perceiver might receive on the basis of a changed attitude; thirdly, any effect that a changed or an unchanged attitude might have upon the reputation (image) of

Exhibit 16.1

> When I was a little boy, Christmas days and birthdays brought me gifts such as toy train sets, carpentry kits and Meccano, while my sisters received dolls, nurses' outfits and cookery sets. Then, when I went to school, I was given woodwork and metalwork lessons, while my sisters were taught 'domestic science'. I couldn't help thinking that someone was getting us ready for something. Thankfully, that kind of thing is beginning to change, but it is a very slow process.

the perceiver; and fourthly, the kind of experiential situation in which an attitude change might take place. People who set out deliberately to change the attitudes of others do so by attempting to produce (or reproduce) such situational factors.

It is worth noting that certain social and legal factors can interfere with our efforts to measure attitudes accurately and change them as a result. Legislation, for example, disallows behaviour that demonstrates an unfavourable attitude towards certain ethnic groups, religious orders, skin colour, nationalities, sex and marital status. Such legislation, coupled with the social changes that have resulted from the efforts of a variety of campaigning groups, has created a society in which some genuine attitudes are not allowed out. Socially, of course, this can only be a good thing, but on the technical front, when we are trying to identify certain attitudes, 'politically correct', rather than genuine, responses may cause us to bypass areas where there is a need for changes to be made.

Such changes in behaviour do ultimately bring about changes in attitudes, but it is a slow process. At present, I believe we are in a kind of 'attitude limbo', in which the behaviour that is carried out is socially, rather than attitudinally, driven (see exhibit 16.1).

FACTORS INFLUENCING ATTITUDE CHANGE

Training, when it is effective, will cause a change in the trainee's behaviour. To the trainer, changes in behaviour are an indication that learning has taken place; in other words, the development of new knowledge and skills within the person produces the *ability* to behave differently. But it also motivates the individual to carry out the new behaviour and, as we know, changes in behaviour can cause changes in attitudes.

One of the factors of the training situation that increases the effectiveness of this development is the credibility of the person who is communicating the new information and inculcating the new skills. If, for example, I said that I was going to give a talk on association football, everyone would yawn, but if I said that I had arranged for Kenny Dalglish to give the talk, the lecture theatre would be full long before that great man appeared. An individual's assessment of the value of an item of communication is determined by his or her attitude towards the communicator.

A considerable amount of research has been carried out into changing attitudes, the main result of which is a number of descriptions of situations in which attitude change is likely to take place. It is said that there are three ways in which attitudes can be changed: (1) through the use of persuasive information, (2) through training and (3), through group work.

Persuasive information   Probably the most well-known example of the use of persuasive information is advertising. In the workplace, advertising is used extensively in the never-ending campaign to reduce accidents. If you look at the 'Accidents at Work' advertising posters, you will see that the pictures and slogans exhibit the after-effects of accidents. Sometimes, these campaigns target just one specific item of working practice, such as the wearing of hard hats on building sites. Humour is often used to compel attention and make people remember the message in the advertisement. One poster I recall exhorted workers to 'protect themselves against "flying bricks" '. The poster depicted a building site worker without his hard hat. Flying through the air, directly towards the back of his head, was a brick. The man is shaking hands with someone who is just leaving the site. The imminent victim is saying to his friend, 'ring me this afternoon, I'm sure I'll have got my brain into gear by then'. His anxious friend is trying to pull away from the handshake.

Training   The development of new knowledge and skills almost always modifies the individual's attitude towards the subject in which he or she is being trained. A change in behaviour might mean that the individual can (and does) now do something that he or she could not do before the training took place. On the other hand, it might be that, before the training, the person *was able* to carry out particular tasks, but did not do them because he or she did not enjoy doing them. New skills and new information, however, delivered during the training may alter the individual's view of the training subject from unfavourable to favourable. From this, we can see that when training changes attitudes, it also motivates a change in behaviour. Finally, it is important to understand that an individual's attitude towards a specific task will be unfavourable if he or she does not possess the skill to carry it out. As a result, the individual will relegate such a task towards the bottom of his or her job description and try to avoid doing it. If, however, the individual is then trained in the task up to the point where he or she feels confident in the necessary ability, the resultant change in attitude and behaviour is very marked and often quite dramatic. It can be seen, therefore that when training is effective in developing new skills and knowledge, it also changes attitudes.

Group work   In simple terms, putting people into small groups and giving them a problem to solve often changes attitudes, but this is not as simple as it sounds. The problem that is given to the group has to focus upon something towards which *some* of the group members have a negative attitude. The underlying idea is that if they analyse the problem and attempt to arrive at a solution, then their attitude towards the matter will change.

One approach to presenting the problem is to form a *Creative Problem-Solving Group* (CPSG). This is a technique in which there are about eight people in a leaderless group. What happens is that each individual is given a written statement of the problem, to which he or she has to produce a solution within a given period of time. How much time is allocated is determined by the size and complexity of the problem. Ideally, the group will be seated around a table, so that when the time limit is reached, each participant passes his or her solution to the person seated to the left. As a participant, for example, you would receive the written solution produced by the person on your right and give your written solution to the person on your left. On receiving the solution from the right, your task would be to extend it, by following the other person's ideas. In other words, you must not try to substitute it with your own solution; rather, you should try to analyse the other person's ideas and solution with a view to expanding and enlarging upon them. Passing solutions around continues until your own solution comes back to you, having been analysed and extended by everyone else. After that, the group sits as a panel to select the solutions that they think will be most likely to solve the problem.

The CPSG system forces all group members, including those who have an unfavourable attitude towards a particular problem/subject, to focus their attention upon it and to have their ideas for solutions analysed by their group colleagues. Even people who have a negative attitude towards something will usually conform to the norms of group behaviour when they are put into the kind of situation that is described above.

Summary

Finally, it should be borne in mind that attitudes are an intangible and complex subject. Attitudes are abstract and, therefore, have to be measured and changed by indirect techniques. Our attitudes *towards other people* are always very important in the workplace.

References

Bem, D.J. 1972: Self-perception theory. In: *Advances in Experimental Social Psychology*, Vol. 6. New York: Academic Press.

Droba, D.D. 1933: The nature of attitude. *Journal of Social Psychology*, 4 (reprinted in N. Warren and M. Jahoda (eds), *Attitudes*, 2nd edn. Harmondsworth: Penguin, 1973).

Festinger, L.A. 1957: *Theory of Cognitive Dissonance*. Evanston, IL: Row, Peterson.

Krech, D., Crutchfield, R.S. and Ballachey, E. 1962: *Individual in Society*. New York: McGraw-Hill.

Likert, R.A. 1932: Technique for the measurement of attitudes. *Archives of Psychology* (reprinted in E. McKenna (ed.), *Business Psychology and Organisational Behaviour*, Hove: Lawrence Erlbaum, 1994).

Petty, R.E., Ostrom, T.M. and Brock, T.C. (eds) 1981: *Cognitive Responses in Persuasion*. Hillsdale, NJ: Lawrence Erlbaum.

Thurstone, L.L. and Chave, E.J. 1933: *The Measurement of Attitudes*. Chicago, IL: University of Chicago Press.

17

Groups in Organizations

Introduction

To sociologists and social psychologists, the terms 'groups' represents a large and complex part of their study, which is of the whole of society. In this chapter, we are interested in the behaviour of people in groups at work. In particular, we will attempt to define the work group, and look at how groups form, the various kinds of groups in organizations, how group members interact with each other and how groups interact with other groups.

What Is a Group?

Few individuals work in isolation. To most people, work is a social activity; even those who regard themselves as solitary workers, such as authors and certain researchers, sooner or later have to contact other people. In the normal work situation, individuals are put into positions in which they have to work together. As we know, all individuals are different from each other; and each brings a unique set of aspirations, expectations, preferences, prejudices and personal needs.

When people are in this situation, they do not behave as they do when they are alone. If the job is going to be done, people have to work in harmony. This means that they have to modify what they perceive as their needs and adjust their behaviour to take account of the needs and activities of others. Individuals learn to work at the group's pace and to its standards of performance. In other words, they learn the 'norms' of the group and conform to them in order to be accepted and, get the job done.

DEFINITION OF A GROUP

When writers define 'the group' they normally are concerned with small groups, each of which is of a size that does not hinder interaction between and among its members. When we refer to large groups, we usually mean the people in a whole organization. For our purposes, we will say that a group is:

> A number of people who are together because of some common or shared interest, who interact with and are aware of each other, and regard themselves as members of the group.

FORMAL GROUPS

A formal group is a number of people who have been put into position by the organization to carry out a particular task or function. It can be identified on the official organizational structure, and the work that it does makes a contribution to the achievement of the organization's overall objectives. The work of one formal group is often dependent upon the work of another. Groups working in a factory, for example, may depend upon the productivity of other groups for their supply of work.

INFORMAL GROUPS

Formal groups, however, are made up of human beings, whose natural tendency is to socialize and relate to each other over non-technical matters. They elaborate upon their relationships, which evolve beyond those that are required formally by the organization. The organization, for example, does not put people into group situations so that they can talk about what was on television last night, or the problems they are having at home. Nor are they there to discuss the terms and conditions of employment, but they do. Informal groups also develop when individuals from different parts of the organization socialize because of common interests, or mutual aims.

Informal groups can have a major effect upon formal operations. We saw, for example, that the problems that prompted the Hawthorne Studies were due largely to the attitudes and behaviour of groups as informal entities. The person who leads the informal group is not necessarily the leader of the formal group. In this context, leaders are accountable to those who put them in leadership positions. Office supervisors, for example, report to the managers who appointed them, whereas shop stewards and other informal leaders are accountable to the trade union or group members who elected them.

PRIMARY GROUPS

A formal group, as we have described it, is a primary group. A primary group is the main group, of which individuals regard themselves as members. Primary groups are of critical importance to the effective working of the organization, and if they fail to achieve their formal objectives, the organization also will fail to achieve its overall objectives. Primary groups are the basic operational units to which employees feel they belong.

A primary group can be described as one that perceives itself to be a separate entity, with an identity that is different from that of all other groups and individuals. It is a working group of individuals who regularly work together, and who accept each other as group members, an acceptance that manifests itself in the form of frequent and habitual interpersonal interaction. Large and medium-sized organizations have many such groups, each an entity, each cohesive and relatively self-contained.

One of the most difficult managerial tasks in organizations is to get the primary groups to work in harmony with each other. Partly, this is a problem of the managers' own making. On the one hand they attempt to build tight, cohesive teams, which is a strategy that pulls people together and generates pride in achievement. It is a strategy, however, that breeds competition between and among teams; and it is likely that the more bonded, cohesive and effective a team is, the more difficult it will be to stimulate cooperation with other teams, towards the broader objectives of the whole organization.

SECONDARY GROUPS

A secondary group is one in which the members do not have such close, habitual and frequent interpersonal contact with each other. One example of a secondary group is when individuals with particular knowledge and skills are selected from a number of groups, to form a separate project group, the purpose of which may be to carry out a special assignment, which is totally unrelated to their regular work. It is also significant that in those circumstances, the members will be working to a different leader. Another example, is that of a team leader; obviously, the leader is a member of the team, but he or she also is a member of a secondary group, the group of team leaders, all of whom report to the departmental manager.

Group Norms

Individuals place a high value on their acceptance into the group. Obviously, if the organization has thrust them upon the group, they will be aware of that, and their formal acceptance will have little personal value. But personal acceptance is a different matter. Individuals rate their group membership so highly that they have been known to moderate, or even sur-render, elements of their own personal values, in order to pre-serve acceptance. All groups develop particular attitudinal and behavioural patterns, to which they expect members to conform. Socially, an individual may be drawn to a group because he or she approves of its 'norms' anyway; that is to say, the group's values and behavioural patterns do not conflict with those held by the individual. In organizations, however, people usually are placed into formal groups because they possess appropriate knowledge and skills; but the group's respect for a newcomer's knowledge and skills does not carry with it a guarantee of *personal* acceptance. This means that a person could be a member of a formal group, but excluded from the informal group, which is made up of the same people.

If a group member perceives that there is conflict between his or her own values and beliefs and those of the group, the result will be cognitive dissonance. Individuals can rationalize this by re-thinking their values and beliefs, by conforming to norms against their own principles, simply to sustain acceptance, or by giving up membership of the group. What individuals do is determined by their ability to achieve a balance between the importance and strength of the particular value or belief, and the degree to which they value their group membership. At Haw-thorne, Elton Mayo discovered that those who failed to conform to group norms, were punished. Informally, the group set pro-ductivity standards, which were usually less than those demanded by the managers. Anyone who over-produced was referred to as a 'rate buster', and producing less than other group members earned the dub, 'chiseller'. The group had its own system of regulating this kind of behaviour, and the punishment for failing to conform to the informally set standards could range from sarcasm and ostracism to threats of physical violence. Members knew they were close to violence when they were 'binged', a 'bing' being a sharp blow to the upper arm. The groups preferred internal harmony in terms of social relations, and binging was often used to control interpersonal friction and other potentially disharmonious behaviour.

A group norm can be regarded as an unwritten, mentally held perception that identifies limits for members' behaviour. The amount of importance that different individuals attribute to the norms (they have to be worth conforming to) are also an influence upon conformity. To a great extent, the group sees the survival of its unique identity as dependent upon its members' conformity; each group, therefore, develops a unique set of norms, by which it is identified. Teenage groups, for example, have norms relating to how they style their hair, how they dress, their esoteric 'streetwise' vocabulary, and so forth. Non-conformity produces ridicule; persistent non-conformity produces expulsion.

All groups have different norms, and these will change over time and in changing conditions. The norm regarding streetwise expressions, for example, may not apply in other, more serious teenage groups, whose values lie in different directions. The notion that group members value their own peculiar norms does not mean necessarily that they oppose or challenge the norms of other groups. It means simply that within the group, they expect conformity from their own members.

Reference Groups

A reference group is a group that has the power to influence an individual, regardless of whether he or she is a member. In our developmental years, reference groups shape our values and beliefs, give us our perceptions and attitudes, and ultimately, therefore, influence our behaviour. The family usually is our first reference group and we tend to adopt its values and beliefs. In time, these values and beliefs are modified by the influence of other reference groups, such as local and school friends, teachers, and leaders of youth clubs. What is said above relates to groups to which we belong, but groups to which we do not belong may also influence us and, therefore, may be reference groups.

How Groups Are Formed

Groups that follow the normal pattern of development may eventually become 'teams'. Most of the theories about how this happens focus upon 'stages' of development. Here, we will examine one of them.

According to Tuckman (1996),[1] the path that leads from when group members first come together to team status is characterized by four key stages:

1   *Forming.* A number of individuals, the prospective group members, are brought together. They consider the purposes of the group, assess its resources and any incoming information, begin to establish a structure for the group, and eventually look upon one of the members as the leader. This can be a stressful stage for the members as they jockey for position, and try to attain some kind of perception of the roles they are expected to play.
2   *Storming.* Familiarity between and among the members has begun to develop at this stage, and they feel confident enough to be blunt and open about particular issues. Any internal conflict that develops can turn out to be productive, in the sense that verbal interchanges, even though forceful at the time, can result in improved structures and more effective rules and procedures.
3   *Norming.* As the word implies, this is the stage at which group values, standards and acceptable behavioural patterns (norms) are established. Any conflicts that may have arisen at earlier stages are resolved, working harmony begins to appear and group members focus more on the task(s), rather than on the establishment and identity of the group.
4   *Performing.* This is the stage at which teamwork appears. The group has become cohesive and flexible enough to manage its tasks efficiently and effectively.

It is important to understand that this is not a 'mechanistic' process; the four stages are not clear-cut, intact entities, each with its own beginning and end. The stages overlap as they run into each other, and the group members, who do not all develop at the same rate, are not aware of being at a particular stage. The development that takes place is naturally human, and it happens without the members' conscious control.

What Groups Are For

The purposes of groups are twofold: formal and informal/ social.

Managers tend to employ people because they have the kinds of knowledge, skills and experience that match the demands of a particular job. But when the person starts work in a group, it is not just the bits that the manager wants that come in; what the manager (and the group) gets is the *whole person*, with all of his or her unique perceptions, attitudes, preferences, prejudices and motivations. These unique personality characteristics manifest themselves in the form of individual needs, and it is the meeting of these needs that bring us to the informal or social purposes of the group. According to Edgar Schein (1980), the group helps to fulfil a number of psychological functions for the individual. Schein lists them as:

1 *Affiliation.* The group fulfils the individual's needs for love, friendship and support. The individual perceives the group as an outlet for such fulfilment.
2 *Self-esteem.* In this context, the individual perceives the group as a means of developing and validating a sense of identity, and sustaining and enhancing a satisfactory level of self-esteem.
3 *Security.* The group satisfies the need to increase the individual's feeling of security and confers the perceived power to cope with a common and powerful enemy or threat.
4 *Mutual dependence.* Experience of the group members' interrelated activities that are required to get the job done develops the notion of mutual dependence within the group.

The individual will be more or less satisfied with the degree to which his or her needs are met by the group; in return, the influence of his or her personality will, to some degree, alter the character of the group. The nature and extent of this change will be determined by the type and strength of the newcomer's personality.

Constraints upon Group Activities

Groups do not always pass through the stages of development without problems. If, for example, a manager wishes a group to develop, then clear and attainable objectives need to be set and agreed with the group members. Furthermore, a knowledgeable manager will realize that even when objectives have been set and agreed, the various group members will vary in terms of their commitment to achieving them.

IMPORTANCE OF OBJECTIVES

Perceptions of the importance of the objectives and the amount of effort required to achieve them may also vary from one individual to another. One approach to heading off or reducing the effect of this problem is for managers, when they are involved in setting objectives and reaching agreement with the group, to stress the importance of each objective to the group, the department and the organization as a whole. The group members should be made aware of any factors that might inhibit progress towards cohesiveness and teamwork. It is worth remembering that informal leaders emerge from within groups, and making them aware of any developmental constraints probably would head off disagreements and difficulties between and among other group members.

GROUP COHESIVENESS

Factors that generate group cohesiveness include: the existence, and adherence to, common values and goals; successfully achieving goals, especially its important goals; the group's status in relation to that of other groups – high status produces greater cohesiveness; the use of effective interpersonal contact to resolve differences between members; conforming to group norms. What we are saying here, is that 'more equals more cohesiveness'; that is to say, for example, the more frequently the group achieves its goals, the more cohesive it will be.

GROUP COMMUNICATION

This is a particularly important feature of intra-group activity. There is a structure or network of links which are in the most frequent use during group activity. The pattern of the communication structure, and the direction of its lines, is especially important for the informal group's activities and interactions. Most often, the information that the structure carries comes first from the leader, from where it flows from one member to another, down the hierarchical order. But communication structures vary, depending upon the specific needs of the group members. Information is categorized on a 'need to know' basis. For example, there is information that all members should have, while on the other hand, there is information that is aimed at one or two particular roles. Items of information that would not interest some members would command the interest of others.

It is important, therefore, to have a communication structure that is most effective, in the light of the group's current situation. As a result of his laboratory experiments, Bavelos (1994) suggested a number of structural designs. He tested several structures to see if they had characteristics that limited or facilitated communication between group members. He concluded that all of the structures were adequate, in the sense that

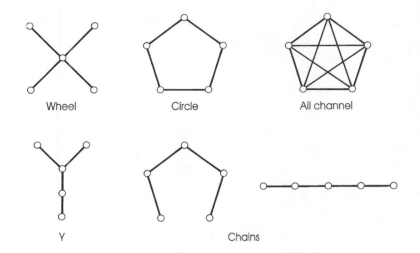

Figure 17.1 Alex Bavelos' patterns of communication.

they did the job, but that some produced more effective communication than others (see figure 17.1).

Summary

Research has produced a large bank of information about group and team formation and behaviour, which is an indication of the importance that is attributed to achieving understanding in this area. As the internal patterns of organizations continue to change, and the human resource is variously deployed within them, group working and teamwork continue to increase in importance.

Notes

1   The item referred to originated in the *Psychological Bulletin* in 1965, by B.W. Tuckman and M.C. Jensen. The concept was then modified, as 'Stages of small group development revisited', in *Group and Organisational Studies* in 1977, and, finally, in 1988, by M.F. Maples, 'Group Development: Extending Tuckman's theory', in the *Journal for Specialists in Group Work*.

References

Bavelos, A. 1994: Communication patterns in task-orientated groups. In D.A. Buchanan and A.A. Huczynski (eds), *Organisational Behaviour*. London: Prentice Hall.
Schein, E.H. 1980: *Organizational Psychology*, 3rd edn. Englewood Cliffs, NJ: Prentice Hall.
Tuckman, B.W. 1996: Developmental sequences in small groups. In S.P. Robbins (ed.), *Organizational Behavior*. Englewood Cliffs, NJ: Prentice Hall.

18

Systems of Appraisal

Introduction

Reviewing people's performance is one of the managerial activities through which the performance of the whole organization is managed. Monitoring the performance of the organization is a vital process, since it is only through the realization of at least an adequate performance that the organization will achieve its objectives and continue to survive and develop. In fact, monitoring is part of a larger process that gathers information about performance and, by implication, it should be assumed that an analysis of the information carries with it recommendations for specific actions that are designed to correct or improve situations where necessary.

Ultimately, the level and quality of an organization's performance is determined by the levels and standards that are achieved by its employees. The argument that external pressures have a strong influence on an organization's performance is a powerful one, but what we are saying here is that the delivery of a good performance by its employees must enhance the organization's chances of survival, even under the most dire market and economic constraints. Putting it negatively, we could say that a poor performance by the employees could cause the demise of the organization, regardless of external influences. It is, therefore, important to assess employees' performance formally, and to have a set of follow-up systems that are designed to solve any problems that might inhibit a good performance.

Performance Appraisal

The appraisal of individuals' performance is an essential component of employee development. The techniques employed within systems of appraisal represent some of the means through which we are able to keep our finger on the pulse of the effectiveness of the training and development plans and strategies.

There are several approaches to appraising employees' performance, but the one most frequently found involves a manager in carrying out an annual review of the performance of his or her staff. In this well-used system, the manager and the employee both complete a form in advance of an interview, in which the two reach agreement over the degree to which the employee has met the required standards of performance and achieved the objectives that were agreed at the previous review. Any problems that might have appeared since then are also reviewed, the causes identified and decisions reached about solutions. The issues we have touched upon so far relate to the past, and while it is essential for both parties to have similar perceptions and understanding of past performance, the manager should ensure that in the whole process, most of the emphasis is on what is going to happen in the future. The identification of problems, for example, gives the manager the opportunity to discuss solutions, which, of course, can only be applied in the future. It may be that coaching, counselling or training are the answers to the employee's problems. Whatever kind of solution is discussed, agreement should be reached about the employee's future objectives and standards of performance in the job.

About two weeks before the interview, the employee is given a 'self-appraisal' or 'self-assessment' form; at this stage he or she already has been informed of the time, date and place of the interview. The structure of the form gives the employee a measured way of considering his or her performance over the past year. The nature of the questions on the form also provides the employee with guidance about the kind of things that he or she should be thinking about. The form used by the manager is usually an extended version of the one given to the employee.

From his or her normal day-to-day monitoring of employee performance throughout the year, the manager will have a broad perception of how each particular employee is performing. He or she will have handled any grievances that may have arisen, be aware of the nature of any problems that were beyond the employee's control, and, through informal contact, will have developed perceptions of the personalities and motivations of the staff. In fact, since managers have this kind of contact with their staff, some argue against the need for formal systems of performance appraisal. 'Managers,' they say, 'should *know* how their staff are performing because they are with them all day, every day; they should be able to assess their performance off the top of their head . . . and if they don't know, . . . well then, they shouldn't be managers.'

This well-known argument completely misses the point of performance appraisal. And in any case, talking 'off the top of one's head' can easily lead to talking through one's hat. Today's managers carry a hefty administrative load which, among other things, makes it physically impossible to be with all of the staff all of the time. The fact, is that a manager who *is* doing the job properly cannot continuously be aware of the performance of all staff.

Managing performance can be *informal* or *formal*. Attempting to appraise performance in the day-to-day context is referred to as informal appraisal. By its very nature, this may be done only in an ad hoc fashion and it relies totally on the manager's perceptions of random and isolated events and situations. The process is very similar to the natural human way in which everyone assesses everyone else, so that the so-called 'assessment' that results must be the product of subjective perception.

In this chapter we are interested in formal appraisal, which is carried out regularly as the central part of a specifically designed system which also contains follow-up components such as training, coaching and counselling. It is worth commenting at this point that a system of appraisal should be custom-built to meet the organization's particular requirements; it should be flexible and capable of adapting to the changing needs of the organization, which means that the appraisal system itself should be monitored for its continuing effectiveness. Performance appraisal is criticized as one of those things that 'looks like a good idea on paper, but seldom works in practice'. It is the failure to monitor and alter the system in accordance with changing needs that causes it to fall into disrepute within the organization.

The Objectives of Appraisal

As we have seen, the *purposes* of appraisal are to raise the likelihood that the organization will achieve its strategic goals and specific objectives, by virtue of its staff performing well, and within the organization's policies and systems. In addition to these organization-wide purposes, however, performance appraisal also has the objectives of (1) assessing past performance, (2) identifying training needs, (3) setting and agreeing future objectives and standards, and (4) motivating (see table 18.1).

It is tempting for the person carrying out the appraisal to wander away from these four central objectives of performance appraisal, but those who carry out appraisals should beware of this, since the more one digresses, the less effective the appraisal session becomes. Some managers take advantage of the one-to-one situation and treat the event almost as if it is part of the disciplinary procedure. Others, particularly those who lack confidence in the system or who have not received adequate training in how to conduct an appraisal, treat it as if it is some extra duty that they will get down to when they have done the rest of the job. A system that is abused in this way will become nothing more than a form-filling exercise and, of course, totally ineffective.

The contention here is that performance appraisal is about how the employee has performed *within the context of his or her job* and nowhere else. Performance appraisal is not about how an individual has conducted him or herself in general around the organization; it is not about how well he or she organized the office party; and for most jobs, it is nothing to do with the personality of the individual. The organization should have specific procedures in place for dealing with matters that are outside of employees' job-related performance. The assessment criteria on the appraisal forms, therefore, should be based upon the contents of the personnel specification for the job, and managers should base their findings on an objective assessment of the degree to which the performance criteria have been met.

Managers who relegate performance appraisal to the lower divisions of their priorities should seriously reconsider their attitude. Let us look at this more closely. A manager is an employee who has been given responsibility for achieving objectives in a particular area of the organization. He or she is also

Table 18.1 The objectives of performance appraisal

Objective	Related actions and decisions
1 Assessing past performance	The appraisal form contains assessment scales on which a level of past performance is recorded. This reflects the degree to which the individual has met required standards and achieved the objectives that were set and agreed at the previous review.
2 Identifying training needs	It may be that any shortfalls that were found in the person's performance indicate a need for training (to fill the gaps in knowledge and skills) or counselling (to motivate the individual towards an improved effort). At the interview, the manager and the employee together may work out a performance improvement programme.
3 Setting and agreeing future standards and objectives	Setting and agreeing future standards of performance and objectives provides another opportunity to identify training needs. This is done in a positive way, in that the training input will enable the employee to gain new insights and skills, increasing his or her versatility and, thereby, the ability to carry out more complex work.
4 Motivating	The one-to-one nature of the appraisal interview gives the manager and the employee the opportunity to have an extended, confidential chat about the employee's total job situation. Talk, for example, about the employee's future with the organization will help him or her to feel secure and motivated to perform well and perhaps, plan a career.

given commensurate autonomy, authority and resources to enable him or her actually to achieve those objectives. One of the resources is the human resource and, since things are done through people, the manager cannot possibly achieve his or her objectives without the cooperation of the staff in the form of a performance which, at least, meets the minimum required standards. The manager's primary concerns, therefore, should be about the staff's work performance.

The Appraisal Interview

SETTING

If an appraisal interview is to be successful, particular attention should be paid to the venue. The interview should be held where both parties can be certain that they will not be disturbed. A comfortable room in a quiet area should be reserved well in advance of the interview.

IMPORTANCE

The manager should attribute due importance to the appraisal interview and should be seen to do so. To the employee, the appraisal interview is an important event in the working year. Employees talk to each other about the event, they ensure that they return the form they have completed in plenty of time for the manager to read it before the interview and then, when the day comes, they make a special effort with their appearance and other aspects of preparation. When employees show their regard for the event by making this kind of special effort, how must they feel if, when they enter the room, they find that the manager appears to be short of time, hell-bent on 'getting the forms filled in' and – the most crushing factor – appears not to be listening, but thinking about something else when the employee is talking?

Appraisal interviews have great potential for enhancing and maintaining good human relations and managers should regard them as important events. They should be planned in advance and an appropriate amount of time should be reserved. All of the relevant documentation and information should be studied and any static information entered on the form before the interview commences, thus heading off the need for copious notes to be made during the interview, so that full attention may be paid to the employee.

APPROACH

It is probably true to say that the appraisal interview, more than any other organizational situation, exposes a manager's leadership abilities. At the end of the interview, the employee should leave the room:

1   believing that the manager is aware of his or her total job situation and that there is a mutual perception of the level of importance attributable to the event;
2   knowing exactly what lies ahead in terms of the standards and objectives to be achieved and that those standards and objectives are attainable;
3   understanding that arrangements will be made to fill in any gaps in knowledge or skills that were identified;
4   with a general feeling that the perceptions, decisions and agreed action were fair and reasonable;
5   motivated to perform well.

It could be said, of course, that these five points describe an idealistic conclusion to an appraisal interview, but they do provide an appraisor with a set of goals to aim for, even when the interviewee is the most recalcitrant of employees.

The degree to which the process and the outcome of an appraisal interview is successful depends on several factors: (1) the personality of the manager, (2) the personality of the interviewee, (3) the situation in which the interview takes place and (4) the nature of the content that is to be discussed.

Managers have been known to have difficulty when faced with the prospect of having to tell someone that their performance is not all that it should be. Many question their right to be judge and jury, making decisions that can seriously affect the future of other people. Douglas McGregor (1957) says that the answer to this is to adopt a different approach. Instead of 'sitting back in judgement' on another person's performance, pointing out weaknesses and the consequent shortfalls in performance, the manager should take up the role of coach and counsellor, approaching the problem as a 'change agent', a person who is willing to help employees and show them how to improve their performance. In this way, says McGregor, 'He [the appraised employee] becomes an active agent, not a passive "object".'

The interview then may be seen as part of an ongoing, progressive movement in which the manager and the employee are working together towards improvement. It is a process that may involve the manager in coaching or recommending training for the employee and it may also involve him or her in using counselling techniques.

Armstrong (1994), in his comprehensive work, outlines three main approaches to this kind of counselling: the 'tell and sell method', the 'tell and listen method' and the 'problem solving approach':

1   *The tell and sell method*, in which the manager seeks first to let the employee know how he is doing, then to gain his acceptance of the evaluation and, finally, to get him to follow the plan outlined for his improvement. The problem with this method is that considerable and unusual skill is required to get people to accept criticisms and to change in the required manner. There are occasions when people have to be told, but it may not always be possible to provide the motivation required for change, unless resort is made to crude threats or inducements.

2   *The tell and listen method*, in which the evaluation is communicated to the employee, who is then allowed to respond to it. Instead of the interviewer dominating the discussion he sits back and becomes a non-directive counsellor during the second part of the interview. The employee is encouraged to think things out for himself and to decide on what needs to be done, and the assumption is that he is more likely to change in these circumstances than if he had been told what to do. A further advantage of this approach is that the interviewer will profit more from the interview by receiving feedback from the employee on how the job may be improved with regard to supervision, work methods and job assignments. But the method requires considerable skill on the part of the interviewer in listening, reflecting feelings and summarizing opinions.

3   *The problem solving approach*, in which the interviewer abandons the role of judge and becomes a helper. The appraisal is not communicated to the employee. Instead, a discussion takes place of the work problems of the employee, who is

encouraged to think through his own solutions to them, including the changes he has to make to his behaviour to achieve improvement. This approach motivates original thinking because it stimulates curiosity. It also provides the intrinsic motivation that can be derived from work itself and the process of tackling work problems. Job satisfaction can be improved by reorganizing or enlarging the job, by changing the employee's perception of his role and by increasing the superior's ability to provide guidance and help in the form it is needed. Again, this approach needs skill, but it is the most fruitful method and it is one that can clearly be linked to results-orientated review techniques.

FOLLOWING UP

Since the performance appraisal process includes identifying training, motivational and maintenance needs, and agreeing upon plans to improve performance, managers should ensure that the actions necessary to invoke training, counselling, machine maintenance and whatever else is necessary are actually taken. It has been known for busy managers to conduct very successful appraisal interviews, in which good information and ideas are exchanged, but then, either the manager neglects to enter the appropriate information on the forms, or the completed forms that carry all of this valuable data are placed on a shelf in the personnel department and allowed to gather dust. Appraisal without effective follow-up is almost a complete waste of time. The information that is gathered at an appraisal interview should be entered on the forms and copies should be sent to the appraisor's superior and the personnel department for action.

INDIVIDUAL DEVELOPMENT PLAN

There is an increasing tendency, during the appraisal interview, for managers to counsel individuals about the management of their own development. The 'follow-ups' that were decided upon during the interview are converted into action plans for individuals to implement, with the manager's guidance.

Potential and Reward Reviews

The arguments for and against combining the processes of performance appraisal with those of potential and reward reviews have been going on for many years. I said above that the objectives of performance appraisal are fourfold and are exclusively related to the degree to which the employee has achieved his or her performance standards and objectives, *within the job*. In this context, I am saying that performance appraisal has nothing whatever to do with pay or promotion and that there should be separate systems for dealing with those issues.

Some organizations draw up lengthy forms, which attempt to integrate performance, reward and potential reviews. The underlying implication here is that a person who out-performs another will receive a greater reward and will be more likely to be offered promotion. While one agrees wholeheartedly with the principle of rewarding good performance, one has to say that it is inappropriate to use the *performance* appraisal system for this purpose. Clearly, if an employee, whose performance is being appraised, thinks that the outcome of his or her appraisal will determine the size of a forthcoming salary increase, then *money*, rather than performance, will dominate the discussion. The information that is gathered from a performance review may be used later, as *one* of the factors influencing a salary increase. It should be remembered that not all rewards come in the shape of notes and coins and that money is not always the reward that the employee anticipates for his or her performance.

The case against linking performance to *potential* reviews is different. In Britain, we tend to promote people at work as a reward for putting in a good performance in their jobs. In certain occupations there are good grounds for this, especially if the nature of the work to be carried out is similar, but at a different level. A production line operator, for example, might make a good leading hand, a job in which he or she carries on doing the same work, but adopts some responsibility for productivity on his or her line. Similarly, a Grade 2 College Lecturer might make a good Senior Lecturer. In these instances, the work at the higher level is similar to that previously carried out, but it is more than likely that the person was promoted through having demonstrated leadership qualities and a sense of responsibility.

On the other hand, a good performance in one job does not carry with it the guarantee of an equal or better performance in another job, such as when a person is promoted to a more senior position, in which the requirements for knowledge, skills and attitudes are different. People are often promoted into managerial positions, having had no training or preparation for the job.

This is often done in an ad hoc way, especially in an organization that lack policies and strategies for employee development and career management.

A system of potential appraisal is there so that the manager and the employee can attain a mutually acceptable perception of where the employee is going in career terms and the rate and nature of the development that will be needed in order to get there. If the organization is to survive and develop, it needs to have a continuing succession of properly trained and experienced managers moving up the organization to take the place of others and to occupy those managerial positions that are created as the result of growth and change.

In a sense, a potential review is a little like the selection process, in that the manager is assessing the current knowledge, skills and attitudes of the person and making decisions about his or her suitability for employment in specific areas of the organization. This means that in a potential appraisal interview, the manager adopts an approach that is entirely different from that of the performance appraisal interview. The information that the manager gathers is different and is to be used for a different purpose. To attempt to link the two kinds of appraisal system is not merely inadvisable, it is counterproductive.

References

Armstrong, M. 1994: *A Handbook of Personnel Management Practice*, 4th edn. London: Kogan Page.

McGregor, D. 1957: An uneasy look at performance appraisal. *Harvard Business Review*, 35 (3).

19

Reward Management

Introduction

The aim of this chapter is to explain the various bases upon which employees are rewarded for their work. This includes reward strategy and policy, and the various approaches to structuring reward systems, such as equity and incentive pay systems. Categories of reward, including salaries and wages, bonus schemes and other kinds of reward, such as non-cash rewards, are also explained. The features that we emphasize, in terms of how rewards are allocated, are that they must be systematic, fair and understood by everyone.

Reward Strategy

Reward strategy addresses the organization's need to obtain, retain and motivate committed, competent, experienced and loyal employees. The ease or difficulty of this task varies from one industry to another and, indeed, from one organization to another, depending, among other things, on the financial health of the place and the state of the relevant labour markets. The availability of labour rises and falls with the economy, and the intensity of competition for the right staff fluctuates accordingly. Even in the most buoyant economic times, however, it is never easy to obtain the kind of staff that are described in the first sentence of this paragraph. Obviously, the size and nature of the rewards offered will determine the organization's ability to compete effectively.

Of course, the organization has to be financially *able* to offer and provide the levels of reward that enable it to compete with other organizations for staff. When formulating reward strategy, therefore, decisions have to be made about how much of the financial resource can be allocated for reward. Such decisions are influenced by the profitability of the organization, the negotiating positions of the relevant parties, and the percentage of overall costs that is represented by pay; today's industrial average for this is around 60 per cent.

FACTORS THAT INFLUENCE REWARD STRATEGY

The organization's freedom to formulate reward strategy and set salary and wage rates is constrained by internal and external influences and obligations, some of which we have already discussed. The main pressures may be summarized as follows:

- the organization's ability to sustain pay levels;
- trade union pressures and bargaining position;
- productivity;
- UK Government and European policies on pay;
- changes in: technology, economy, labour market;
- rates of pay comparable with other organizations;
- cost of living increases;
- levels of skill and competence required.

PERCEPTIONS OF REWARD

Reward as a concept is perceived differently by those who own and run the organization, and those who are employed by it. Managers, for example, see it as a percentage of the organization's total costs, and they want value for money; they see it as a motivator, in that they use it as an incentive to increase employees' performance; and some see it as a power tool, that enables them to favour some and not others. Employees, on the other hand, perceive reward as a return on the investment of their time and skills. We said earlier that reward systems have to be seen to be fair, but fair to whom? The organization and its shareholders? The employees? The question of what is 'fair' will be answered differently by different people. In this respect, organizations continuously have to bear in mind the provisions of the Equal Pay Act and the discrimination laws, including those that have arisen from appeals for legal decisions from the European Community.

THE NATURE OF REWARDS

In the minds of most people, the phrase. 'reward' means money, in the form of a wage or salary. But if that was all that it meant, the word 'pay' would be more appropriate. Reward may take several forms. Money certainly is important; some people say that they work for no other reason. *Wages* are paid weekly, usually to people who are paid an hourly or weekly rate, while *salaries* are paid less frequently, normally on a monthly basis. Money is also used as a performance incentive, and as an indicator of the level of responsibility of the employee.

Because of individual differences, perceptions of what constitutes an appropriate reward for a particular effort vary from one employee to another. Managers who get to know their employees well, therefore, will be able to identify the kinds of reward that will motivate them most effectively.

When considering reward then, individuals have different priorities. But people have to live. According to Goldthorpe (1968), most *manual* workers are motivated by 'extrinsic' rewards. In other words, they see it as the means by which they are able to sustain, and possibly improve, a particular domestic lifestyle, which means that they value the ability to spend money more highly than any intrinsic satisfactions that might be available in the workplace.

Systems of Payment

Basically, there are two philosophical approaches to structuring a system of payment. The first is the *incentive* approach, and the second is the *equity* approach.

INCENTIVE SYSTEMS

Incentive systems are those in which pay is tied to actual performance. *Payment by results* (PBR) schemes, which are usually associated with the factory-floor environment, are a good example of an incentive system. The idea of pay being tied to actual performance is illustrated simply by *piecework*, in which employees, whose job it is to produce a certain number of items daily or weekly, are paid in accordance with an agreed rate per

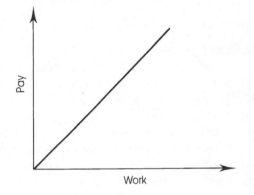

Figure 19.1 Typical piecework scheme.

item, for the number of items produced. When this kind of system was introduced, almost 100 years ago, it worked in a totally direct fashion (see figure 19.1).

This indicates, however, that if the employee produced very few items, perhaps through being unwell, or being absent through sickness, he or she would receive very little pay. In most of the countries in which this system is still used, it has been modified to provide for a guaranteed basic wage, which the worker receives regardless of output. Through limited periods of sickness, the guaranteed wage is sustained, usually with a mixture of state/employer provision, but if the sickness absence is prolonged, other arrangements are made. Beyond the guaranteed wage level, workers are given a target which, when exceeded, makes them eligible for a piece-rate bonus, as shown in figure 19.2.

Note the angle of the curve beyond the 'guaranteed' point. Through the bargaining processes, management and workers negotiate what they call the *steepness* or the *flatness* of the scheme. In a 'steep' scheme, fewer items may be produced in order to obtain a particular bonus, whereas in a 'flat' scheme, a greater number of items would have to be produced to achieve the same bonus. Piecework schemes work very well when there is a need for increased productivity; workers are easily persuaded to give it.

Criticisms of piecework include the idea that it places the productivity effort in the hands of the workers, instead of the managers, and that the 'money-motivated' rush for quantity, adversely affects the quality of the product. Also, workers tend,

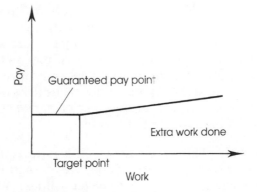

Figure 19.2 Guaranteed wage plus piece-rate bonus.

informally, to standardize productivity beyond the guaranteed point, and that trouble arises when the need for productivity reduces. In the medium to long term, employees do become accustomed to receiving regular weekly piece-rate bonuses, and they incorporate the extra cash into their perception of their 'income'. When they are asked to reduce productivity, therefore, the inevitable slimmer pay packet comes as a shock.

Obviously, the 'direct' workers who are paid in this way have an advantage over the 'indirect' (support) workers, such as clerks and administrators, who have less control over what is in their pay packets. This sometimes creates dissatisfaction among the support workers, and many companies have successfully minimized the discontent by introducing organization-wide bonus schemes, in which all employees benefit from the profitability produced by their efforts, whether they be 'direct' or 'indirect' labour. The main problem with this kind of scheme is that the relationship between the input of the work effort and the receipt of the reward is difficult for the employee to perceive.

There are many more variations on PBR schemes and, indeed, many more pay structures through which hourly paid workers are rewarded. The main purpose here was to explain the principles underlying incentive systems of payment.

EQUITY SYSTEMS

While incentive systems are tied to individuals' actual performance, in that they are rewarded for their productivity, *equity* systems are tied to in-job performance, in that they reward the job-holder at a level that reflects what it is worth to the organization to have that particular job done. This involves the organization in assessing the relative values of jobs, and setting up a pay structure that reflects those values. This means that everyone is rewarded equally for carrying out jobs that have been judged to be of equal value to the organization, regardless of how hard they work and how the quality of their performance compares to that of others in similarly rated positions.

Job evaluation   This is the most well-known equity system. It is a system in which jobs are compared to each other and then graded according to their perceived values. While the given grades do not constitute a payment system, they do provide the basis for one. Job evaluation structures are developed/ suggested by job evaluators and approved by a Job Evaluation Committee or Panel. There are several approaches to job evaluation, some of which are 'non-analytical' and some 'analytical'. This is not to suggest that one approach is better than another, but choosing the most effective method for one particular organization is an important decision, since they vary in their suitability. The organization also must decide which categories of employee they wish to be covered by the scheme. Sometimes, the greatest effectiveness is achieved by using different approaches in different parts of the organization. Here we will discuss three approaches: (1) job ranking, (2) job grading and (3) points rating.

Job ranking   This is quite a simple, non-analytical process, and, like all job evaluation structures, its effectiveness relies on the subjective assessments of those who create and approve it. Evaluators select a sample number of jobs, often called *benchmark* jobs, which are representative of the total range. Benchmark jobs are selected on the basis of such factors as the level of responsibility, the complexity and technical nature of the skills required and the range and number of tasks to be carried out within the job. Using the same criteria, other jobs are then compared to the benchmark jobs and graded accordingly. For example, if we selected four jobs, such as:

- clerk
- VDU operator
- administrator
- junior manager

we can see immediately that each of them has a different value. Other office jobs are then ranked alongside the clerk, slightly higher jobs alongside the VDU operator, and so on. It is a rather crude and basic form of job evaluation, and it is sometimes necessary to grade certain jobs individually, since not all jobs fit neatly into benchmark categories; some jobs, as they say, 'stick out' as isolated entities. Nevertheless, it is probably good enough to be effective in a small company.

Job grading Job grading, or job classification, as it is often called, is another non-analytical approach. A grading scheme is based on the organization's structure, so that the level of work and responsibility is reflected in the job's given grade. Since it is based on the structure, the number of categories in the scheme is determined by the number of levels in the hierarchical order. This can be useful in times of change, since new or redesigned jobs can be assessed according to the criteria, and placed in their appropriate levels. On the other hand, modern thinking about organizational design tends to favour leaner, flatter structures with a reduced number of levels, which can produce difficulties when categorizing jobs.

Another approach to job grading is to categorize the jobs according to criteria, without first considering their potential hierarchical position. In this way, criteria are related more directly to the actual work itself, so that the levels of knowledge and skills required to do the work are taken into account, along with responsibilities and the importance of the decisions the job-holder takes. The Job Evaluation Committee then categorizes the jobs by relating total job descriptions to descriptions of the grades.

The process reveals a similarity between the methods of job grading and those of job ranking, in that when the the committee is making comparisons, it treats jobs as whole entities. The Job Evaluation Committee makes its decisions by reaching a consensus, but they are also open to consider appeals from employees who feel that their jobs have been unfairly or inappropriately graded. In some organizations, appeals are considered by independent panels.

Points rating method This is an analytical method, and probably the most commonly used. The principal feature of points rating is that it analyses and compares jobs on the basis of factors that are common to all jobs. Each of these common factors carries a number of points, and the amount apportioned to each job is determined by the degree to which the factors are present within it. A hierarchical structure is produced on the basis of the points rating of each job. Pay for a particular job is determined according to the number of points it carries.

Job analysis is an essential precursor to a points rating system. If common factors are to be found, job descriptions and specifications need to be revised and perused, and, where necessary, completely rewritten. The ultimate scheme has to be seen to be fair, and, since the differences between jobs is measured in accordance with the degree to which the selected factors are present, great care must be taken over the analysis.

The objective is to assess the 'value' of each job. Each common factor carries a maximum number of points, a proportion of which is allocated commensurately. The factors that typically are considered include: level of decision making; complexity and range of tasks; knowledge and skills required; interpersonal contact; physical effort required.

Deciding how many points to allocate to each factor is a well-known problem in points rating. The factors vary in their importance to each job, and the most important is allocated the greatest number of points. This is called the *weighting* of factors. The factors are placed in order of importance and weighted according to a maximum number of points, bearing in mind the degree of importance that each factor has in a particular job. Each job is then graded, according to the level at which the factors are present.

PERFORMANCE-RELATED PAY

While there are several kinds of performance-related pay (P-rP) scheme, the conceptual basis is the same for all of them. The systems that are used for assessing individuals' performance are also used to relate the value of that performance to commensurately additional pay.

While the main purpose of an 'incentive' scheme is to stimulate productivity, the purpose of a P-rP scheme is to reward, and for this to be successful, the basis upon which awards are made must be seen to be fair. Ideally, the individual will have had a performance appraisal session in advance of the P-rP assessment process. In chapter 18, we stressed the advisability of keeping the two processes apart in time, so that the subject of pay did not predominate over the discussion about performance. Nevertheless, it is legitimate for a manager to use the information gathered from a review of performance as a basis for assessing a P-rP award.

Range of P-rP systems   There is a wide range of P-rP systems, probably about a dozen or so, but some are better known than others. Additionally, there are schemes that have been customized to the specific needs of organizations, some of which are modified versions of conventional schemes, while others are unnecessarily complex, tending to reflect the abilities of those who created them, rather than the needs of the organization. As with any system of payment, a P-rP scheme must be handled with care and continuously monitored for its fairness and effectiveness. The managers' and employees' perceptions of a scheme are of critical importance, and if the basis upon which the scheme is founded is perceived as flawed, or the approach to assessment is regarded as biased, the scheme will fall into disrepute.

A set of guidelines for action designed to achieve a positive attitude towards a P-rP scheme might include:

- integrative bargaining for the optimal scheme;
- the selection or creation of a scheme in which *all* employees may participate;
- employees are included in the scheme as a matter of right and do not, therefore, have to *apply for* P-rP;
- the onus of responsibility to identify the level of an employee's performance in relation to the minimum standard is placed firmly upon the manager;
- managers who operate the scheme are trained to do so, and given a thorough understanding of the *spirit* as well as the *letter* of its regulations;
- steps are taken to ensure that all employees are provided with an explanation of the scheme and access to further explanatory information and advice;
- employees are given the right of reassessment by request.

P-rP schemes were first developed many years ago, but it is only in the past five or six years that the concept has become acceptable to both managers and workers, since when their use has become widespread. It should be noted, however, that P-rP has many factors in common with so-called *merit schemes* which have been in use in industry for most of this century. Here we will discuss briefly one of the more well-known P-rP schemes.

Fixed scales This is a fixed incremental scale, which is the same as that used in job evaluation. Instead of 'rubber-stamping' the employee's automatic progression up the scale, however, the manager is given freedom to use discretion in making awards, so that the employee may be moved two points, rather than one point, up the scale; or, of course, the manager may postpone progression, the ultimate decision being made on the basis of the assessment of the employee's performance.

The HRM Approach

One of the most important features of HRM is that it is committed to improving the relationship with the individual employee. This can be difficult, when about 80 per cent of all pay settlements are reached through collective bargaining; furthermore, most of these settlements are reached on behalf of wage earners, rather than salaried staff; certainly that is the case in the private sector, although it is less so in the public sector. Also, incentive schemes, which are designed to stimulate productivity, tend to provide extra pay through previously agreed production *quantities*, while P-rP rewards past performance through *qualitative* measures. It seems, therefore, that those who benefit most from incentive schemes are the hourly paid workers, while P-P is aimed at managers and specialists who, in most organizations, are a relatively small proportion of the total workforce.

Summary

Reward strategy addresses the organization's need to obtain, retain and motivate committed, competent, experienced and loyal employees. Such staff are hard to come by, regardless of the economic climate, and employers always have to compete for the best staff. Reward strategy is written in the light of internal and external pressures, such as the financial situation, the unions' bargaining powers and government policy on pay. In most organizations, the concept of reward is perceived differently by workers and senior managers.

Wages are paid weekly, usually to workers who receive an agreed hourly rate, while salaries usually are paid monthly, to staff who are on an agreed annual rate. There are two broad categories of payment system: *incentive* and *equity*. Incentive systems are designed to stimulate productivity, in which bonus payments are made according to easily calculated quantities produced, while equity systems reward past performance, on a qualitiative basis. It is easier to recognize and reward individuals' performance through equity systems, and particularly through P-rP, which marks its relationship with the HRM philosophy of improving relationships with employees as individuals.

References

Goldthorpe, J.H. 1968: *The Affluent Worker: Industrial Attitudes and Behaviour.* Cambridge: Cambridge University Press.
Vroom, V.H. 1964: *Work and Motivation.* Chichester: Wiley.

Part V

Personnel Information Handling

The ability to gather, store, retrieve, interpret and present information is one of the most important sets of personnel skills. To do these things efficiently, effectively and at reasonable speed, the computer is an essential tool. This part of the book aims to explain how information technology can assist the personnel practitioner, and the main areas of personnel work in which it may be applied.

20

Personnel Administration

Introduction

The administrative work in a personnel department is of two kinds. Firstly, there are the day-to-day tasks of handling internal and external correspondence, the organization of events, such as interviews, induction sessions, training courses, career conventions and liaising with training centres, schools, colleges and other educational establishments. Personnel departments carry out many daily tasks on behalf of the organization. They also maintain a relationship with the local IPD branch and their specialists are often involved in its activities.

The second part of personnel administration is largely to do with handling information. Information about the human resource is vital to the successful management of the organization. This involves the personnel department in keeping and maintaining records of all events and activities relating to its people. For example, a personal history is kept on every individual employee, starting when they join the organization; this includes all personal details such as: home address and telephone number, state of health on joining, date of joining, National Insurance number, date of birth, sex, ethnic origin, marital status, the job title on joining (updated with any changes), category of employee (staff or hourly paid, etc.), hours of work, department, periods of absence, salary details, academic qualifications on joining, training and further education undertaken since joining, assessments of performance, and suitability for promotions and transfers.

Individual information Obviously, when information such as that described above is held on all employees, collectively it represents an extremely useful data bank for management and planning purposes. But the individual records themselves are also valuable. If, for example, a case arises concerning an individual's current behaviour or future position, his or her personal history will provide background information that will assist in decision making. Similarly, when people are being considered for further training and development, promotion or special assignment work, the personal records provide an ideal information base upon which good quality decisions can be made, to the benefit of the individual and the organization.

Statistical information Most organizations have computerized their personnel records, and there are personnel data systems that enable us to input, manipulate and retrieve information that is used in all personnel specialisms, including human resource planning, recruitment, absence management and control, wages and salary systems, training records, career management and succession systems. Statistical information can also be drawn from accumulated individual records relating to staff turnover, workforce stability, sickness absence, skills inventories, deployment, job analyses, recruitment trends and employment costs. Externally gathered data may also be added to provide information on the availability of labour, including specific skills, local, regional and national employment trends, average earnings and so forth. The information that is derived from such records is indispensable to the organization's senior managers.

Using Personnel Records

Personnel records are a useful and lively tool of management and maintaining them can be a full-time job. If the records are neglected, especially in terms of keeping them up-to-date, they do not become merely useless, they can become dangerous. Clearly, poor decision making will follow the use of 'out-of-date' records as a source of information for something important.

The parts of the records that are used most frequently are those that are used in planning and in control systems:

1   *Wages and salary records*: used for monitoring the normal payment of wages and salaries and for keeping a record of payments made for extra time worked and special duties. Also used for monitoring changes in salaries and wages, such as salary increases, bonuses and piece-rate payments.

2   *'Unapproved' absence*: used for monitoring time taken off by employees through, for example, lateness, leaving work early, absence from the job while still on the premises, etc.

3   *Sickness absence*: essential for monitoring the amount of time taken off work through sickness. Types of sickness are recorded and within these records there are indicators of morale and stress monitoring.

4   *Personal history*: these are the records where all of the employee data mentioned above is kept.

5   *Training records*: an account of training experienced by every employee before and during his or her employment with the organization is vital. Skills developed during training can be compared to the skill demands listed in the job description and training needs can be identified from the comparison.

6   *Job descriptions*: reorganization and frequent changes in technology mean that it is essential for these records in particular to be kept up-to-date. Updating these records should be a continuous process, rather than only when a vacant position arises; the description of the job should always be updated through consultation with the relevant line manager.

7   *Performance appraisal/P-rP records*: this is another means through which training needs may be identified and through which the employee's career development can be monitored. May also be used for assessing operational efficiency.

8   *Application forms*: there are many reasons why the employee's original application forms should be kept. Initially, they will have been used in the original selection process, through which the person was employed, but the form is a rich source of information about the employee's background before he or she joined the organization.

9   *Accident records*: records of accidents and injuries and other forms of industrial illness are a must in any organization. It is from these records that the effectiveness of the health and safety policy can be assessed, and the information may also be used to form not only the basis of future policy, but the

floor upon which 'Healthy Workplace' campaigns can be built.

Legal Requirements

Legislation provides for the protection of individuals, and usually demands information, rather than the keeping of records, but if the data is kept in secure systems, maintained and updated regularly, the information that results is more likely to be accurate and reliable, it can be accessed speedily, and presented clearly and attractively.

CONFIDENTIALITY

This is a legal issue that has been under close scrutiny, not only in employing organizations, but in many areas of our lives, for at least two decades and certainly since the period leading to the Data Protection Act of 1984. Confidentiality is a two-way issue. On the one hand, many managers are reluctant to allow employees access to the information about them that they have on record, while on the other, most employees feel that they ought to have access, even if only to check that the information is correct. Legally, they do have access to their own personal records and, indeed, to any information about them that is stored electronically (Data Protection Act, 1984). Also, most people would object to their personal information being disclosed to others. Clearly, there can be little harm in communicating collective and anonymous data in statistical form to internal and external third parties; the really sensitive area is in passing on personal information from which people can be identified.

Personnel records are confidential and kept under very tight control. As a broad rule, the release of blocks of statistical data normally is acceptable, while the release of personal information about individual employees is not, at least not without the express permission of the employee concerned. A 'safety first' maxim in this respect is: *if in doubt, hold back.*

AUTHORIZED ACCESS

With computerized systems it is very difficult for an unauthorized person to access information to which he or she is not entitled, although 'hacking in' to systems, which is a process whereby unauthorized users gain access, obviously is possible.

While in some organizations the personnel records are kept on the mainframe or other central computing facility, others are kept on a network of PCs that is not accessible from outside of the personnel department. Clearly, a system that is confined exclusively to the personnel department is more secure than one that is centralized. On the other hand, we have seen that the personnel records contain statistical information that is indispensable to the organization's planners. Human resource planning, for example, is implemented in the light of the corporate strategy, because the strategy determines the organization's human resource demands, while the human resource plan attempts to meet them. Corporate and human resource strategists, therefore, need access. Again, the password system is used. The general approach here is to provide a password that allows access to the statistical information, but not to the individual, confidential information. It is encouraging to see the more widespread involvement of personnel specialists in corporate strategy, which in itself, helps to solve the problems outlined above.

The IPD's *Code on Employee Data* (1988 and 1995), contains eight principles that provide excellent material for formulating policy on data protection; it covers specifically the issue of confidentiality in keeping personnel records. Each 'principle' includes a set of recommendations, and is further explained with paragraphs of relevant material.

Summary

Personnel administration is of two main kinds. The first is the day-to-day tasks of dealing with correspondence, organizing events and maintaining relationships with outside bodies; and the second is handling employee information. Records are kept on every individual, which collectively, and with the addition of external information, enables the production of statistical information. Information technology allows most of these tasks to be carried out on the computer. Small organizations, of perhaps 100 people or so, may still use manual systems, although even they now are turning to the computer for greater efficiency and effectiveness.

21

Personnel Information Systems

Introduction

A personnel record system is an organized storage system, in which information about individuals' employment history is categorized according to the organization's needs. When such information is stored in a computer, it provides the database for what generally is referred to as a *Computerized Personnel Information System* (CPIS). Most of today's organizations use a CPIS, and most personnel practitioners are computer literate. The purpose of this chapter is to explain the role of the CPIS, showing the areas of personnel work in which information technology (IT) may be applied, and how IT may be used to increase the efficiency and effectiveness of personnel people.

Role of the CPIS

Carrying the admin burden A computer is a machine that is capable of processing information at a greater speed and with greater repetitive accuracy than any single individual, or group of individuals. When it is used for personnel purposes, it takes the 'chore' element out of the day-to-day administrative work, reduces the demand on resource requirements, and releases personnel specialists for more meaningful tasks.

Providing decision making information The type of data, and the way it is stored, provides access to valid information by those who make decisions relating to corporate strategy, human resource planning, reward management, employee relations and many other organizational issues.

The role of the CPIS, therefore, is to improve efficiency and effectiveness at the activities level of personnel work, and enhance the quality of decision making at managerial levels. Although a CPIS may seem costly to install, the enhancement it provides will ultimately reduce operational costs.

Acquiring the System

Many of the systems in use today are reputed 'packages' that have been developed by software companies and sold to the user. A 'ready-made package' is software that has already been written, and packages have been developed for application in almost any organizational system, although where the requirements are organizationally specific – that is to say, the requirements are exclusive to the user organization – a custom-built package may be developed. There are, therefore, personnel packages on the market, which can be bought and installed, or customized to the particular requirements of your organization. It is also possible to put a CPIS on to the company's main computer, and this may be carried out by the company's own experts. At first glance, the cost of a ready-made package may seem high, but the ultimate cost of a DIY job on your own mainframe, even though it may not appear so at first, usually turns out to be considerably higher.

You have to ensure that you are getting the package that you need, in terms of how the information is stored, the amount that can be stored, and the forms in which it can be retrieved. Software packages, like all systems, have their limitations, and it is a good idea to obtain the advice of an independent software consultant who is capable of analysing your needs and has no commercial axe to grind when advising you on the appropriateness of systems. Ideally, your own in-house experts, if you have them, will be able to help.

Installing the System

There are two ways of doing this. Obviously, when the package is first installed, it carries no information at all. The first job, therefore, is to input the personnel records and any other information that you will need. This can be an arduous task for someone, because of the volume and technical complexity of the information to be input. Also, it is a time-consuming activity that increases the overall cost of installation. If your records are already computerized and you are buying in a new system, it is possible to 'port' the information across from the old to the new system, and it is advisable to ask the supplying software house to do this for you. It does involve an extra cost, but this is considerably less than the cost of doing it yourself. If you are computerizing the records for the first time, it probably is best to delegate the inputting to two or three people (depending on the size of the task), who will do nothing else until the input is complete. Care should be taken over choosing people for this task, since much of the information is confidential.

It is vital that at this stage, you retain your original files and keep both systems running concurrently until the new system is fully operational and a 'back-up' is in existence. There are always teething problems with new systems and it is possible, during the course of solving them, for information to be lost.

Applications

The applications for which a CPIS may be used are many and varied, but the main ones are as follows:

- personnel records
- recruitment
- absenteeism (for whatever reason)
- human resource management
- human resource planning
- human resource development
- performance management
- salaries and wages

As we have seen, the personnel record system provides the database for the CPIS. A database is the accumulated, integrated data, which is stored in the computer and can be accessed. When, therefore, you retrieve the personal record of any individual employee, the information that comes up on the screen contains everything about that person (see figure 21.1). You can scrutinize the total history of the person's employment, including his or her personal details, such as date of birth, sex, marital status, ethnic origin, home address, telephone number, number, sex and ages of children, the job and salary on joining, all of the details about past employment up to and including those for the current job, the employment contract and details of salary, appraisal results, such as those for performance, potential and reward, and the type and amount of training undertaken since joining the company. Normally one will access an individual's record for a specific purpose, perhaps to list the person's absence periods or performance history. For example, if an employee is to be interviewed for some reason by his or her manager, then that manager may wish to gain background information to help in the process.

Details appear on the screen in a frame as indicated in the figure. What appear here are purely the personal details of the individual; job details can be called up on another screen in a few seconds. The advent of 'Windows' allows for extra details to be incorporated into the screen in a smaller frame, which can be enlarged, even to occupy the whole screen if required. 'Windows' is software technology that has been developed to simplify

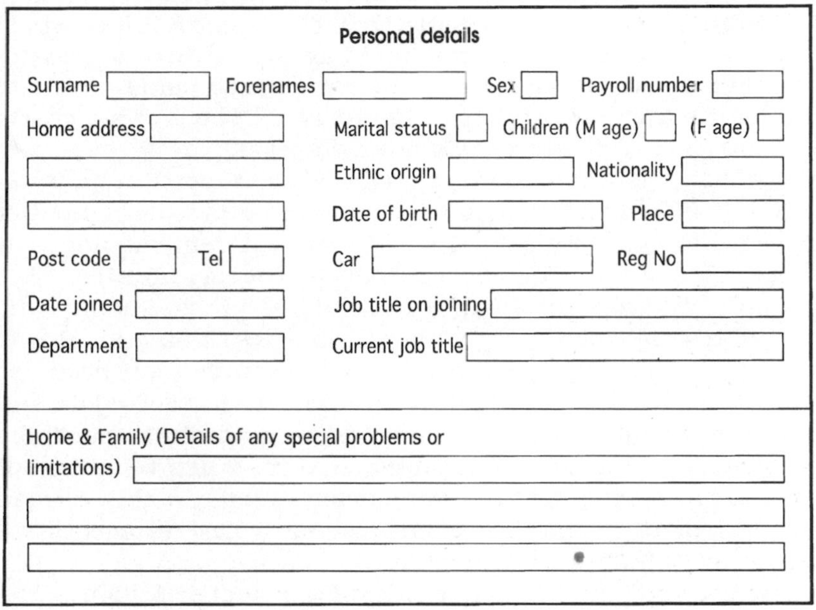

Figure 21.1 Individual employment details.

usage, and modern packages are available with or without windows.

When the data is manipulated collectively, statistical information that aids decision making can be retrieved relating, among other things, to the following areas of human resource planning:

- staff turnover
- workforce stability
- age profiles
- the internal and external labour markets
- skills audit figures.

Statistical information may also be retrieved on:

- equal opportunity monitoring
- comparative salary and wage payments
- annual expenditures on total employment costs
- workforce (rather than individual) performance levels
- annual training costs

The information you need can be retrieved in a variety of graphical and other illustrative forms: bar charts, graphs, histograms, scattergrams, pie charts, tabulations and so forth, all of which enable you to present information in an attractive and easy-to-read form, and, depending on the equipment, using colour to highlight particular points (see figure 21.2). The graphs, charts and tables that illustrate this book, for example, were all produced on a computer. Managers can be provided with information that will enable them to see clearly the trends in manpower movements, and forecasts of manpower requirements and how these relate to the business needs of the organization. For example, we have seen that organizational plans, such as the human resource plan, are rolling programmes. Inputs relating to maintaining and updating the human resource plan occur as and when the corporate strategy changes, when people join and leave the organization, are promoted, given specialized training in readiness for a future need, and so forth. When we carry out these inputs, the CPIS automatically updates the human resource plan, so that the picture we see when we access the plan is always the current picture.

Curve C in figure 21.2 shows that the age distribution of the workforce is skewed towards the more mature members of staff. While this implies that there is probably no shortage of current

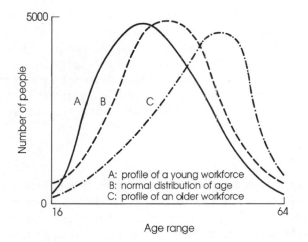

A: profile of a young workforce
B: normal distribution of age
C: profile of an older workforce

Figure 21.2 Screen showing age profile.

experience in the workplace, it also shows that in the medium term, there will be a high number of retirements. This would pose a problem for the uninformed and, therefore, unprepared organization.

Using the Computer

To do this you need keyboard skills and a complete knowledge of the versatility of the package in use. When you buy a package, it comes with manuals containing comprehensive information about the package and instructions for the user. In most cases, the supplier will provide the initial training in the use of the package. Even so, it is still a good idea to undergo training in a variety of packages, especially those for word processing, such as WordPerfect or Word (which you can use for report writing), and those for information analysis, such as Lotus 1–2–3 (which would enable you to analyse the data gathered from, say, an attitude survey, and incoming statistics). Where needed, other packages are available.

Some people feel a little nervous when they first attempt to use a computer; some have never tried to use one, feeling that it would be beyond them. This attitude is inherited from the early days of computing, when comparatively few people understood the technology, and what was available for use was determined by what it was possible to produce, rather than what the user needed. Today, software is specifically developed to be 'user-friendly', which means that those who develop packages do so with ease of use in mind. It is only when you try that you realize just how easy it is. One analogy that comes to mind is that of driving a modern car. The car itself may be the product of complex, high techology, but you don't have to be an automobile engineer to drive it.

Acquiring the skills

Courses approved by the Institute of Personnel and Development, particularly the Certificate in Personnel Practice and the more advanced Professional Management Foundation Programme, contain significant IT elements. It is said that there is no substitute for experience, and in a sense this is true, but you do need to have at least a basic grounding in the use of several packages. Also, proper training, rather than the trial and error of untutored learning, enables you to get the best from a package, since you will be aware of its full capabilities.

After basic introductory training, you will be able to use the keyboard, gather, input, store, collate and retrieve information. These are skills that you should practise at every opportunity. From there, you move on to applications, in which you are shown how to apply a number of packages to personnel work. Concurrently, you will develop knowledge and the skills of statistics, from which you will be able to analyse, manage and present information.

Part VI

Employee Relations

Those who work in the personnel function need to be able to advise and assist line managers in matters affecting the relationship between the organization and its employees. This part of the book addresses recent developments in employee relations, contracts of employment, the rules and procedures relating to matters of grievance and discipline and related interviewing. Elements of employment law relating to individual rights and discrimination are explained. The status and role of trade unions, and questions of conflict and power in organizations are also explored.

22

The Employee Relationship

Introduction

This chapter aims to provide an understanding of how the relationship between the organization and its employees is established, regulated and maintained. While it includes explanations of the important features of industrial relations, such as the legal and behavioural implications, the term 'employee relations' is used here to describe a broader concept than that of industrial relations, since it embraces a scope and spread of activities from which the employer and the employee may derive mutual benefit.

Unitary and Pluralistic Perspectives

The style and quality of employee relations ultimately is determined by the frame of reference through which its top managers perceive the formal employee relationship. The perspective adopted by the senior management group is determined by their values and the strength of their beliefs about such things as managerial authority, power and control. Alan Fox (1966) suggested that managers may adopt one of two philosophical approaches:

1   *The unitary perspective*, in which there is only one source of power, where the managers value and protect the legitimacy of their authority. There is an assumption that all employees

share the common goals of the organization and that they will receive a portion of the rewards, which will come if, through their efforts, the organization functions efficiently and effectively. When conflict occurs, causes are attributed to communication failures, or the foolish temperaments of those involved. Trade unions are unwelcome and the organization fiercely resists their approaches for recognition. The managers retain total command, regard themselves as the 'authoritative management group' and as a 'management team', and assume that is the way they are generally regarded by the employees.

2   *The pluralistic perspective*, in which managers may allow, and actively foster, freedom of expression and the development of groups, which establish their own norms and elect their own informal leaders. In this way, power and control arise in several parts of the organization, and loyalty is commanded by the leaders of groups, which are often in competition with each other for resources. Within this kind of approach, the managers achieve results through joining the groups, encouraging participation, motivating employees and coordinating their work efforts. In this way, the managers are exercising good leadership, although sometimes it can be difficult to achieve the necessary balance, in which the interests of customers, suppliers, shareholders and employees have to be taken into account. However, when employees become involved in solving work-related problems and making decisions, they develop commitment to the achievement of successful outcomes.

Employee Relations Policy

The perspective adopted by the top managers determines the general ambience of an employee relations policy. In formulating policy, they are advised by the personnel director, whose recommendations are influenced by such factors as: the geographic spread, size and scope of the organization; the nature of the industry; the role, strength and status of the trade unions and the collective bargaining arrangements. Two further influential factors are the managerial style and climate of the organization. When the policy is implemented, it will interact with these factors and influence culture, hopefully, to make it conducive to the achievement of objectives.

The 'Psychological' Contract

The employer and the employee have a formal relationship in which the employee 'works for' the employer and is paid for doing so. This formally agreed relationship about work and pay is legally binding, and is described in the employment contract, which is discussed later in this chapter. Also there is a tacit, informal relationship which exists on a social and cultural basis, and in which people relate to each other at a personal, rather than an official, level. It is at this less tangible level that most effective communication takes place, in which people do each other 'favours', turn a 'blind eye' to certain items of behaviour, and carry out work that is not referred to in their job descriptions.

In essence, the psychological contract is made up of all of those aspects of 'being at work' that are outside of the provisions of the employment contract, but have been elaborated upon and extended to rights and privileges, and perceived duties and responsibilities that are powerful determinants of employees' behaviour. It is within the reciprocal spirit of the psychological contract that people are motivated to work, gain satisfaction from what they do, develop feelings of job security and belongingness, and enjoy a culture of trust and mutual respect. All of this implies that the 'exchange' aspect of the psychological contract is manifest in the form of mutual expectancies and need satisfactions (Schein, 1980). More than the formal, it is the psychological contract that causes people to do what they do in organizations.

In recent years, the psychological contract has suffered considerably from the ravages of so-called 'macho-management', in which managers have adopted an authoritarian and, indeed, sometimes threatening, coercive attitude towards their staff. Since the late 1980s and into the 1990s, organizations, driven by fierce competition from overseas and a serious recession at home, have been busy developing leaner, flatter structures, and this process of 'delayering' has created changes in power structures, and produced smaller workforces but with larger internal groups, redeployments and, unfortunately, redundancies. It seems that managers have themselves feared becoming victims of delayering, and other changes, and have adopted these macho attitudes in the hope of protecting their positions by portraying what they perceive as an image of 'strong and effective leadership'.

More recently, expressions such as 'downsizing' and 'rightsizing' have entered corporate jargon. Downsizing means reducing the number of staff at corporate level, while rightsizing means employing the bare minimum number of staff to do the work. The philosophy underlying all of these activities is that 'small is beautiful'. In other words, a small company can be more effective and profitable than a large one. You do not need so many support staff, communications pass through fewer hierarchical layers, and the workforce, through multi-skilling and empowering, can accomplish more. These positive outcomes are moderated by the fact that when redundancies are called for, it is the more mature, experienced, skilled and knowledgeable workers who take the money and run, which can leave the organization virtually bereft of the means of achieving the intended results.

It is clear that this contract is just as susceptible to being breached as is the formal contract. The recent strategic changes mentioned above, and the resultant managerial styles, may well have breached the informal contract in many organizations. Certainly, they have changed it. Terms such as job security, culture, job satisfaction, motivation and morale are never found in the formal contract, since they are features of work and of the workplace that are the product of employees' values and beliefs, which determine behaviour (see exhibit 22.1). Since such values and beliefs are the products of deeply held, even 'taken-for-granted' assumptions about 'how things should be around here', they do not surface visibly unless they come under threat.

Goodwill is one of the mainstays of a positive relationship between employer and employee; it leads to mutually advantageous, informal employee behaviour and, obviously, should be fostered. Rules that regulate employee behaviour clearly are necessary components of good internal order, but the over-regulation of workplace behaviour, particularly that which introduces 'duties' that previously were carried out informally, destroys goodwill, reduces morale, and, incidentally, increases costs.

Exhibit 22.1

Alistair Mant (1995) writes: 'The four components of morale have been variously described as satisfaction that is obtained from what you *do* (the job itself), enjoying the people you are working *with* (the work group), trusting the people you work *for* (management practices), and finally, the economic rewards. Delayering and downsizing disturb these satisfactions.'

The Employment Contract

This describes the formal relationship between the employer and the employee. The employment contract may be seen as a legally binding agreement in which the employer and the employee have agreed to exchange work for pay and other agreed rewards. More than any other person in the organization, the personnel specialist needs to have a thorough understanding of the contract of employment. As soon as an individual has accepted an offer of employment from an employer, or an employer's authorized representative, such as a personnel specialist, a contract of employment exists.

A contract of employment, therefore, can be brought into existence orally at an interview, or on the telephone. Such contracts can also be in writing, or obtained by conduct, although it is normal for the offer to be made and accepted in writing. The details of the contract of employment are referred to as the *terms and conditions*, and the employer must issue a statement of them in writing, to the employee, within 13 weeks of commencing employment. The statement should contain certain items, which include:

- the employer's name
- date of commencement
- the job title
- rates and conditions relating to pay
- working hours
- amount of notice of termination to be given by either side

- sick pay and related procedures
- holiday entitlement
- pension rights
- disciplinary and grievance procedures.

The statement does not normally include the terms and conditions in detail. In most organizations, there is a collective agreement that provides for a precis of them to be issued, as long as (1) the full details are made freely available for the employee to study, and (2) the statement contains information about how and where this can be done. Neither the terms and conditions, nor the statement, constitutes the Contract of Employment. The contract may be seen as a legally binding agreement in which the employer and the employee have agreed to exchange work for pay and other agreed rewards.

The Contract of Employment contains 'express conditions', which are those that have been expressed orally or agreed in writing; and 'implied terms', which are those that may be assumed to be constituents of every contract of employment, according to common law. The contract provides for obligations on both sides, which on the part of the employee relate to his or her duties, including showing good faith to the employer, being ready and willing to work, obeying reasonable orders and conducting him or herself in the interest of the employer; while on the part of the employer, they relate to the responsibility to provide work, pay agreed wages, not to make unreasonable deductions from wages without the employee's agreement, and to conform to the law.

The Status of Contracts

'The extent to which an employer can unilaterally change working arrangements or the terms of a contract depend entirely on the terms themselves. The employer has no inherent or implied power to change the contract terms, no matter how unreasonable or inconvenient they may be' (Aiken, 1992). A contract of employment, therefore, is a legally binding instrument, and any changes to it may be made only with the freely given consent and agreement of the employee. The law on contracts, and particularly that on contracts of employment, is complex, and there is no intention of providing great legal detail here.

It is, however, important to note that the nature of contracts in employment is changing as a result of changes in employers' demands for particular skills. The fact that an employer needs to access certain skills for limited periods, or for specific purposes, for example, does not necessarily give rise to a conventional offer of a contract of employment. Changes in the ways that organizations are managed mean that there are variations in the status of job-holders, in that some are more important than others. Long-term or open-ended contracts are offered to key staff, who also enjoy superior terms and conditions of employment, while less important, or ancillary staff are given less favourable terms and conditions. Others are given part-time contracts, while yet others come in to work on an 'as-and-when-required' basis. The need for organizations to change to remain competitive, coupled with high unemployment, has led employers towards this kind of solution.

References

Aiken, O. 1992: *Contracts*. Law and Employment Series. London: Institute of Personnel and Development.

Fox, A. 1966: *Industrial Sociology and Industrial Relations*. Royal Commission on Trade Unions and Employers' Associations research paper no.3. London: HMSO.

Mant, A. 1995: Changing work roles. In S. Tyson (ed.), *Strategic Prospects for HRM*. London: Institute of Personnel and Development.

Schein, E. 1980: *Organisational Psychology*, 3rd edn. Englewood Cliffs, NJ: Prentice Hall.

23

Industrial Relations

Introduction

The term 'both sides of industry' is used to refer to employers and trade unions, who bargain with each other over the terms and conditions of employment. Employers and unions use systems, rules and procedures to regulate this process and to protect their respective interests. Industrial relations encompasses these systems, and defines the roles of the managers and trade union representatives involved in operating them.

Today, industrial disputes are far less frequent than they were 20 years ago. Negotiations between management and unions are taking place somewhere in the country every day, and most are carried out in a friendly and businesslike fashion, resulting in agreement.

The present framework provides managers and unions with a medium through which they can communicate with each other and reach agreement over the terms and conditions of employment. The agreements that are reached between the two sides cover a wide variety of issues, which can be analysed to form two kinds of agreement:

1 Procedural agreements, which describe the methods to be used in, for example, handling disciplinary matters, grievances, disputes and redundancies.
2 Substantive agreements, which describe the rights and obligations relating to the individual's contract of employment, such as pay, hours of work and so forth.

It may be said that procedural agreements provide methods and rules to govern 'how we shall go about doing things'. They result from what is called *integrative bargaining*, in which both sides, rather than being in conflict, acknowledge that they have common problems which, if resolved, would produce mutual benefit. The approach in integrative bargaining sessions, therefore, is one of informality and cooperative problem solving.

Substantive agreements arise from *distributive bargaining*, in which there is a climate of 'my gain is your loss'. Here, there is negotiation over how much of a particular element each side should have, or give. Factors such as time and pay, for example, are limited and it is obvious that the less one side gives, the more the other side keeps. Distributive bargaining sessions are carried on in a more formal manner, and usually there is just one item on the agenda: money or time. So-called '*mixed bargaining*' is partly integrative and partly distributive. This produces the need for the parties to alternate between cooperative and unyielding approaches in the same session, which some negotiators find difficult.

Personnel specialists frequently become involved in industrial relations negotiations, and if they are to be successful, they need to develop sophisticated skills in interpersonal communication, particularly in the more subtle aspects of non-verbal communication.

Negotiation has been described as 'the art of achieving a mutually acceptable compromise', and a successful negotiation may be assessed by the degree to which one has achieved one's objectives, rather than by 'winning' or 'losing'. Negotiators who are totally unyielding put themselves in a *win–lose* situation, and might come out with nothing. Inflexibility on the part of one side often produces a confrontational attitude, which makes the other side equally unyielding, producing a *lose–lose* situation, in which nobody gains anything. Ideally, there will be reasonable give and take on both sides, which is the recipe for a *win–win* situation.

Occasionally, however, people feel very strongly about a particular issue and remain so steadfast in their demands that they are prepared to take industrial action, perhaps even in the form of a strike, in order to achieve their objectives. The British Rail strikes of 1994 are an example of this kind of incident.

Rules, Procedures and Codes of Practice

As we have seen, formal behaviour in organizations is regulated by systems of rules, procedures and codes of practice. Most organizations produce an 'Employee Handbook', which contains employment policies and procedures relating to discipline, grievances, disputes, severance, and health and safety at work. There is a legal obligation to provide employees with written explanations of these procedures. The company handbook also contains details of payment systems and general entitlements, such as holidays, overtime payments, time off, etc., and regulations relating to conduct within the organization. Usually, the handbook is produced by the personnel department and approved by senior managers.

Where trade unions are recognized, rules and procedures are produced within the agreed framework of collective bargaining. But not all of the rules and procedures that govern employee conduct are as clear as those that are written into internal and external legislation, and not all are agreed formally. On the one hand, managers may decide to draft rules and procedures without referring to the trade unions, while on the other hand, employees may behave in ways that have not been planned by managers. Workplace traditions, 'on-the-hoof' decisions, social habits and so-called 'accepted custom and practice' all result in conduct which, although not unruly, seems in parts to lack procedural clarity.

The extent to which the organization may go, when drafting rules about certain issues, are limited by legislation. Employee rights and the law on health and safety at work, for example, must not be breached. New laws supersede old ones, and legal cases create new interpretations of the law. An essential part of the personnel role today, therefore, is the careful monitoring of all new UK and European legislation. Employment legislation tends to set minimum standards of conformity to regulations relating to certain industrial practices, such as health and safety at work, and it provides protection and rights for individuals.

CODES OF PRACTICE

Codes of Practice are issued by several bodies, including government departments, government-funded bodies, and such professional institutions as the IPD. They are related to legislation, but are not legal requirements in themselves. Their purpose is to provide a framework through which employers can achieve good employment and personnel practices in areas such as discipline, the handling of grievances and disputes, dismissals and other procedures. Usually, they are contained in booklets, the format of which follows the structures of the procedures to which they relate. While it is not illegal to breach a code of practice, hard evidence of a breach can weigh heavily against an employer who is defending an action.

The Role of ACAS

The Advisory Conciliation and Arbitration Service (ACAS) is a body that was established under the provisions of the Employment Protection Act, 1975, to promote the improvement of industrial relations.

Advisory   As an advisory body, ACAS offers advice to individuals and organizations who either perceive themselves to have been treated inequitably, or lack the knowledge and skills that would enable them to cope with a particular process or situation. ACAS also publishes Codes of Practice and advisory handbooks, relating to such employment procedures as discipline, grievance, industrial disputes, redundancy, dismissal and many others. Each of the recommended procedures has an acknowledged structure, which is generally recognized as one that leads to good practice. Many organizations have incorporated the ACAS principles into their own practices and procedures.

Conciliation   In this role, ACAS attempts to settle impending tribunal actions before they reach the 'hearing' stage. When, for example, someone feels that they have been unfairly dismissed, they may ask for their case to be heard by an industrial tribunal. Firstly, they lodge their complaint, usually within three months of the dismissal. They do this by completing a Form IT1, which is sent to the Central Office of Industrial Tribunals. ACAS receive copies of all such claims (except for those in respect of compensation for redundancy). ACAS is organized regionally, so that its conciliation specialists are close at hand to help employees and employers to resolve problems, and in many cases, heading off industrial tribunals. The experienced conciliation officer can advise both parties of the likely outcome of a tribunal.

Arbitration   Arbitration occurs when an external third party is brought in to address a problem which internal dialogue has failed to resolve. Most organizations' procedures relating to discipline, grievance and disputes take account of the possible need for arbitration, and many identify ACAS as the prospective arbitrator. The ACAS approach to the structure of arbitration can take several forms, ranging from the appointment of a sole arbitrator, to the convening of a board of arbitration, depending upon the size and complexity of the problem. A board of arbitration consists of an independent ACAS arbitrator, who takes the chair, and equal numbers of employer and employee representatives. When two parties agree to take a problem to arbitration, there is a strong implication that both sides will accept the solution that is recommended by the arbitrator.

Employee Rights

When we refer to 'employee rights' usually we mean those that are embodied in the provisions of UK employment legislation, although recent history shows that in specific cases, interpretations given by the European Court may override our own legal decisions. Certain legislated rights are activated as soon as a recruitment advertisement appears, and they remain in force for the duration of employment. Further rights come into effect as the length of the employee's service increases. Rights are established to protect individuals from being exploited or mistreated by dissolute employers, and to provide for a number of entitlements, including:

Payment
- equal pay, regardless of race or sex
- paid time off for antenatal care
- redundancy pay after two years' service, and further compensation if notice of redundancy falls short of statutory requirement, regardless of length of service
- pay for time spent looking for employment after notice of redundancy
- pay for time spent on trade union duties
- compensation in the event of the employer going into liquidation or becoming insolvent
- guaranteed pay, in which the employee is entitled to full pay when there is a shortage of work

- maternity pay at the lower rate after six months' service, and at the higher rate after two years
- statutory sick pay for those earning above the 'low pay limit'
- an itemized payslip

Rights

- time off for public duties
- protection against unfavourable treatment or being placed at a disadvantage in relation to other workers, on the grounds of race or sex, for example, from redundancy, selection for training, promotion, allocation of holiday times, etc.
- a minimum period of notice
- protection from dismissal during suspension on medical grounds
- a written statement of the terms and conditions of employment within the first 13 weeks of service
- protection from unfair dismissal after two years' service (if the organization has more than 20 employees)
- maternity leave (after two years)
- reasons for dismissal given in writing, for those with more than six months' service.

The main sources of protection and individual rights that are given above are in (1) legislation, and (2) legal decisions that have been made by the Employment Appeals Tribunal. The Acts of Parliament that contain the relevant provisions include: the Equal Pay Act,1970; the Trade Union and Labour Relations Act (TULRA), 1974; the Employment Protection Act, 1975; the Sex Discrimination Act, 1975; the Race Relations Act, 1976 and the Employment Protection (Consolidation) Act, 1979. Several subsequent Acts of Parliament amended those referred to above: the TULRA (Amendment) Act, 1976 and the Employment Acts of 1980 and 1981.

Most of these Acts are in the form of 'enabling' legislation, which is legislation that provides relevant Secretaries of State with the authority to draw up regulations and codes of practice, set up advisory and authoritative bodies, and appoint individuals to administer and enforce the requirements of the legislation. Implementation of these Acts by relevant Secretaries of State has resulted in establishing and providing legal status to the following organizations:

- The Advisory Conciliation and Arbitration Service (ACAS)
- Industrial Tribunals (ITs)
- Employment Appeals Tribunal (EAT)
- The Equal Opportunities Commission (EOC)
- The Commission for Racial Equality (CRE)

Employee relations involves us in carrying out the personnel policies of the organization, relating to such matters as recruitment, selection, training and appraising employees. But the organization has to be managed on a day-to-day basis too, and procedures should be in place to enable us to deal with particular events and issues, such as discipline, handling grievances, redundancies and other dismissals, and manpower movements, such as promotions and transferring employees from one part of the organization to another.

Discipline

Exhibit 23.1 is an example of a structure for a disciplinary procedure. Invoking the formal disciplinary procedure ultimately can lead to dismissing an employee, usually for breaching one or more of the organization's rules on several occasions. Offences are categorized from minor offences, through to serious, or gross misconduct. This last often carries the penalty of immediate dismissal without compensation.

HANDLING THE DISCIPLINARY PROCEDURE

Because of its ultimate implications, a disciplinary procedure has to be seen to be fair to all who are involved. Fairness and justice should prevail, and the approach, rules and practices surrounding the procedure should reflect this. Disciplinary procedures that are in use now generally have been formulated with the law on unfair dismissal in mind. The structure that will be familiar to most practitioners provides for repeated offences and has three stages:

1   For a minor offence, an employee will be given a formal warning by the manager. This may be delivered orally, or in writing; usually it is given orally. However it is given, it must advise the employee of the nature of the offence he or she has committed, and of the possible consequences of repeating the offence.

Exhibit 23.1 Structure of a disciplinary procedure

Preamble:	In which the immediate manager and the employee get together to discuss why the alleged offence took place. This may result in no further action.
Stage 1:	In which the manager delivers a formal warning to the employee. This may be given orally or in writing. Usually, a first warning is given orally, although the event is noted, including the date and the nature of the offence. In the warning, the manager points out the nature of the offence and the possible consequences of repeating it.
Stage 2:	In which a second formal warning is given, almost always in writing, stating the time, date, place and nature of the offence. Again, the possible consequences of repeating the offence are pointed out, and in particular circumstances, the employee may be referred for counselling.
Stage 3:	In which the third and final formal warning is delivered in writing. At this stage, the employee is in danger of receiving a severe penalty in the event of repeating the offence again, and this should be made very clear by the manager. The removal of privileges, suspension or even dismissal could result from a repeated offence after a final written warning.
Stage 4:	This takes the form of a hearing, usually by a panel consisting of senior managers, including the personnel manager. After the hearing, decisions are made about the culpability of the employee and, where appropriate, the penalty to be applied.

2 If the offence is repeated, a second warning is issued in writing, stating the time, date and place of the offence, its nature, and the possible consequences of repeating it.

3 If the offence is committed for a third time, a final written warning is delivered. This particularly important warning should point out that a further repeated offence would result in a severe penalty, such as the removal of privileges, suspension or dismissal.

The role of the personnel specialist in disciplinary matters varies from one organization to another, but usually it is to ensure that the procedure, and the law, are strictly adhered to. In cases where a dismissal looks possible, the matter should be referred to a senior manager, to gain approval for the proposed action. Normally, managers and supervisors have *some* authority in disciplinary matters, but in the absence of a senior manager, it is recommended that they do not dismiss the person, even in cases of gross misconduct. The procedure should allow for an employee to be accompanied by a colleague when the formal warnings are issued, and the manager too is advised to issue them in the presence of another manager.

It is important that a thorough inquiry is carried out at every stage of the procedure, and all of the facts collected and recorded, along with details of what happened when the procedure was implemented. If the dismissal of an employee was to result in an industrial tribunal, one of the first questions asked would relate to whether a thorough investigation was carried out.

Managers and supervisors should not be too quick to invoke the procedure. Often, a manager under pressure, making a superficial assessment of the situation, does not get the whole story. For example, being late for work is against the rules in most organizations, but if an employee who has a good record for punctuality suddenly starts coming in late, the manager should investigate the cause, rather than go straight for the rule book. Good workers are hard to find, and if a manager can counsel an employee, or guide him or her towards the solution to a problem, even though that problem may be at home, a good worker can be turned into an even better, more loyal and motivated worker.

Disciplinary processes should begin with a *preamble*, in which the manager and the employee get together to discuss the reasons why a rule has been broken. This gives the manager an opportunity to discover any problems, assess the employee's attitude towards his or her behaviour, and to decide what action might be taken. The result could be to counsel the employee into more appropriate behaviour; the transgression might have been due to a lack of knowledge or a skill, in which case training or coaching might produce the desired results.

Handling Grievances and Disputes

The formal grievance procedure provides a channel through which employees can have their grievances heard by managers. The grievance procedure, which is used for handling individuals' dissatisfactions and complaints, has a structure that comprises several stages, so that if an aggrieved employee does not obtain satisfaction at one stage, the grievance can move on to the next. There are three stages, and in the event of repeated dissatisfaction, or if the issue is beyond the manager's control or authoritative scope, the grievance is heard at successively higher levels, ranging from the supervisor to a board member, such as the managing director or personnel director. Each stage takes the form of an interview between the employee, who may be accompanied by a friend, and the manager (see exhibit 23.2).

Note from exhibit 23.2 that the personnel department does not get involved at the initial stage; experience shows that most grievances are resolved at that level. The procedure provides for a maximum amount of time to pass between the stages, the objective being to deal with a grievance speedily. Speed, and fairness to all concerned, are said to be the most essential ingredients of a good procedure.

GRIEVANCE INTERVIEWS

Individuals may feel aggrieved for a variety of reasons. Grievances vary in their complexity and so, therefore, do the interviews. Grievance interviews have two purposes: firstly, for the employee to state the grievance, and secondly, for the manager to analyse what is being said, identify the cause and, where possible, eliminate it. Employees are usually well prepared for such events, and the manager should also prepare. Before the interview, the manager should obtain an understanding of the problem at the root of the grievance. In a small organization,

Exhibit 23.2 A formal grievance procedure

Stage 1: The employee, who may be accompanied by a friend, airs the grievance to the immediate manager/supervisor, and an attempt is made to resolve the issue.

Stage 2: This takes place if the issue was not resolved at Stage 1, and usually involves a more senior manager. Again, the employee states the grievance and a second attempt is made to resolve it.

Stage 3: This takes place if the issue was not resolved at the previous stages and usually involves the senior managers and the personnel manager/director. The grievance receives a full hearing and a final attempt is made to resolve it.

Few grievances reach Stage 3. Most are resolved at Stage 1 and many at Stage 2. In extreme circumstances, however, special panels may be set up, including the involvement of experienced external arbitrators, where appropriate, in attempts to resolve serious or complex grievances.

---

the employee is probably well known to the manager and, indeed, may be known to be an inveterate griper. In large organizations, however, where it is not possible to get to know everyone personally, it is a good idea to check such matters with associates, and take a look at the employee's record. Making enquiries will provide the manager with several perceptions of the circumstances and produce information about the individual concerned, so that when the employee's version is expressed at the interview, the manager can put it into some kind of context, taking care not to jump to conclusions.

At the interview, the manager should listen attentively and allow the person to speak freely. There is no better way of getting the employee's perception of the situation. After the manager has heard the grievance and established mutual agreement with the employee over its nature, both parties can adopt a joint problem solving approach to it, in which the employee is encouraged to suggest solutions to the problem. Some such suggestions may be impracticable, or outside of the limitations of the organization's policy, but the manager can offer the employee guidance on what is and is not possible. If agreement is reached over the solution to the problem, it is important for the manager to follow this up and ensure that the agreed action is taken.

Those who draft procedures try to write them in language that makes them watertight, so that the possibility of misinterpretation is reduced to a bare minimum. On the other hand, every case is different, and where a grievance has been shown to be justified, it often is possible for the manager, using common sense, to 'wriggle within the skin' of a procedure, in order to be fair to the employee and any others who may be involved.

DISPUTES

A grievance becomes a dispute when several (rather than just one) employees feel that they have been unjustly treated, or are dissatisfied in some way with a particular situation. Generally, it may be said that a dispute has arisen when a number of employees are in disagreement with the organization over a particular decision or action.

There are both local and national procedures for handling disputes. Local procedures involve the trade unions, where they are recognized, while national procedures always involve the trade unions. In broad terms, disputes that are handled at national level are those that have occurred industry-wide, rather than in a single organization, and those that include matters which are the subject of national agreements.

At a local level, disputes that do not lend themselves to simple or speedy resolution would be handled through negotiation or joint consultation which, in a large organization, would take place internally. In the absence of agreement, the employees may take the matter to their local representatives, who will try to negotiate with management. If the parties still fail to reach agreement, they may decide to go to arbitration.

The Trade Unions

The trade unions have a long and colourful history, in which the episodes are punctuated by civil disturbances, Acts of

Parliament, and Appeals Court and House of Lords' decisions. Over the years, they have demonstrated not only the depth and strength of the feelings of employees over particular issues, but the risks they were prepared to take and the extremes of deprivation they were willing to endure, in pursuance of what they perceived to be justice and their rights at work.

Trade union structures

Since the middle of the nineteenth century, trade unions have grown and become an integral part of society. Their popularity and influence rises and falls alternately, in accordance with the effects of economic conditions, the size of their membership, the nature of the issues at stake and the ideology of the party in government. Since the early 1980s, the number of trade unions has fallen, mostly owing to amalgamations, and membership has declined. There are four different kinds of trade union, and each kind is organized differently:

1   *Craft* unions are those whose members are employed in a variety of industries as skilled operatives, such as electricians, draughtsmen, boilermakers, etc. These are the oldest unions, and were started by the craftsmen themselves, each union representing one craft. Entry to the union was gained through apprenticeship to a particular craft, but now, most such unions have amalgamated.
2   *General workers'* unions. Originally, these unions represented semi-skilled and unskilled workers, although now their members are from a wide variety of occupations, including health workers, local government employees and the professions. These unions, which again are the result of several amalgamations, recruit members from every kind of trade, profession, industry and organization.
3   *Industrial* unions. As their name suggests, industrial unions represent workers in specific industries. The National Union of Mineworkers (NUM) and the National Union of Railwaymen (NUR) are two examples. The distinctive feature of such unions is that all of the members work in the same industry, regardless of their trade or profession.
4   *White collar* unions. Here, membership is made up of non-manual workers. White collar unions were started early this century. Now, they have grown to embrace many industries

and professions, with membership categories ranging from clerical workers to senior executives.

THE PURPOSES OF TRADE UNIONS

Trade unions exist to represent the best interests of their members. Through the processes of collective bargaining, they attempt to improve the quality of the working lives and general standard of living of their members, by negotiating with employers for the best possible terms and conditions of employment. Negotiations take place at local level, in the form of workplace bargaining, and at national level, where agreements that affect whole industries, craft and professional groups are reached. Recent, well-publicized national agreements were reached in the health service and railway industries.

The future role of the trade unions seems to be in some doubt. We have seen that the privatization of national industries produces smaller workforces, and when people lose their jobs, they usually give up trade union membership. Traditionally, the trade unions have acquired their power and influence through numbers, and recent history has shown that when their numbers dwindle, they amalgamate, not only in order to sustain power through size, but for financial reasons too. There are more privatizations to come, and so one should expect to see more dwindling numbers and more amalgamations.

Summary

The nature and conduct of industrial relations in Britain has changed significantly since the early 1980s. Legislation, reductions in trade union membership and amalgamations, the false boom of the 1980s and the long recession that followed consolidated the already appalling unemployment situation, reduced the power of the trade unions and forced companies to change the way they managed the relationship with their employees. Also, the advent of human resource management, as an influence that determines the corporate managerial style, has reduced the degree to which trade unions participate in decisions relating to work activity and reward management. The system is still governed by the same rules and procedures, but in the main, power has switched to management, who now prefer to deal directly with individual employees. High unemployment and economically influential remnants of the recession are still with us, and it is a good idea to follow trends in these respects, since they have an important influence on domestic industrial relations.

24

Workplace Health and Safety

Introduction

Common sense and a humane attitude should tell us that a healthy and safe workplace will help to produce a pleasant atmosphere, and a more productive and profitable organization. Yet historically, our track record for ensuring the health and safety of employees is poor. During the industrial revolution, apart from the attitudes and actions of a handful of paternalistically motivated Victorian employers, little was done to protect employees, visitors, local residents or passers by from the hazards that arose from the activities, or even the very existence, of a firm. Those most likely to be the victims of health and safety risks were the employees, and this still is the case. Several Factories Acts were passed in the nineteenth century but mostly, employees' protection was derived from the common law, although there was no such thing as Legal Aid, and employees had to rely on the goodwill of their 'masters' to compensate them for injuries or health problems that were attributable to work.

Today's Legal Framework

Several Acts of Parliament were passed in the middle of the twentieth century, but these targeted specific industries, rather than the general panoply of industrial activity. Today, the policies and procedures that govern health and safety practices in the workplace are the result of the findings of the Robens Committee of Inquiry on Safety and Health. The Committee carried out a major review of health and safety at work, and the publication of its recommendations in 1972 gave rise to the Health and Safety at Work etc. Act, 1974 (HASAWA). This was the first Act of its kind to *require* people to be proactive in health and safety matters. Under previous legislation, those responsible risked prosecution for causing or allowing something to happen. Now, under the 1974 Act, they run the extra risk of failing to take particular actions; for example, failing to:

* prepare and keep updated a written safety policy
* establish a safety committee
* introduce safe working systems

The HASAWA sets out to involve employees, as well as employers, in health and safety. To secure the implementation of its provisions, the Act enabled, *inter alia*, the creation of two organizations: the Health and Safety Commission (HSC) and the Health and Safety Executive (HSE).

THE HEALTH AND SAFETY COMMISSION

This is the senior body and it has wide-ranging powers that enable it to carry out its duties and responsibilities. There is an appointed Chair, and the membership of between six to nine people is shared between employers, the trade unions and third parties. The general duties of the HSC are related to:

1 the health, safety and welfare of persons at work;
2 protecting persons other than employees against risks to health and safety;
3 controlling the use of explosives or highly flammable or otherwise dangerous substances;
4 controlling the emission into the atmosphere of noxious or offensive substances from prescribed premises.

Additionally, the HSC has a number of specific duties, which can be listed as follows:

1 assist and encourage the furtherance of the above general duties by persons concerned;
2 make appropriate arrangements for research into health and safety matters;
3 provide an information and advisory service to employers, trade unions and others;
4 submit proposals for the making of Regulations;
5 maintain regular links with the Minister concerned and carry out his directions.

To enable the HSC to carry out these general and specific duties, the HASAWA provided for the establishment of several Advisory Committees and the HSE, which is the enforcement agency of the HSC. This has produced an organizational structure, through which the provisions of the Act are enforced, and research and advice provided.

The Health and Safety Executive

The HSE is headed by the Director General and a Deputy Director General, appointed by the HSC. The HSE appoints 'Inspectors', who work under the control of one of its various branches, which include: The Field Operations Directorate, the Nuclear Safety Directorate, the Offshore Safety Division, the Chemicals and Hazardous Installations Division, the Railways Inspectorate, the Mines Inspectorate and the Health and Safety Laboratory.

The law confers substantial powers on HSE Inspectors, which include the right to enter premises and examine records, provided the grounds for doing so are reasonable; they may make inspections at any time, without giving notice, so long as they are carried out at reasonable times; and they can issue *enforcement notices* and prosecute serious or persistent offenders. These powers suggest that HSE Inspectors might behave like a kind of 'industrial Gestapo', but this is not the case. They have the powers *in case* they need them, rather than to 'snap check' premises and fill the courts with minor and accidental offenders. The HSE Inspector has to be knowledgeable, so that he or she may advise people on their health and safety at work, and persuade them to behave in a responsible way.

At this point it is worth noting that European legislation has become an important influence on our own, especially in respect of such matters as health and safety at work. For example, one of the main aspirations of the European legislators is to harmonize such laws throughout the member states.

Health and Safety in Practice

Health and safety at work starts at policy level. Under the provisions of the Act, all organizations must prepare and keep up to date a written statement of policy relating to health and safety. The policy should include a general statement, along with specific organizational arrangements for its implementation. Ideally, the general statement will be a reflection of the wording of Section 2 of the HASAWA, which says, among other things, that: 'It shall be the duty of every employer to ensure, so far as is reasonably practicable, the health, safety and welfare at work of all his employees.'

Workplace Accidents

References to accidents at work may invoke a variety of recollections ranging from those of our own individual experiences of witnessing or being personally involved in minor accidents or 'close shaves', to those major incidents that remain in our minds forever, such as large scale factory fires, explosions in chemical plants or mining disasters. Even since the 1974 Act came into force, thousands of people have been killed or injured as a result of minor and major industrial accidents, including children and other members of the public.

Discovering the causes of accidents, therefore, is an extremely important aspect of accident prevention; the causes identified through accident investigations may lead to appropriate preventive measures. Explanations for accidents are many and varied, and attempts have been made to categorize them. These include: (1) environmental, (2) behavioural and (3) physiological (Molander and Winterton, 1994). It is important to regard the three sources of explanation as interrelated and interactive. For example, individuals' responses to the environment and the factors within it are both behavioural and physiological; also, particular items of behaviour, such as alcohol or drug abuse, cause perceptive and physiological disorders that produce a negative, and often dangerous, psychological state.

ENVIRONMENTAL CAUSES

Obviously, the working environment is extremely important, especially in industries that clearly are very hazardous, such as working at sea on ships and oil rigs, chemical factories and mining operations. In such industries, however, companies' and employees' 'risk awareness' is high, and significant progress has been made in training and the provision of safety equipment.

While this high level of 'safety consciousness' has resulted in fewer accidents, such industries are still regarded as 'high risk', although industries which clearly are less hazardous by their nature have a higher incidence of accidents. With many people, environmental causes of accidents are thought of as 'factory floor' phenomena, but the point has to be made that an office environment, with computer wires laid across the floor, faulty electrical fittings and insufficient working space, can be a very dangerous place indeed. Office workers often attempt to make minor repairs and adjustments to their electrical equipment, lighting and so forth, without switching off the power supply and without the right equipment to reach the area where they think the fault is. Thus we find people standing on chairs to reach ceiling fittings, bending under desks to fiddle with connection boxes and so forth. Often, even the chairs they sit on are unsafe in some way.

BEHAVIOURAL CAUSES

Particular aspects of social learning are responsible for accidents at work. This refers to learning that has not been developed through formal education and training, but picked up from copying the behaviour of others, conformity to 'norms', and trial and error. A new operative, for example, may notice that in order to achieve particular production levels, which carry extra pay, some workers breach Health and Safety Regulations, by removing machine guards or using other unsafe practices, which enable them to reach bonus figures.

Also, people experiencing stress undergo changes in behaviour; when they are worried about their marriage, home and family, money, job security and career prospects, they are thinking about these things when they should be concentrating on what they are doing. It has long been known that so-called 'daydreaming' is a cause of accidents at work.

PHYSIOLOGICAL CAUSES

In addition to those referred to above, there are several specific physiological causes of accidents. Poor eyesight, poor hearing, a limited sense of smell and other non-induced physiological problems can cause slow reactions to situations, and might turn a prospective 'near miss' into an accident. Not everyone is fit and healthy, and managers and supervisors should be aware of their employees' state of health and fitness, in relation to the nature of the work that they assign to them.

Other Health and Safety Problems

Not all health and safety problems are accident-related. When we think of accidents we think of the physical injuries that can result from them. Serious damage to health, however, can be caused in the workplace by inhaling/ingesting noxious gases and substances, perhaps caused by a failure to use safety equipment, or, alternatively, caused by incorrect storage or faults in production machinery and equipment. Office workers may experience visual problems when using computer terminals, and those who sit for long periods may not have the ideal chair. Repetitive strain injury is the result of over-use of the same part of the body for too long a period. Smoking while using solvents can cause serious health problems. None of these effects is accident-related.

Healthy Workplace Initiatives

'Healthy Workplace' initiatives are a comparatively recent arrival on to the workplace scene. They are the result of the national initiative *The Health of the Nation*, which was introduced by the Department of Health in a White Paper of 1992. The White Paper recognized that the increasing concern of employers and their workforces over health issues provided opportunities to intensify health promotion in the workplace. A 'Task Force' was set up to examine and expand this activity. The Task Force carried out a nationwide survey and the results were set out in a report, *Health Promotion in the Workplace*, published by the Health Education Authority (HEA). The survey was designed to gather information about the nature and frequency of 'Health-at-Work' activities, in terms of track record, the present situation and future plans. In total, 1344 organizations were examined.

One general conclusion was that the larger the organization, the greater was the probability of frequent and relevant activity.

The survey questionnaire was based on a wide range of questions in order to obtain an accurate picture of what was happening in workplaces. Many aspects of workplace activity were covered by these questions, including:

- smoking and tobacco products
- alcohol and sensible drinking
- healthy eating
- weight control
- exercise/fitness/activity
- stress management and relaxation
- health screening
- cholesterol testing
- blood pressure control

- drugs/substance abuse
- back care
- HIV/AIDS
- heart health and heart disease
- breast screening
- cervical screening
- lifestyle assessment
- repetitive strain injury
- eyesight testing
- hearing
- women's health

Obviously, not all organizations reported problems in every single area, so that the 'healthy workplace' activities that were set up each dealt with their own respective areas of concern. The initiative taken in the Health Service, for example, 'Health at Work in the NHS', was based on five main areas of concern: (1) occupational stress, (2) sexual health (HIV/AIDS, etc.), (3) smoking, (4) drug/substance abuse and (5) healthy lifestyle (eating habits etc.).

While the HEA Report did not offer advice on specific actions to be taken, nor indeed, on how to audit the health of the workplace, it did tell organizations what to look for.

Stress at Work

Stress occurs when an individual is pushed or pressurized beyond the level of his or her natural coping capacity. Occupational stress is one example of 'non-accident related' workplace factors that can lead to ill-health. What follows is an explanation of the sources and causes of workplace stress, and some indications of what organizations and individuals might do about it.

SOURCES AND CAUSES OF STRESS

Sources of stress are those areas of life from which stress arises. Research shows that there are six main sources of stress, or

stress theatres: (1) the workplace, (2) one's marriage, (3) home
and family, (4) personal finances, (5) living accommodation and
(6) social relationships and leisure. Each stress theatre contains
a number of causes of stress, or *stressors*. A literature search,
ranging from 1970 to 1993, which, *inter alia*, examined survey
reports from within that period, revealed that more than half of
all stressors reside within the theatre of work. Some stressors
cause more concern than others and, therefore, are reported
more frequently. To identify the areas of greatest concern, the
researcher classified stressors as high-, medium- and low-fre-
quency stressors. Of the thousands of stressors examined, 116
emerged as those most often reported by questionnaire respon-
dents. Of these 116 'high-frequency' stressors, 59 originated in
the workplace (Currie, 1993).

While the main concern is with workplace stress, it is clear
that the effects of stressors that originate in one theatre travel
around with the person to the others. For example, people take
their workplace stress home with them, where its effects are
communicated to the family. If there are additional pressures at
home, perhaps over finances, or the accommodation itself, then
they will be added to the load and carried back to the workplace.
In a severe case, when stress commutes with the individual, the
load becomes too much to bear and ill-health follows. In these
circumstances, marriages may break down, the person's work
performance may suffer and the job is lost as a result. Ill-health,
induced or exacerbated by stress, can develop into serious
conditions, causing mental problems, stomach ulcers and heart
disease.

STRESS AND PRODUCTIVITY

Stress adversely affects productivity. It has been estimated that
around 92 million working days are lost annually through
stress-related factors, such as sickness absence and reduced
work performance. It is worth bearing in mind that these losses
are thirty times greater than those associated with industrial
relations problems, especially when one compares the national
and corporate investments that have gone into industrial relations with those dedicated to stress problems.

Summary

Health and safety at work is a complex and wide-ranging subject. Here, we have explained the fundamentals of the subject, including those relating to health and safety policy and the main legal obligations. While in the workplace there is, quite rightly, considerable emphasis on *safety*, particularly regarding accident prevention and the storage and use of specific substances, it is also important to pay attention to the physical and mental health of employees. Finally, it is worth bearing in mind that the human being develops and evolves at Nature's pace, which is considerably slower than the rate of change that Man's ingenuity and capability has brought about. Mankind has changed the environment in which we live and work, and in addition to the resultant advantages, people have to contend with the stresses and strains of modern living conditions. The 'fight-or-flight reaction', which developed as we adapted to the natural environment, is all we have to combat man-made conditions.

Note

1   This is sometimes known as an Employee Assistance Programme (EAP), and there are firms who provide access to confidential counselling and support. Very often, employees are more ready to discharge information about themselves and their feelings to an outsider, rather than to another employee, such as a personnel specialist. When considering the engagement of such a firm, it is a good idea to ensure that the service offered is acceptable to both employees and managers.

References

Currie, D. 1993: *Stress in the Health Service*. Southampton: Southampton Institute.
Molander, C and Winterton, J. 1994: *Managing Human Resources*. London: Routledge.

Index